EVERY TICKET TELLS A STORY

Volume 1

Mark Baxter & Stuart Deabill

SOUL DEEP

Published in Great Britain in 2023
by Soul Deep Books
www.souldeep.co.uk
SD005
Manufactured and Printed in the UK

ISBN 978-1-7397586-2-2

Dedication

The phrase 'honour thy father' struck a real chord with me when I first heard it. Since my dad died in the year 2000, I have thought on many occasions "what would the old man do here?" as I've made my through the last twenty-odd years. In truth, my dad's way of going about life was pretty 'unshowy'. Sure, he loved his clobber, football and a game of darts, singing a song in a pub and a light ale. But that was pretty much it. The rest of the time, he kept it simple, and he kept it classy. As I've got older, I've also realised more and more that he led by example. "Earn your own money son. Get a job and stick with it, don't be late, never go sick, provide for the family. Graft son, it's all about the graft." And you know what, he was right. You can claim to be anything nowadays, but without the graft to back it up, it's a load of empty noise.

As we were putting the finishing touches on this book, Stuart's dad, Derek, sadly died. Poignantly, Stu had asked his dad to contribute a story for it and this Derek did, expressing his love for the jazz greats, Ella Fitzgerald and Count Basie. The words he wrote now mean so much more of course, and I can only guess of how proud Derek would be, to see his son once again producing graft of a high standard and, once again, use his own publishing oompany to let that graft see the light of day.

I'd say we were lucky boys growing up. We had fathers who taught us by example, and what an example they set.

'Honour thy father', eh?

Amen to that.

“LADIES AND
WOULD YO
WELCOME TO

GENTLEMEN
OU PLEASE
THE STAGE...

CONTENTS

OI FRANK!

I have mentioned before, I wasn't much of a gig-goer in my mid to late teens. No, any spare money I had went on football, but that all changed when I got a job in the glorious world of the 'print', working for a news agency on Fleet Street, aged nineteen, in the summer of 1982. My first role was opening mail in the editorial department. While doing that, I regularly spotted gig tickets, usually in pairs, sent in complementary style for the attention of the music journalist to attend the various shows. Only, I also noticed that most of them ended up in the bin. The truth was, none of the journos were bothered unless it was big gig, like the Stones or Bowie. Of course, being of the 'mumper' persuasion, I quickly dug the tickets out of said bin, and those I didn't fancy personally, I'd sell on. Truth is, though, as I hadn't been to many gigs before, I started to use the tickets myself, and to say they were for a mixed bag of 'acts' was an understatement to say the least.

Over the next year or so, I was seeing at least a gig a week, mainly at Hammersmith Odeon, but also The Dominion and Wembley Arena. Off the top of my head, I can recall seeing, in no particular order, Wham, Yazoo, Kid Creole & The Coconuts, Depeche Mode, UB40, Japan, The Police, Gary Numan, The Style Council, Lynx, Madness, Frankie Beverly & Maze, Luther Vandross and many, many more who obviously failed to make a lasting impression on my fading memory. I'd take a variety of people along with me to each show: new mates from work, old mates from our estate, cousins, and an old girlfriend or two. It has to be said, the anticipation of each gig was great, though not having to pay a tanner for the privilege certainly added to the occasion.

As for the really special gigs that have stuck in my mind over the last forty years, I'd say Anita Baker at Wembley Arena was a great night, a really mixed crowd with a very soul boy/soul girl vibe. There was Miles Davis at the Royal Festival Hall, Weller at Crystal Palace, The Verve at Earls Court, Slim Gaillard at the Seven Dials Club in Covent Garden, Oasis at Knebworth, The Who and Dionne Warwick at the Albert Hall (not on the same bill), Madness at Finsbury Park the first time around, and the one I write about in here, Francis Albert Sinatra at the Albert Hall with my mum and dad and Uncle Bob, all of whom are no longer with us.

That was simply a remarkable night.

So, with so many gigs under my belt, I was delighted to be asked by Stu and Steve to get on board this project. Thanks, chaps, and I'm equally chuffed that so many of those I asked for their memories also loved the idea and contributed.

God bless the lot of 'em.

So, get that last trip to the khazi in, grab yourself a light ale on the way back to your spot, and let the sweet music that follows take you over...

Mark Baxter
London
Summer 2022

THE JAM
blur
THE ASTORIA
Monday 10th February 1997
7:00pm
Tickets £14.00
00578
Solo - ITG proudly present
SEX PISTOLS
+ SPECIAL GUESTS
The Shepherds Bush Empire
Wednesday 17th July 1996
Doors 7:00pm
£15.00 in advance
S.J.M.
CONCERTS
PHOTO
LIAM GALLAGHER
MANCHESTER ETIHAD
01/06/2022
HUGGY BEAR
SUNDAY 14th MARCH
EMPIRE POOL, WEMBLEY
DANNY O'DONOVAN presents
THE JACKSON FIVE
and Supporting Artistes
SUNDAY, 12th NOVEMBER
at 7 p.m.
ARENA
£2.00
DEL MAR FAIRGROUNDS
CYPRESS HILL
SHARON JONES
AND THE DAP-KINGS
THE FILLMORE
OPEN DANCE FLOOR/DRS 8PM
Wed., June 16th, 1976
U.K. SUBS
ITB and THE MEAN FIDDLER present
Neil Young
WITH BOOKER T. & THE M.G.'S
Finsbury Park - London
SUNDAY 11th JULY 1993
Harvey Goldsmith Entertainments &
Trinifold Mgt Proudly Present
THE WHO
performing
QUADROPHENIA
plus support
SAT 07 DEC 96 7.30pm
BLK ROW SEAT
3 Y 46
Price £27.50
Sold to GOUDIE
on 201196
HAMMERSMITH Tel. 01-748-4081
Manager: Philip Leivers
EVENING 7-30 p.m.
May 6th, 1983
THE GARDEN
PENZANCE
THURS 1ST SEPT
MYSTERY APPEARANCE
OF A TOP INTERNATIONAL
BRITISH GROUP
?
PLUS DISCO
BIBA
RAINBOW RESTAURANT
NEW YORK
Celia Cruz
Tito Puente
ORCHESTRA
EL SONIDO DE LONDRES
Hammersmith Palais
Thursday 10th July at 7:30pm
DANMEN LTD PRESENT
FRANK SINATRA
IN CONCERT
MAY 31/92 AT 8:00 PM
THE MODETTES
THE LOW NUMBERS
LUSU ENTS present
PLUS SUPPORT
QUEEN'S HALL
Percy Gee Building
CONFLICT
SAT 19 DEC
MANIC
STREET
PREACHERS
CUBA 17-02-01
KARL MARX THEATRE
TEENAGE
CANCER
TRUST
The Who
Plus special guest
Wilko Johnson
Thu, 26 March 2015
HAROLD DAVISON presents
FOR THE FIRST TIME IN GREAT BRITAIN
THE
THELONIOUS MONK
QUARTET featuring CHARLIE ROUSE
Plus
ART BLAKEY'S
JAZZ MESSENGERS
ROYAL FESTIVAL HALL
PAUL WELLER

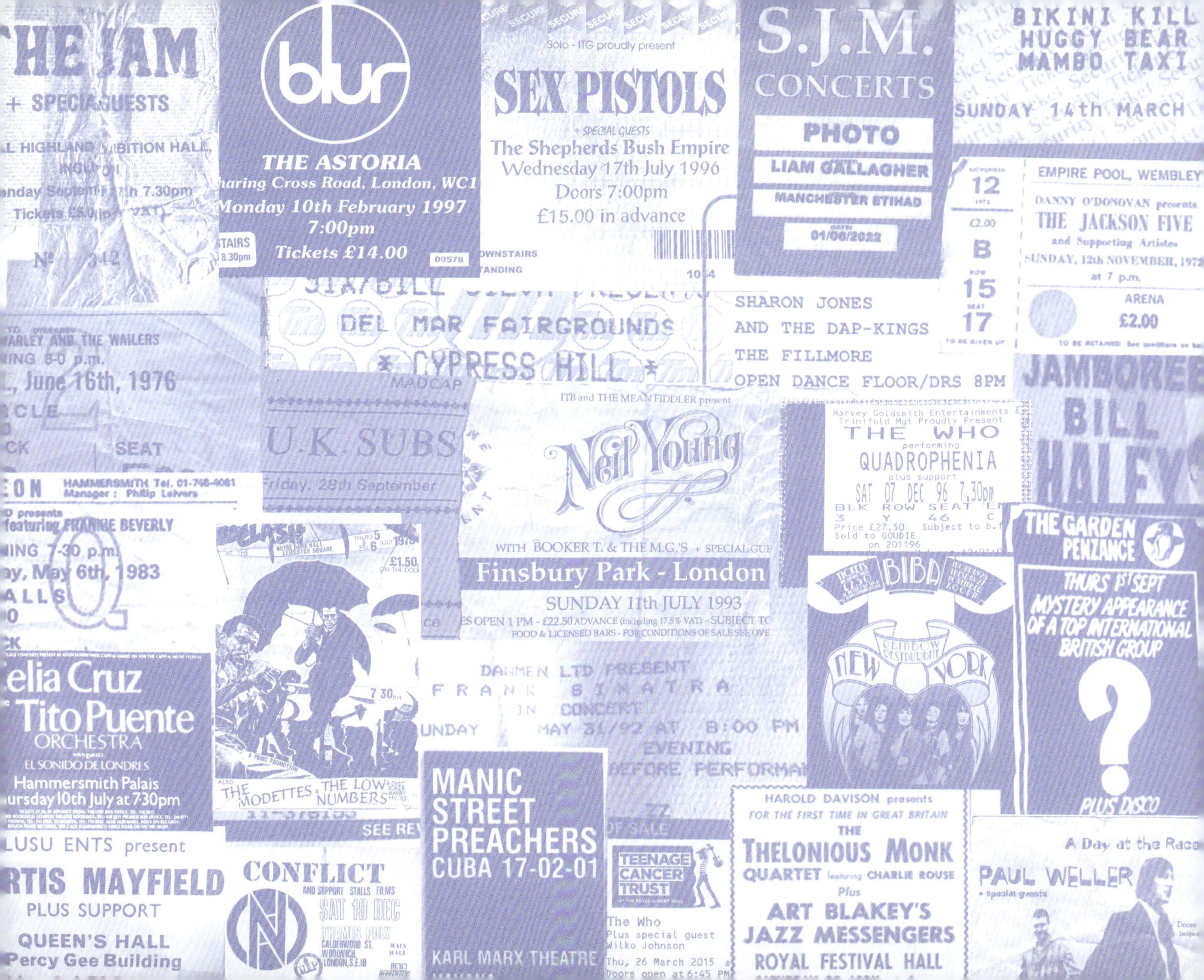

+ SPECIAL GUESTS
Tickets £5.00
blur
THE ASTORIA
Charing Cross Road, London, WC1
Monday 10th February 1997
7:00pm
Tickets £14.00
Solo - ITG proudly present
SEX PISTOLS
+ SPECIAL GUESTS
The Shepherds Bush Empire
Wednesday 17th July 1996
Doors 7:00pm
£15.00 in advance
S.J.M. CONCERTS
PHOTO
LIAM GALLAGHER
MANCHESTER ETIHAD
01/06/2022
BIKINI KILL
HUGGY BEAR
MAMBO TAXI
SUNDAY 14th MARCH
EMPIRE POOL, WEMBLEY
DANNY O'DONOVAN presents
THE JACKSON FIVE
and Supporting Artistes
SUNDAY, 12th NOVEMBER, 1972
at 7 p.m.
ARENA
£2.00
DEL MAR FAIRGROUNDS
* CYPRESS HILL *
SHARON JONES
AND THE DAP-KINGS
THE FILLMORE
OPEN DANCE FLOOR/DRS 8PM
MARLEY AND THE WAILERS
June 16th, 1976
U.K. SUBS
Friday, 28th September
ITB and THE MEAN FIDDLER present
Neil Young
WITH BOOKER T. & THE M.G.'S
Finsbury Park - London
SUNDAY 11th JULY 1993
Harvey Goldsmith Entertainments &
Trinifold Mgt Proudly Present
THE WHO
performing
QUADROPHENIA
plus support
SAT 07 DEC 96 7.30pm
JAMBOREE
BILL HALEY
HAMMERSMITH
featuring FRANKIE BEVERLY
May 6th, 1983
THE CLASH
THE MODETTES
THE LOW NUMBERS
THE GARDEN PENZANCE
THURS 1st SEPT
MYSTERY APPEARANCE OF A TOP INTERNATIONAL BRITISH GROUP
?
PLUS DISCO
BIBA
RAINBOW RESTAURANT
NEW YORK
Celia Cruz
Tito Puente
ORCHESTRA
EL SONIDO DE LONDRES
Hammersmith Palais
Thursday 10th July at 7:30pm
DANMEN LTD PRESENT
FRANK SINATRA
IN CONCERT
SUNDAY MAY 31/92 AT 8:00 PM
MANIC STREET PREACHERS
CUBA 17-02-01
KARL MARX THEATRE
LUSU ENTS present
CURTIS MAYFIELD
PLUS SUPPORT
QUEEN'S HALL
Percy Gee Building
CONFLICT
SAT 19 DEC
THAMES POLY
TEENAGE CANCER TRUST
The Who
Plus special guest
Wilko Johnson
Thu, 26 March 2015
Doors open at 6:45 PM
HAROLD DAVISON presents
FOR THE FIRST TIME IN GREAT BRITAIN
THE THELONIOUS MONK QUARTET featuring CHARLIE ROUSE
Plus
ART BLAKEY'S JAZZ MESSENGERS
ROYAL FESTIVAL HALL
A Day at the Races
PAUL WELLER

LOAD IN

I love a gig. Live music is in my blood. After the first show I attended back in 1982 aged sixteen (The Jam, Wembley Arena), life changed forever. Discovering bands that lit my consciousness at the age of twelve was enormous enough to my being, but to then hear it amplified through a sound system so large it caused my body to shake (partly excitement, mainly volume), alongside thousands of other fanatics in the famous old north-west London barn – I was hooked! Suddenly going to a gig became discovery, a new journey, something more personal – and I wanted more!

As I became more intrigued and captivated by the experience, and got a few shows under my belt, I started spreading my wings and attending shows outside of London with like-minded pals. There is always a new venue, a new band, a support band or three to fall in love with, or not. The frontman thanking everyone for coming while the drummer plays the hi-hat, or in Miles Hunt from The Wonder Stuff's case, calling the audience c***s before leaping into another high-octane classic. And the audiences – who varied from the wasted (Lou Reed) to high-spirited, respectful followers (Echo And The Bunnymen) and abusive, drunken arseholes, looking to fight or throw piss about (Oasis), it all adds to the occasion. Throw in the lighting, backdrops, intro song, rotund blokes in faded tees untangling leads or changing guitars for the axe hero and it is always an all-encompassing experience.

At each show I was capturing moments for posterity in real time and replaying the songs, the in-between banter in my head for days, weeks, months and, as you'll find out, years after.

The best live music connects in a way you can't even explain at times. Watching an artist I love rocking a concert hall, a student union bar, a pub, a sweaty basement, an arena, a stadium or a park (1,2, 1,2, hello LOOONDDDONNN!), with my mates or even on my own is one of life's absolute pleasures. It may damage your hearing (fuck you, tinnitus), but it's healthy for the soul. I've seen The Stone Roses play to less than 200 in Cologne. I've seen Billy Bragg play to 150,000 in Hyde Park. Both had their merits in totally different ways. I've been to the venues – from Portsmouth to Paris, Hammersmith to Hamburg, Dundee to Dundalk and many others in pursuit of the ringing chord.

I've also promoted gigs, DJ'd at them, roadied, tour managed, and I've even played one, at the age of twenty-two (my guitar amp blew on the first song while my arse was flapping; somehow I managed to hang on by going through a replacement, with gentle applause from a crowd of forty followed by early retirement…).

SOUND CHECK

It's rare for me to have a book title before I'd written a word. I usually agonise over the right 'frame' for months, during and after the full process. But I'd had the idea of compiling a book like Every Ticket Tells A Story for the best part of the last decade. It's a simple idea with an endless scope. "Hey you! Pick out a gig, concert, festival or event ticket stub, from any year, any genre, any venue, a nywhere in the world, and tell us your story!"

So, a book like this should have been a straightforward one. No dramas or ego wars behind the scenes. Just a slow, methodical walk through the near and far. However, distractions are plenty and, as it does, life got in the way and the idea stayed in an old metal Christmas sweet tin along with all the tickets I've collected over the last forty years (I would have had a lot more if I hadn't stupidly disposed of most of my Eighties briefs, as I was consumed by the Madchester and Acid House zeitgeist before the turn of the decade and rejected the past. Ho hum.).

In the spring of 2022, myself, co-author Mark Baxter, designer Steve Rowland and another character talked about working on a different book, which due to various reasons, didn't get further than the initial Zoom call. After that idea quickly faded away, I said to Mark (or Bax, to his many friends) "I've got this idea…".

And here we are! Many different stories, all ages, genre-fluid and all told with passion – some with humour, some with regret, some with life-changing beauty but every one with heart and soul. I'm pleased that we've managed to entice so many different and diverse people to share these wonderful accounts. Not all have kept their original paper or card stub, and in more recent times the humble paper or card entry has now become a digital non-descript, so we've sourced tickets or gig posters elsewhere where possible. Many contributors have allowed us to use their 'brief' and paint a veritable picture, of a life-lasting moment of their time, lost in music. And there's no turning back.

Stuart Deabill
Watford
Autumn 2022

PAUL WELLER
CRYSTAL PALACE NATIONAL SPORTS CENTRE
LONDON
2 AUGUST 1997
PAUL ANDERSON, WRITER/POSTMAN

Blimey, it seems like a million years ago now. The details are hazy, but this gig will remain memorable for one reason alone.

1997 was a strange period. It felt like the world was in limbo. Britpop had peaked and was now in decline. Hip hop had lost its jazz overtones and had reverted to gangsta style. The whole 'new lad' thing, which had come along with magazines like *Loaded*, felt a bit stale too. We'd also waited an eternity for a Labour government, and it had arrived in the form of Tony Blair. Only a few months into his tenure, it already felt like we were getting Tory-Lite. Only one thing had remained a constant throughout all this; a certain Mr Weller, who had helped shape our lives for the last couple of decades.

For a few of us, the Eighties had been an era of retro Mod purity in the form of tailormade clothing and rare vintage Sixties vinyl. This had gradually given way to a journey of real Modernism with the advent of acid jazz, clubs like Sunday Afternoons at Dingwalls and the opening of boutiques such as Duffer St. George in D'Arblay Street, Covent Garden. New sounds, new clobber and new horizons.

One person who'd taken the same direction as me was my mate Matt Ashman. In our minds, forging ahead with the Mod ideals of taking the best and most sussed from the past and mixing it with the best that today or tomorrow has to offer was the only way. Forever moving forwards.

It tells you something that I can pretty much remember what I was wearing that day: a Lacoste button-down shirt, Paul Smith 'speedometer' watch, white Levi's 501s and either Adidas Gazelles or Patrick Cox loafers, while Matt was sporting a vintage Italia away top and off-white canvas Gazelles. I think there was a pair of girls with us too, but sadly can't remember who, which kind of seems Mod. They say that the devil is in the detail.

It was a fantastic, sunny day and on our travels around the site we bumped into a few other like-minded souls who had also taken Curtis's advice and moved on up. A Dat at the Races was a long one too, as we would have to sit through nine support acts, most of whom I wasn't really bothered about, although I seem to remember them all doing very short sets. The £23.50 a ticket had seemed like a king's ransom at the time for what was basically a mini festival incorporating lots of bands that I was quite happy to swerve on any other day. Skunk Anansie, Republica… not for me really. But I was happy to see the Real People, Travis and The Supernaturals. In truth, it was all just a build-up to the main event.

By the time Paul Weller hit the stage, the crowd were more than ready for it.

Looking healthy and toned, he bounced around the stage sporting a short-sleeved white grandad-style collarless shirt. His cardigan had been demoted from the European chic style of being draped over the shoulder and sleeves knotted, to being tied around his waist, umpire-style. He kicked off with the anthemic 'The Changingman', and for us old ex-purist Mods, it seemed kind of apt. Weller's third solo album, *Stanley Road*, had provided him with an entire album of live favourites, and 'The Changingman' was up there with the best. His then recently released fourth album, Heavy Soul, dominated the set and two of my favourite tracks from it, 'Up In Suzes' Room' and 'Mermaids', sounded fantastic. Other crowd pleasers included 'Broken Stones', 'Sunflower', 'Peacock Suit' and 'Into Tomorrow'. Although 'You Do Something To Me' had given us some calming respite, while still singing along. I remember the show didn't end on a big single, but instead he opted for 'Woodcutter's Son', which the crowd were pleased with, as the band were joined by the ever-fantastic Mick Talbot on keyboard duties.

All in all, this gig remains one of my favourite Weller gigs. But none of this is the reason it remains memorable.

At some point during the day we ventured over to one of the beer tents. On such a hot day it was obvious they'd be really busy and the queues were horrendous. Somehow, I drew the short straw and offered to join the crowd that was slowly shuffling towards a distant bar. There were four of us, and as nobody wanted to go through this trial again, I'd stupidly offered to buy all the rounds at once. They all gave me their share of the money, and I stepped into the long chain of people, with Matty offering to later check on my progress and help me carry the sixteen drinks back.

The atmosphere in the tent was one of hot, bothered, frustration. Everybody was getting a bit impatient and tetchy. I got chatting to the girl next to me, and we made a pact that whoever got served first we would order the other's drinks. Time rolled on and looking at the sea of people behind me, I realised that there would be no way Matty could come to my rescue. I started to work out how exactly I was going to balance all these drinks in a secure way and get them back to everyone. Finally, after what seemed an eternity, a voice suddenly said, "Can I help you love?"

"Sixteen pints of lager please," I said, while looking over my shoulder to a mass of people, none of whom was Matty. "Er, I think I'm gonna need a tray or two," I added.

"Sorry, we've run out of trays," the barmaid replied.

The girl next to me gave me a ten-pound note, and I added her drinks order to mine. As she wasn't buying that many, she offered to help me carry my order. In the meantime, the barmaid had come up with a solution that looked destined to fail. She'd started to put the first eight full plastic pint glasses onto a piece of cardboard that I'm sure was the base packaging for shrink-wrapped cans. Christ, it looked flimsy. And as she picked it up, it was already wobbling. As I stood there, wondering how exactly I was going to navigate a path through the mob, plus get the other lot on there too, a voice broke my concentration.

"Ooh, I think I'll have one of those!"

A cheeky chancer on the other side of the bar, as I was stood at a corner, proceeded to lean over and liberate one of my purchases. Now 'cheeky chancer' is me being really polite here, because at the time I just saw red. And, as he stood there smiling at me with one of my pints hovering in front of my eyes, it was all a bit too much.

"Well. If you're gonna take one, why not take the whole fuckin' lot?" I just snapped and launched the entire tray of beer at him, soaking him head to foot.

He threw a punch, but I ducked, and he hit the geezer directly behind me. Before I could do anything, he's smacked the lager-thief himself. Suddenly, it's a Wild West-style free-for-all. Bodies and beer everywhere. Somehow, I got pushed over in the melée and lay there laughing my head off. I got up and headed back to my mates, who by this point were watching in awe. As I was explaining the lack of drinks, as well as the pivotal role I had played in the skirmish, several security guards ran past us to de-escalate the battle. More bodies flying out of the tent, as it began to subside.

It was time to walk off whistling, albeit thirsty and minus quite a lot of money. Later, we passed the tent, which was closed, collapsed and all taped off. Suddenly a woman shouted. "Hey, you were in that fight, weren't you?"

Here we go, I thought.

The woman, who I hadn't recognised, turned out to be the barmaid who'd served me.

"I saw what happened," she said. "Shocking. I saw it wasn't your fault. Would you like your money back?"

I couldn't believe it! Not only did she give me our money back, but also the tenner the other girl stood next to me had given over. There was no chance of seeing her again, so we bought food with it. Somehow, I'd kind of started a fight, not got a mark on me and ended up quid's in.

Whenever I see Matty, which sadly isn't often enough these days, he's always quick to remind me of when I started the Great Weller Beer Riot in Crystal Palace!

R.E.M.
ROYAL COURT THEATRE, LIVERPOOL
21 MAY 1989
AAQIL AHMED, ORGANISER/
BROADCASTER/FILMMAKER

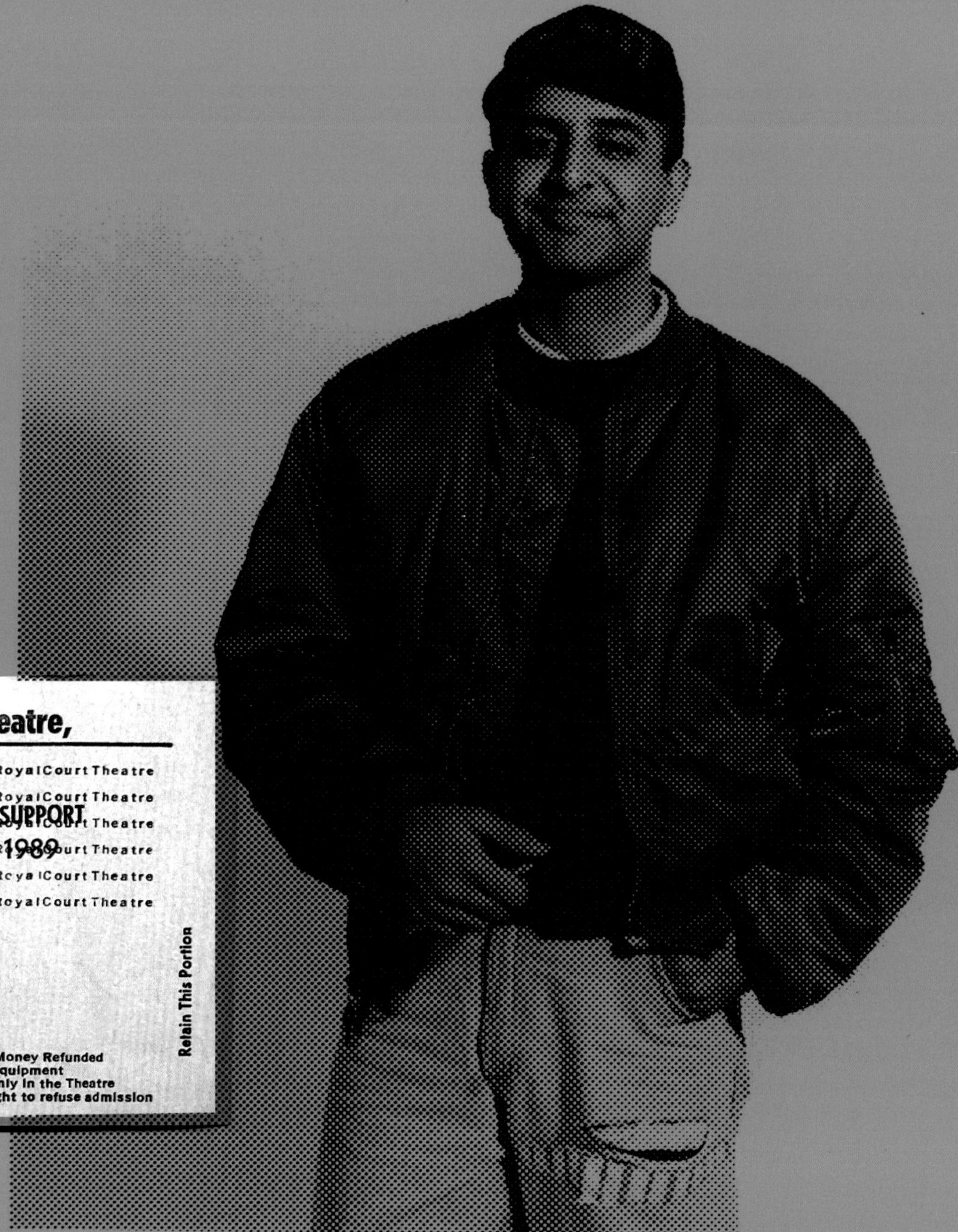

Think of a gig, Stu said – it'll be easy, we both agreed. Three months later I've bored family and friends going through the list. Would it be Nirvana at the Astoria in 1989, the countless Weller gigs from 1984 onwards or The Redskins' last gig at Manchester Polytechnic student union that actually never happened as they split up backstage…? Problem with these and many others is I can't remember much, or they were just what they were meant to be: a good gig and there isn't much to add.

I thought about writing about a Selector gig at the Sir George Robey in Finsbury Park when it got attacked by Combat 18 and we all ended up outside throwing up after a pepper spray cannister was let off, before resuming a sweaty night of skanking, of course. But in the end, I went for a night I have never forgotten because it was a right place, right time moment that can never be replicated – R.E.M. at the Royal Court Theatre in Liverpool.

Back then I was an art student and living that year in West Yorkshire. The 'jangly guitar' indie scene of the past few years had been a perfect haven for someone still pining the loss of all the bands I'd loved throughout the Eighties. I'd discovered R.E.M. around 1986, liked them and had copies of their albums *Lifes Rich Pageant* (1986) and *Document* (1987). They were, though, a band most of us followed in the pages of the *NME* or *Melody Maker* and by the time of *Document* they had even had a few indie disco stalwarts in 'The One I Love' and 'It's The End Of The World As We Know It (And I Feel Fine)'.

At art school in Dewsbury, I'd met a couple of people who were big R.E.M. fans. One was a guy who wore dirty jeans with the band's name on them and the other a lovely girl called Vicky. Vicky was normal, in that she hadn't marker-penned R.E.M. down the side of one leg. So when she said they were going to tour and did I fancy it, the answer was obvious – get two tickets and ditch marker-pen jeans boy.

There was no gig in Yorkshire, and Manchester Apollo had sold out, but I could get two tickets to Liverpool. No brainer at the time. I can't remember how I got the tickets, just that I had them and was excited – I was finally going to see them live! Then the doubts crept in. I was, as a Manc, about to watch a gig in Liverpool, and I was sure that Morrissey had been attacked as we were told for being a Manc on stage in the same venue. We now know it wasn't that he was a Manc but probably for simply being him, but that's another story. Also, Liverpool wasn't the most welcoming place for an Asian lad, and then I realised I would be with Vicky and that, back then, that would go down great with some of the numpties. I hatched a plan; I would drive to Liverpool and try and get in and out as soon as I could.

I asked my mate how to do it and he of course told me the worst place to park, so I had to walk through Liverpool to get to the venue, trying not to be spotted or to speak to anyone with my accent that would mark me out as someone to chase through the street (I'd had previous experience of that happening at a footie game). Vicky, of course, was oblivious to my inner turmoil as she was immune from all the tribalism, coming as she did from Hampshire.

Back then, gigs in Manchester, Liverpool and Glasgow were raucous events and the atmosphere inside the venue was electric. The sense of anticipation was crazy. I have zero recollection of the support band, The Blue Aeroplanes, but unlike at other gigs from that time they must have been OK, as I don't remember them being bottled off.

But I do remember R.E.M.'s entrance, or should I say Michael Stipe's. They came onto the stage and straight into 'Pop Song 89', Stipe in a straitjacket with thick black eyeliner. You couldn't take your eyes off him. The band were as tight as they were on record and the set list was full of bangers. Stipe was released from the straitjacket, and I remember him singing at one point through a loudhailer. We were fairly near the front and, being a young lad, I gallantly ran off and decided to join the craziness in the mosh pit. That craziness then to spread and pretty soon there was no front or mosh pit – it was a sea of people being crushed. I'd like to make a pun about the song 'Orange Crush', but this was a gig in Liverpool, a few weeks after the Hillsborough disaster. Audience members were being carried over our heads from the crush at the front, and it was a heavy time.

The band stopped playing and I think we were all told to sit down. I found Vicky and decided I wasn't going near that mosh pit again, as it was out of control. I'm not sure which member or members of the band lectured us about Hillsborough but it calmed things down. We were all told to stand back and behave, or they wouldn't play anymore. Eventually, a calm of sorts was restored, and the band resumed with 'End Of The World As We Know It…' – probably not the best choice in the circumstances, as everyone surged forward once more! I remember on the drive home, and for the year or so after that I knew Vicky, I would say, "Wouldn't you have come back on with 'You Are The Everything' or something similarly as slow?"

After all the madness had died down, I waited patiently for them to play my favourite song, 'Radio Free Europe', but I suppose even by then it was a song too far back in their history so it was a no-show. They were so good that night I didn't want the gig to end, but eventually it did, of course.

I looked at the set list recently and we were definitely lucky to see them that day, and in that venue. The *Green* album (1988) had already been released by that point, and the band were way too big for the Royal Court Theatre, and even then we all knew it. They were on their way to becoming a stadium band and this was a 'last hurrah'. A set list they couldn't really replicate within two albums, as by then they had worldwide hits and played aircraft hangers full of yuppies who only knew them from 'Losing My Religion' onwards. *Green* was the last classical R.E.M. guitar album and, for me, the end of my fandom.

I've seen better bands since, and I've been lucky to be backstage or in the green room. But seeing R.E.M. on the cusp of world domination, in a small venue with the drama of being an Asian Manc in hostile territory and the audience crush weeks after Hillsborough, can't be replicated, and for me, this has to be my most memorable gig ever for all that.

I can even let them off for not playing 'Radio Free Europe'. Just.

PRINCE
MADISON SQUARE GARDEN, NEW YORK CITY
18 DECEMBER 2010
SANJIV AHLUWALIA, WRITER

I have to find my ticket. The premise for this book is to describe a significant gig and, importantly, provide a visual memory in the form of a ticket. No evidence of a ticket, then no story of the late, great Prince in New York, playing, even by his high standards, an outstanding live gig at the legendary Madison Square Garden. And a story of New York in the early 2010s, an era of change and of a city's new identity.

But I need to find the ticket, otherwise the story lives in my head.

The irony is that I have hundreds maybe thousands of ticket stubs. My wife reminds me periodically that these tickets have no value apart from sentimental, clutter our home and are of no use. But. Here we are.

Prince is my favourite ever artist, up there with Mozart, The Beatles, Miles Davis and John Coltrane. More personally, Prince was a part of my teenage years, saw me through college, adulthood and married life. And Prince's late-notice New York show in December 2010 at the esteemed Madison Square Garden was majestic.

But we nearly never made it. There was snow…

The night before my wife and I flew from London to New York, snow was forecast. It didn't feel real; a relatively mild winter's evening with not a hint of a snowflake. There was also a sense of disbelief on my part; snowfall could mean transport disruption, which could lead to – horror of horrors – flight cancellations and not attending the show!

My blasé attitude would come back to haunt me the next morning. I drew open the curtains and outside was a blanket of virgin snow. Six hours later, we sit on a delayed Virgin flight waiting on the tarmac to depart. A de-icing vehicle has been working its magic, allowing aircraft to be airbound, my purple dream reliant on a piece of mechanical engineering. The de-icer worked on the planes ahead of us, each lingering minute one step closer to our flight being cancelled. The tension on the plane was apparent. Passengers shifted in their seats; the attendants gazed emptily and the pilot's hopeful announcements masked the inevitably of a cancellation. The snow fell heavily. I looked out of the window, full of hope. And the plane began to move…

Around 7.30 p.m., in a three-quarters empty arena, a person dressed all in black, draped in a cape and wearing a pointed hat jumped onstage to join the support band, Larry Graham and Graham Central Station. Graham and his band were good, including a handful of Sly and the Family Stone tracks (the band, in essence, were Sly and the Family Stone without Sly). The forty-five minute set turned into an excellent one, as the dark figure and Graham duetted on 'I Want To Take You Higher'. The two of them, little and large, dancing down the runaway, was a sight to behold. The few thousand in the arena, looked at one another … and roared.

New York in 2010 was a handful of years into what we now know as the hipster takeover. There were the beginnings of locals with facial hair, tattoos and lumberjack shirts. In cafes, freshly ground coffee slowly began to replace the black liquid that was often served, a concoction left to stew on a hot plate until the bitterness wrapped around your mouth. There was craft beer, natural wine – artisan and hand-crafted; a blueprint for metropolitan areas the world over.

We would stay in Rivington Street in the Lower East Side, an area built on Jewish and Latin emigres – tailors and clothing wholesalers; tenements and basketball courts. Splendid graffiti pieces were my view while dining in a tiny deli on a mighty New York breakfast of ham and eggs, over easy. The lexicon was catching.

Two weeks earlier Prince had announced the gig at Madison Square Garden. My wife and I had visited New York annually since 2007, but this year would be a year off – Christmas shopping and preparation for a big family party were the or der of the day. But I managed to persuade my wife that New York was the perfect place for that Christmas shopping and preparation. She smiled; I had mentioned Prince a million times in our eight years together. The million and first time would be in New York.

"New York, are you ready?"

Twenty-thousand fans at a sold out Madison Square Garden shout YES. With the lights down, under a cloak of darkness, the opening lines of a new track, 'Welcome To America', ring out. Prince, in his deep baritone voice, chants the title. Then a snatch of Sylvester's 'Disco Heat' quickly follows, and the chorus of 'Get Up, Get Up Everybody' gets the crowd into the groove. Still darkness.

And then, like an apparition, Prince materialises, standing in the middle of the stage. The musical magician shouts, "Give me one, two, three … New York are you ready?" And this is the band's cue; over the next two hours something very special is to occur.

The whirlwind funk explosion of 'Baby I'm A Star' signals the beginning of the concert proper, and Purple Rain-era hits follow: the soulful 'The Beautiful Ones' complete with a piano intro and a ballet dancer; 'Let's Go Crazy', which gives us our first electrifying guitar solo. Out goes the 'everything and the kitchen sink' sound productions of previous tours. A big and bold sound has been replaced with simplicity and intricate playing. and a show spectacle has been eschewed for longer, crowd-pleasing songs.

From the 1999 album, the rock'n'roll 'Delirious' follows, and it is apparent that Prince is enjoying himself, alongside his band, with the amazing Esperanza Spalding on keys – the best he's had for years. 'Delirious' is accompanied by Elvis-like hip twists, with tongue firmly in cheek. Prince plays the showman and quickly has the crowd on his side (a whole section of the arena gets up and joins in en masse to synchronised steps, à la The Time, an amazing group of musicians from Minneapolis who had world class producers Jam and Lewis in their line up).

Within twenty minutes I am ready to catch my breath, blown away by the ferocity of the music, but this is just the warm-up. I catch my breath again and think about sitting down to savour the moment, but I can't … there's more … much, much more to come.

"Anyone under twenty-five? Well, you won't know this one". 'Uptown' from the 1980 funk album *Dirty Mind* follows, confirming then, as is now, that Prince is a master funkateer. 'Raspberry Beret', sung sweet, soul-style with the crowd filling in most of the lyrics, is equal to the 1986 Parade Tour version. The thrill and adrenaline of the show reaches from the stage and into my legs; I look around and the crowd are going crazy. Smiling, happy people, dancing and singing.

The next forty-five minutes reveal an artist at the top of his game, a Prince returning to his palace, playing to a court of subjects. The 1982 B-side 'Let's Work' is aired, and the predominately old-school black audience roars its approval (it is no coincidence that Prince announced the concert dates at the Harlem Apollo). To see Prince at the legendary Madison Square Garden is one thing (its ugly 'office block exterior' aside), but to hear Prince playing obscure funk experiments is entirely another. They say the New York crowd is the hardest to please. Well, there must be something in the water (that does not compute), for the excitement and crowd delirium rises to new heights, and it's apparent to the band, who match the crowd's exuberance with a riot/party on the stage.

The bare-boned funk of Sheila E.'s 'A Love Bizarre', a fan favourite, completes the evening. The band captures the sultry, seedy and wonderfully hypnotically groove of the original, with guest stars Sheila E. herself on percussion and Roots drummer ?uestlove. ?uestlove, who is reported to own one of the biggest collection of Prince bootlegs, drummed like his life depends on it and is chuffed enough to be on stage with his hero that he holds his phone aloft and catches the scene on his camera.

A cast of well-knowns including Spike Lee, Jamie Foxx, Naomi Campbell and Whoopi Goldberg are then pulled on stage to dance. Reluctant at first, they dance admirably, Jamie Foxx in particular. The ten-minute finale is a masterclass in funk.

And then it's over. Concert of the year? Easily. Best concert of the 2000s? Probably. Prince back to his best? Definitely.

"New York, my name is Prince and this is my house." And then he was gone.

Postscript: I found my ticket. It's Willy Wonka-esque 'chocolate factory' golden, with just a hint of purple.

TROUBLE FUNK
TOWN AND COUNTRY CLUB, KENTISH TOWN, LONDON
DATE UNKNOWN, 1986
PARTHA BANERJEA, CONSULTANT CHILD AND ADOLESCENT PSYCHIATRIST

There's Trouble in the Land…

Militant memories: for months, years after his passing, Double would appear through my sleep to bump a lesser dream, still bopping with armed resistance of his dedication to 'jazz', which he said was "two, say three broad-crooked jumps off to the side of the mainstream straight and narrow, out to where sound becomes sight, as it should be!" (Cartier, 1987)

The A-Team always had one, and I needed that plan, in the full knowledge the high-wire act playing out between the dilemma of gig vs exam was only ever going to have one glistening winner. But, inherent within the structure of all plans are the fledgling seeds of their own failure and desire. Hannibal and his crack squad knew that, and so did I. As F. Scott Fitzgerald reminds us, no second acts, and not just in American lives.

Case in point; a transplanted South Londoner, treading water at Birmingham Medical School. I had already toyed with the idea of quitting my medical degree, but really what I was describing to myself, with a plan in mind, was the wish for a 'home', masquerading as my angst's self-cancelling feints against boredom. I was out of love with learning lists but held on to the belief that life could be sought and made meaningful through music (itself a vapour trail of a dissipating dream). And I held on to this for dear life. A proselytiser for that coda, whereby the truth and light – indeed, salvation – arrived in the form of jazz (Pharoah Sanders, anyone?), soul (obscurantist to a fault), funk and the Afro-Latin concrete of the barrio. And of course, like any taste worth its salt, it was elitism, pure and simple, but a pared-back version, sharp with an edge of insouciance designed to keep the masses at bay.

Into this, and the 'this' was mid-Eighties London, landed the sounds of mutated next-instalment disco. With a little help from Kraftwerk, black science fiction poured out of Detroit and the Bronx (which had been paring it all down for some time anyway, ever since Kool Herc tricked the mutant switch on JA sound-system culture). And way beyond the projects and block parties of its birth, it started to reverberate in other cities too, each time with a local twist. The London version nodded to the imaginary of Marley's 'concrete jungle', remixed with boogie and for all those that just missed out, rare groove. Cold Crush Brothers meeting The Rockers, and Clarence Wheeler, uptown. There was more life in an average night out in London than a year spent at Birmingham medical school wondering if that was it (happily, it wasn't).

So, back to the plan. 2 p.m. start, a three-hour statistics exam, then leave after thirty-five minutes, having displayed both wisdom and acumen (this would be optimistic since I had resolutely failed to turn up to any of the requisite lectures); jump on the noddy train to New Street and then Intercity myself down to Euston, Northern line to Kentish Town, and a quick stroll to the Town and Country Club for Trouble Funk. Ah yes, DC (Dee See) go-go – a sound which, with the benefit of hindsight, never packed quite the charge on vinyl as it did in person, where it tore the roof off live. A sound with way too many congas, harking back to a time before the ships came, or to the call and response of black low church, the swing and looseness of a New Orleans second line. It was funk and then some. And yes, statistics would have to pay the price. And yes, there's a woman, but more of that later.

Leaving 160 other souls wondering whether 'regression analysis' would suffice for question 52 was easy and obscurely thrilling: to his astonishment, I muttered "piece of piss" at the chinless wonder who sat behind me (to note, medicine had been and mostly continues to be the preserve of the middle classes). The excitement on the train down to London was not even dented by the formless, baggy-jumpered, heaven-knows-I'm-miserable-now student, destined to be a social worker in Slough. I'd seen him around the Union, told him about the upcoming gig in an effort to make conversation, yet suspected deep down that nothing I could say would shift him from shoegazing. Heaven knows what he makes of Morrissey now.

Kentish Town was having the shakes; a warm night, the sound of whistles greeting those exiting the Tube. Janis's Mercedes Benz's were being relieved of their logos. B-boys, wide boys, soul boys, and just the plain curious. A London particular. It smelled of excitement and possibilities, and suddenly there it was: the legend, emblazoned in bold for all to see just across the road at the Town and Country Club: "Trouble Funk, Sold Out".

For one night only, forget Groucho Marx! This was the exception that proved the rule. A club I'd have happily traded a hundred Benz logos to gain admission to. I was ecstatic. These moments don't come around too often, I thought to myself. Savour them. Looking back now, a few more have been added to that list. Sakura, Jill Scott many years later at the Jazz Cafe, D'Angelo at the same, the sound of a word (san), or the ineffable beauty of a look all had this quality. And then with obscene haste, it's gone.

My idyll was punctured by the gothic beauty who had decided sometime before that I might be a good catch (I could have told her that goths and soul boys are an odd mixture, but who was I to quibble with beauty). There was a look on her face that could only speak to a number of upcoming difficulties. She'd evidently worked out this gig was going to be nothing like the Sisters of Mercy-style revue I'd promised her. (That I may have proposed a passing similarity between DC funkateers and the long dark night of the gothic soul, in a punt to see whether she'd come along, was in fairness the least of my sins). My mates were being insufferable (nothing new), but as evidenced in her increasingly severe expression, their antics must have added further to the nature of my choices, and hence character, in her eyes. To top it all, I was late (the wonders of British rail, so again nothing new). The pre-gig mood music, then, was, at best, strained.

There was trouble ahead, so instead of dealing with it, I did the honourable thing and piled straight into the gig. And there it was – that sound coming in from all sides. Congas, drums and a tight horn section, call and response, but most of all that rolling syncopation, slightly off but so on with space and time to play (check J. Dilla for another sonic interpretation of this, or the short stories of Somerset Maugham). In the sweat and heat, with the goth's eyeliner heading south, the shouts of "Drop the bomb!", the lock groove and the stabs of Cameo-style synth, the Town and Country resembled less a gig, more a fevered dream whereby I started to feel that I'd arrived or had a sense that this was what I'd been waiting for all along. Home in sound, and sound as home.

I had missed Parker playing double time, Miles in his heyday, Alice Coltrane in India or even Chuck Brown and the Soul Searchers, the Godfather of go-go (by a few months), but somehow this warm London night had managed to align with the musical universe. I'd caught up with myself, and British Rail notwithstanding, I was finally on time. In a sense, like the John Holt lyric "Time is the master". And here I was, in this maelstrom of 'now', of bodies and sweat and 'Let's Get Small', sensing the future and true witness to the past even as I dissolved into an intense present. I was watching sakura blossom gently fall to the floor in a gust of wind in Ueno Park, Tokyo, prompting a very different crowd to applaud spontaneously, or walking at the right speed behind the coffin in *Camus's L'Étranger*, absorbing a look that would launch a thousand ships.

But above all, in the melée, in the percussive time signatures, an idea was forming; that I was finally part of a club, I like to think as Groucho had always intended. It is one that has grown over time and served me well, be that in nurturing an international view, or a minimalist nod to clean, sharp schmutter (peace go with you, George). It's a club with kindreds in far-flung places and one that has given me the confidence to live with the idea that to choose is also to exclude, for in not having it all, we move forward. Discernment, no less. The clear price to pay (and how cheap a price this was really – market-stall seconds, in fact) was giving up food for funk and, for now, an exam had been sacrificed at the altar. The smudged eyeliner attested to the way in which all relationships tended to end in those days, afraid of the deafening silence at the edge of the notes. I walked.

The fevered dream took a long time to break, eventually prising apart the tired chord arrangements of what was expected to create something new. System vs soul, though of course the interstice, the liminal, call it what you will, is a complicated shadow. That sweaty, sulky, delicate night in Kentish Town started a journey that has continued to this day. From bars in Tokyo listening to Leon Thomas, to lining up on Sundays outside Vinyl in the meatpacking district of New York, or to those greeted at the top of the stairs in Soho by Muriel Belcher with the hallowed phrase "Hello, Cunty!", we all heard the welcome of home.

NEIL YOUNG
FINSBURY PARK, LONDON
11 JULY 1993
ALEX BANKS, ART GALLERY CLOTHING

I must admit that I didn't appreciate Neil Young until I was twenty-three; before then he had just been another 'old rocker' (Amusing to think that in 1993, when I saw him in Finsbury Park, he was five years younger than I am now.)

To be honest, like many of my peers on the Mod scene, a lot of my cultural loves have come through Paul Weller leading me in the right direction. On this occasion, I seemed to have tuned my ear to Young just as PW was recording *Wild Wood*, an album heavily influenced by the great Canadian singer-songwriter. In fact, PW's cover of 'Ohio' appear on *The Weaver* EP later in the year, and to me, the universe was aligning and confirming I was going in the right musical direction.

Back to the summer of 1993, when Britpop was in its infancy (although the term was yet to be coined by the media), and my hair was long – longer than Neil Young's. The gig was a day event in Finsbury Park. Watching bands in daylight in the open air is not my favourite way to experience live music, but I went in hope anyway.

Some fans were disappointed that Crazy Horse weren't backing Neil for this gig. More surprisingly, neither were The Stray Gators, who had played on Neil's recently released studio album Harvest Moon and backed Young on his *MTV Unplugged* performance. However, with my Mod roots, I was intrigued that Booker T. & the M.G.'s was the band on the day.

It was an overcast day, if memory serves me right; the type you get a damp backside sitting on the grass, which I'm sure I did. Before the main event, support came from 4 Non Blondes, Teenage Fanclub, James and Pearl Jam. When Neil Young eventually came on stage, the band kicked off, aptly enough, I thought, with 'Mr. Soul', a tune from Neil's in Buffalo Springfield. It was a blistering start to the set and had my pulse racing.

After another tune written in the Springfield era, 'The Loner' (released on Young's first self-titled solo album in 1968), the highlights for me resumed with 'Southern Man', which is still one of my favourite Neil Young songs to this day.

Following 'Helpless', a track that means much more to me as I've grown older, the show continued with another song I love: the powerful 'Like A Hurricane' from the 1977 long player *American Stars 'N Bars*.

Next up was 'Motorcycle Mam', displaying the impressive vocals of Astrid Young (Neil's half-sister) and Nicolette Larson, who would sadly pass away just four years later.

My memory fails me for the next three tunes, 'Love To Burn', 'Separate Ways' and 'Powderfinger'. A mix of unfamiliarity with the songs at the time and alcohol consumption on the day may have had something to do with it. It's worth mentioning that 'Separate Ways', recorded between June 1974 and January 1975 but not released until 2020, would later become my favourite track.

For 'Only Love Can Break Your Heart', a beautiful composition first brought to my attention by Saint Etienne a few years earlier when they covered the song on their album Foxbase Alpha (1991), Neil swapped his guitar for the piano. Next, he took to his acoustic guitar to play a faultless rendition of 'Harvest Moon'. With what seemed like a significant shift in mood, he then went straight into 'The Needle And The Damage Done', a dark and sobering, intimate description of heroin addiction.

Before the encores and after 'Live To Ride', he ended the set with 'Down By The River', another stone-cold classic that had the crowd baying for more. For the first encore we were treated to a cover of the Otis Redding classic '(Sittin' On) The Dock Of The Bay'. It was a truly beautiful rendition, and the fact that three of the backing band – Booker T. Jones, Steve Cropper and Donal 'Duck' Dunn – had played on the original Volt recording made the experience even sweeter. Bob Dylan's 'All Along The Watchtower' followed and was the perfect soundtrack to the day's drab weather. For the finale Neil was joined on stage by Pearl Jam for a triumphant singalong of 'Rockin' In the Free World'. A fitting end to the day and any Pearl Jam fan who had slipped away earlier would have surely come to regret their choice.

What a miserable day for a concert, as the man himself said towards the end of the set. However, I left North London with an uplifted soul, such is the power of great live music.

Over the following years I would collect Neil Young's entire back catalogue, and what a magnificent body of work it is too.

FRANK SINATRA
ROYAL ALBERT HALL, LONDON
31 MAY 1992
MARK BAXTER, AUTHOR/FILM PRODUCTION

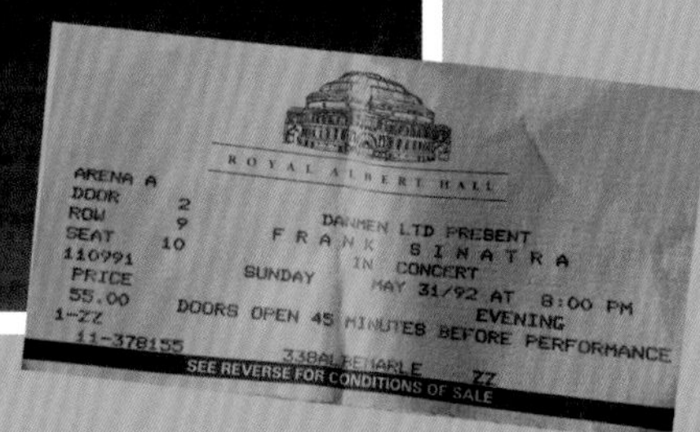

For as far back as I can remember, Sunday mornings in my old family home, reverberated to the sound of my old man warming up his tonsils in preparation for a performance at The Flying Dutchman pub, London SE5 a few hours later. He'd sing along with his mates – Nat, Sammy, Tony and of course Francis Albert – and cover all their great tunes as he limbered up.

From the fragments of mind that are still in working order, I can remember him telling me that as a boy he was soprano in a church choir, so he always had a decent set of pipes, and once his voice had broken, he carried that love of singing on to different places of worship, namely working men's clubs and south-east London boozers. He'd be out a couple of nights' a week and nearly every weekend on a stage somewhere as I grew up. Even on holiday, he'd enter the singing competitions at holiday camps and invariably come in the top three.

From the age of twelve or so I'd be allowed to accompany him on Sunday lunchtime sessions, where, once we'd landed at that particular day's venue, there'd quickly form a queue of men and women by the piano player, all looking to give a song over. They knew they'd all get one song, maybe two if they were any good, and three, if they'd slipped the landlord a couple of quid...

I'd be sitting there with my bags of crisps, a pint of prawns or whelks, and necking the dregs of my dad's numerous bottles of pale ale, having tailor-made Old Holborn smoke blown all over me. When I was caught having a crafty swig, I'd hear, "Oi, bollock chops – school in the morning," before he'd soon forget I was there and I'd be off drinking again.

My favourite venue to go to was the Pembroke Club, which sat just behind the Old Kent Road, as I liked the band that turned up each week to accompany the singers. There was 'Harry the Milkman' on the drums and Mr Patel on the piano. As his name suggests, he was an Indian gentleman and how he ended up playing the Joanna in a back-street drinker in the mid-Seventies is one of life's sweet mysteries.

When he got on stage, my dad would turn slightly to a sort of side-on stance. Some people thought it was because he was a little shy, but actually, it was because of the perforated ear drum (which got him out of National Service, much to his delight) he suffered as a kid. By standing like that he found he could hear the piano better in his 'good' ear.

As I got older, I'd often lay in my bed upstairs on those Sundays, suffering from my previous night's shenanigans, and would try shouting, "Dad, give it a break, dying here mate," but to no avail. He couldn't be stopped; that was his time. In truth, because of the exposure I was then getting to that Great American Songbook, from these wonderful singers, I was finding myself lying there, feeling as sick as a dog, singing along. My personal favourite performer was always Frank Sinatra. On his up-tempo numbers, Frank swung like an outdoor khazi door in a hurricane, and on the slower ballads, he'd break your heart with his tender delivery. He was simply The Guvnor.

Then, in 1992, it was announced that Frank was coming to London to play the Royal Albert Hall. I managed to get four tickets, with the intention of taking my mum, my dad and my Uncle Bob. Bob also sung in clubs and pubs. With him being twenty years younger than the old man, however, his repertoire tended to pull more from the likes of Neil Diamond, Neil Sedaka and Vic Damone. Bob even auditioned for the TV show New Faces, where he used his stage name of Bob Morgan & The Pendants. Sadly, he didn't get selected to appear on telly, and took it very well as I remember: "Fucking carve-up son – there was definitely a fiddle going on." All the members of his band wore pendants, as their name implies, though Bob's was larger than the rest, because he was the frontman. In fact, it was so large, it sort of weighed him down, so he stooped forward as he sung. I reckon someone, somewhere is still trying to work out what happened to their brass lion's head door knocker that was nicked in 1977 – they'd need look no further than around my uncle's neck!

Our big night finally came around and we got there early and hung around the stage door area, along with hundreds of others. Suddenly a black people carrier pulled up and out stepped Frank. "Oi Frank!" shouted my Uncle Bob, as loud as it would humanly be possible to do so. As he did that, I had my camera poised and got a shot of Frank looking round thinking, "Sweet Jesus, what the fuck was that?"

The beautiful Royal Albert Hall then welcomed us in and we found our seats right up in the Gods, as my dear old mum would have called them. In all honesty, it mattered not where we were sitting. The looks of anticipation on the faces of my dad and uncle will never leave me. Finally, Frank wandered out on stage and, yes, he was looking old and a little heavy, and he was using an autocue to remind him of the words, but who gave a fuck, it was Frank 'Flipping' Sinatra!

His first words were, "What are all you people doing in my room?", which brought a round of applause, and then we were off. With Frank's son, Frank Sinatra Jr. leading the orchestra, we were treated to songs like 'A Foggy Day In London Town', 'The Lady Is A Tramp', 'My Funny Valentine', 'The Best Is Yet To Come', 'My Way' and he finished the night with 'New York, New York'.

By then the venue was in raptures, but in truth he could have sung the words out of the Yellow Pages and got the same reaction. This wasn't just your usual gig: this was much deeper than that. No, this was paying homage to a legend, and I don't use that word lightly. To top it off, it also turned out to be Frank's last ever concert in London. Quite a thing to be present at, I think you'll agree.

Sadly, Bob died in March 2022, aged sixty-nine, and he has now joined my old man and mum, Johnny and Jeannie, up in the saloon bar of God's version of The Flying Dutchman, where no doubt him and my dad are queueing up to give a song or three. I sincerely hope they saved me a chair up there, for when my time comes.

THE CLASH
SHEFFIELD TOP RANK
27 JANUARY 1980
TONY BEESLEY, AUTHOR

By the release of *London Calling* (1979), The Clash had become a finely tuned raucous and formidable rock'n'roll band; their star was on the ascendency, touching upon worldwide acclaim. I had all of their records, avidly read their music press interviews and was heavily influenced by their look, often trying to create my own versions of Clash-styled shirts. I would later own Joe Strummer's White Riot Tour shirt, which originated from a girl called Sharon, who had attained it from Joe at a Sheffield Top Rank gig in 1977. I wore that shirt with pride. I was a huge fan. Just one thing was missing for this young teenage Clash City Rocker and that was to be able to see The Clash live on stage. That yearning would soon be fulfilled.

Coinciding with the news of the impending double album, a lengthy quota of tour dates was announced in the music press and I keenly spotted a date for the first month of the new decade at Sheffield Top Rank, a venue I had seen The Damned, 999 and The Stranglers play. I certainly wasn't going to miss this opportunity. Nothing on earth was going to stand in my way.

The tickets were soon snapped up, the excitement dial switched to the max, and when the day arrived, my two mates and I set off to the gig on the number sixty-nine bus to Sheffield. I had dyed my mate's hair blue with food colouring before we set off and later, during the gig, it ran all down his face, the temperature was that hot in the venue. I can still recall that nervous excitement and anticipation on the bus ride to the gig; I was finally going to see my heroes, The Clash.

When we arrived, outside of the venue was packed with punk rockers queuing up, all a good few years older than us three – we being among the youngest punk kids there at a mere fourteen years old. How we managed to get into those scores of gigs back then is a small miracle. Thankfully, we were rarely questioned about our age throughout that time – a period that ranks among the best and most exciting of my life.

On entering, I went to the merch stand and bought a copy of the Clash zine, *The Armagideon Times*. The place was rapidly filling up and the excitement levels were increasing as we stood around listening to the dub reggae being played; a genre we also enjoyed via the likes of Steel Pulse and *The Front Line* compilation LP. Reggae artist Mikey Dread was the support. I hadn't heard him before, but did feel that it added that extra touch to the atmosphere.

Soon afterwards, a few figures appeared on stage dressed in Crombies with collars turned up and bandanas partially covering their faces beneath their trilby-style hats. They joined Mikey Dread, skanking to the reggae sound, and the crowd soon began to realise who these figures were: it was The Clash themselves. The lights went down followed by a short break in the music as the crowd slowly began to cheer and chant in unison, knowing what was to come next. Then… the guitar intro to 'Clash City Rockers' kicked in and the place erupted. The entire venue seemed electrified.

The Clash were dynamic and on fire – I was awestruck! First album faves such as 'Protex Blue', 'Janie Jones', 'Garageland' and 'Police And Thieves' merged with 'Safe European Home', 'Complete Control', 'Tommy Gun', '(White Man) In Hammersmith Palais', and a selection of tracks from the brand new album, *London Calling*, which we were already familiar with and had our own personal favourites. 'Brand New Cadillac' almost blew the roof off, and renditions of 'Spanish Bombs', 'Hateful' and 'Jimmy Jazz' were equally memorable, as was 'Guns of Brixton', when Joe and Paul swapped guitar and vocal duties.

I placed my copy of *The Armagideon Times* under my soaking shirt, as we frantically dived around. It's a wonder I didn't get crushed by the huge, heaving crowd as we were swept along in a wave of packed-tight bodies, yet I was transformed. I felt older than my years and as though this experience was everything my life had been heading towards – an epiphany and a life-defining event. I watched as Joe introduced songs, keeping a keen eye on Mick and Paul, and also Topper back there pounding away at his drum kit: the human drum machine himself. The three-pronged attack of Joe, Mick and Paul, jumping up in the air, swerving and just missing each over, with slashing guitar chords and a thumping bass reverbing out of the huge speaker stacks, this truly was an experience. Visually, The Clash looked amazing too. The punk look had merged with an American rock'n'roll style; they were the epitome of cool as far as I was concerned.

I seem to recall that The Clash finished their encores with 'Armagideon Time', concluding a gig that had completely blown me away with its sheer intensity. The crowd slowly began to filter out of the venue and as we approached the exit, a tough-looking, older punk girl snatched my mate's zine and tore off the back page with Elvis on, scorning the band for the mere association: a sign of the division between their fans, I duly noted. Mine stayed safely tucked under my T-shirt.

We went to that gig as young and naïve punk rock kids obsessed with the music and the do-it-yourself creativity and attitude of the recent punk revolution, and returned with a whole new stance; punk was not so much over in my life, more a case of taking a new direction and having a different mindset. The future was for the taking. That gig and the associated double LP, *London Calling*, along with *Sandinista* which soon followed, completely changed my attitude towards music; they opened me up to so many different musical styles and genres that I had previously been mostly dulled to, or unaware of. The influence on my life is almost indescribable, such was its huge impact. In due course, across time, my tastes would embrace a wide variety of music so tantalisingly eclectic that I would never look back, and much of it thanks to The Clash.

SHARON JONES & THE DAP-KINGS
THE FILLMORE, SAN FRANCISCO
29 MARCH 2014
REUBEN BILLINGHAM, DESIGNER/OWNER ANGLOZINE LONDON

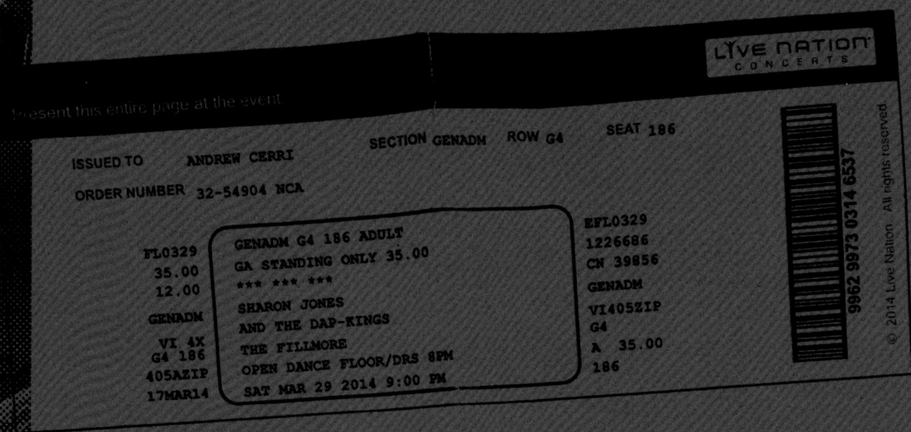

In my infinite wisdom, going to a gig in San Francisco four hours after landing seemed liked the right thing to do. My wife Pascale and I got out of the airport, jumped in the cab and headed to The Phoenix motel in the Tenderloin. There are various stories as to how and why the Tenderloin area got its handle. Most boil down to the fact that the police who worked the area got so much money in bribes, they could eat tenderloin every night. Or for walking the beat in the area, you got a hefty sum of danger money. It was that edgy.

We sort of took it to heed when reading the guidebooks, but I'm a Brummie living in Homerton, East London and so… Looking at the ticket we are not named, and I'm guessing I bought it from a second party sell-on ticket company, fully legit of course. I was most probably toying with the idea for some time about how wise it was to buy a ticket for a gig hours after a transatlantic flight, taking so long to decide that by then the kosher ones had sold out.

A quick shower and change of clobber, and we decided to walk to The Fillmore for the gig. Stretch the legs on the pleasant spring evening after a ten-hour plus flight and to hopefully keep us awake. As the first of San Francisco's hills took us away from the lights of the hotel the street fell darker and tree-lined streets grew thicker, the scent of wet leaves and number ones greeted us. The street community in SF is no laughing matter and a sad tale. Some explain it away as a hangover from the city's hippie past. In an instant, almost hallucinogenic jet-lagged state, we got very windy, sensing imminent danger. Much like the village of the damned, a cracked twig, we spun round and in the street were easily half a dozen humans in crooked silhouettes that were not there a millisecond prior. They were silhouettes, as they seemed to have switched off all of the streetlights with only a back-lit moon to guide us. Terrorised, we picked up the pace to The Fillmore. The first pint did not touch the sides.

Once suitably medicated at the Fillmore bar, we headed up to the gallery at the iconic venue to check out the famous film poster archive, the swirly Day-Glo artwork for The Who, The Yardbirds, Otis and the Grateful Dead further playing havoc with our jet lag-addled brains.

The gig, as you'd expect, was superb. Having seen Sharon Jones many times, she never ceased to amaze. There were no seats in the stalls, and the bouncers wouldn't let us lean on the bins to rest our weary legs, so we danced – sort of. For those lucky enough to have seen the excellent Sharon Jones & The Dap-Kings live, you will know that the woman was an absolute force of nature, and no song was a dud. I'm pretty sure she's the only act that has successfully managed to muster crowd 'participation' out of me, and in honour of her passing I promised never to holler or clap above my head ever again – thanks Sharon.

Naturally we got a cab back to the Phoenix motel after the gig to avoid the village of the damned, and enjoyed the rest of our trip along the Californian coast. When we got back to London – again suffering from jet lag on the Sunday sofa – news of another Sharon Jones gig popped up on our Instagram feed (we'd only landed in the UK that very morning, so a pattern was developing – surely a sign?). Sharon and a handful of The Dap-Kings were doing an impromptu gig at Rough Trade East that afternoon. The record shop was just five bus stops away from our home – so we got a cab, just in case.

There were maybe forty people in the store's stage area, and we seemed to know half of the room. The gig was short and sweet. Sharon was there to promote the latest album, Give The People What They Want, and she also did a Q&A and album signing. We dutifully bought a second LP to get signed and waited to meet the well-travelled singer. While having our selfie taken, we explained we'd seen her at the San Francisco Fillmore ten days before. My wife nodded at her in a confirming the fact manner, while taking the iPhone shot. Sharon pulled the same horrified face I pulled on that first evening stroll in the Tenderloin – security!

BOB MARLEY & THE WAILERS
HAMMERSMITH ODEON, LONDON
16 JUNE 1976
PEARL BOATSWAIN, AKA DUBPLATE PEARL, DJ

I grew up with music; there was always music in the house. On weekends after work, my dad, who was a builder, would go to the pub and afterwards he'd come home and play his Ray Charles records on the old-fashioned GEC radiogram, LOUD! My mum worked part-time when we were at primary school, and we'd go home for lunch and she'd have the radio on. So wherever we were, there'd be music. Added to that, there was the music I heard at weddings, christenings, so music was all around. This was the ska era, then rocksteady, then into the reggae. I also grew up listening to pop music, with my mum being a Beatles fan, though her favourite artist is Rod Stewart. The first soul single I bought was 'Sugar Pie Guy' by The Joneses, and the first soul album was *Keep On Steppin* by The Fatback Band in 1974, which had 'Wicky Wacky' on it. I bought the album with money I received for my birthday.

DJing started for me by chance. I would often visit my friends Ossie and Lennox, who had a in Shepherds Bush, where I would take some records – mainly soul and jazz. Ossie is a big soul and jazz DJ, and Lennox was really into reggae. They'd organised a dance in Hammersmith and asked me if I wanted to do the warm-up. I put them off for as long as I could, but then I got cornered by Lennox (RIP), and I said OK, I'll do it. So, I did the two-hour warm-up, and I was the only female. The other DJs on the night kept saying they had no idea I had those kinds of records, because me being a girl they'd expect you to have soft, lovey-dovey type tunes, but I had hardcore stuff. Even today, when I play out, I get guys saying how come she's got those records? I'm representing the females!

From the mid-Seventies, I was heavily into reggae, then had a break when the music changed in the mid-Eighties, but commenced buying again once I started DJing in 2012. I grew up in West London, with guys in sound systems, and I used to go to loads of concerts. I also listened to pirate stations coming out of South and West London. Some of my friends now say, "Pearl, we can't understand how you ended up in that sort of culture." But I grew up with two families who lived on the same road, and in those days they all wanted to build their own sound systems. One family, the Frasers, had a sound system that regularly played in Acton Town Hall. They asked me along to one of the events. I had to ask my dad first for permission – I told him that Tyrone was going and when we come back, we'll come back together. That was the only way I could attend. So, I went early and helped them wire up, or "string up" as they called it back then. What an experience.

I've been attending the Notting Hill Carnival since the early Seventies with my parents, but in 1974 I went with friends instead; this was around the time when sound systems were introduced to the carnival and I thought, "this is where I want to be".

The Bob Marley concert came back to me as soon as I was asked to contribute to this book, because of my proximity to Bob on the night. I was basically on the stage.

I went to the concert – one of three shows at the Hammersmith Odeon – by myself, as I couldn't get anyone to come with me. I was seventeen, eighteen at the time – kind of nervous. I was in sixth form or maybe just left. I was thinking that people would stare at me, wondering why I was on my own. But when I think back, no one said anything. Because we lived in Shepherds Bush and the Hammersmith Odeon was just down the road, I used to walk it. Concerts in those days used to finish around 11 p.m., so I got a bus straight home afterwards.

I had thought this gig was later, 1980 or so, but turns out it was actually 1976. The tour was for the *Rastaman Vibration* LP, which I have and it's my absolute favourite Bob Marley album. This was a big album and a big thing at the time. It was all going on that year. We had the hot weather, the riots at the carnival and there was a lot of tension – rather tough. I had strong parents and they gave me good guidance, though I wasn't so much overprotected (although I was speaking to my dad last night; he's in his eighties now and he still thinks he can tell me what to do!).

I can still see myself on the right-hand side of the stage for that gig, standing by the speakers. I didn't have a seat; the stalls were cheaper than the rest of the theatre, so I got in for something like £2 or £3. I even remember what I was wearing: a white sweatshirt, with a number one on the back, and flared jeans and platforms. I was looking up at Bob Marley and The I-Threes (the all-female singing group that backed Bob) on the stage and I had a great vantage point. Bob did quite a few tracks from the album, but he didn't do my favourite track, 'Johnny Was', so I was quite disappointed. I can still remember him walking on stage with The Wailers.

You can't beat the sound quality at Hammersmith Odeon – you still can't, actually. The atmosphere was electric, and it wasn't one race or the other, it was really mixed. It was also packed and it was hot. It was such a brilliant concert. When you heard Bob sing, it was just like the records. Just brilliant – my number one reggae concert, ever.

On our way out of the auditorium, after the gig, the track 'Johnny Was' played out on the PA. I remember sitting there listening to it as everyone was leaving. I also remember getting a poster on the night and a drawing of Bob, which my brother still has.

BLACK SABBATH/FAITH NO MORE
MOTÖRHEAD/SOUNDGARDEN
HYDE PARK, LONDON
4 JULY 2014
FIONA BRENNAN,
EX-SOUTHERN STUDIO MANAGER

Like many of the people you'll come across in this book, live music has been a huge part of my life since I was a teenager. It's far too difficult to name one ticket stub that made the biggest impact on my life.

It would be easy to talk about stepping into the throngs of my first live show, aged thirteen, in the impressive St George's Hall in my hometown of Bradford. It was the late Nineties and Terrorvision were playing a homecoming gig, thrashing about on stage to their latest – and most popular – songs.

Or how three years later, I'd attend that same venue to see the American nu-metal band Fear Factory play, where I'd also meet the man who would later become my husband.

I could also talk about how, in 2005, I sat with my future husband on the hill at Glastonbury, watching Brian Wilson play in the glorious sunshine as it dried up another year of mud. A festival that marks a coming of age for me when, two weeks later on 7 July 2005, I step on to a Piccadilly Line train that would not make it past Russell Square in one of the most notorious terror attacks on British soil.

Instead, I feel the most notable live show that is seared into my memory is the British Summer Time gig in Hyde Park on 4 July 2014.

It was billed at the time as Black Sabbath's last ever live show. It wasn't. However, it was my only time I saw two of the bands on the bill perform live: Motörhead and Soundgarden.

I'm much more at ease at small gigs in the back room of an East London pub than I am at big corporate events. Preferring the better sound and intimate nature of smaller shows, I tend to keep any ticket stubs I get because you never know which support band might go on to do great things. And it's fun to look back and see who you saw before they "made it big".

Also, I worked in the music industry during most of my time living in London. Gig tickets were swiftly replaced by a guest pass stamp on the hand or sticker attached to my jeans. But the line-up of Sabbath, Faith No More, Mötörhead and Soundgarden playing their seminal album *Superunknown* (1994) in full, was a big enough pull to spend a day drinking overpriced lager in Hyde Park.

We bought the tickets nearly a year before the performance date, so it was less than ideal that I was thirty-nine weeks pregnant with my second child by the time the show came around. However, I'd spent most of my first pregnancy watching underground bands play in shoebox venues across the city, where your trainers made Velcro with the floor. Spending the hottest day of the year in Hyde Park where I could sit and hop on the Tube back home was an easy decision.

We arrived as Motörhead smashed through their pneumatic set. Lemmy pressed against the microphone like it was holding him up. They were seasoned performers, rhythmically moving through their set in the blazing heat.

Faith No More were next to take the stage. Another band on the wish list of wanting to see them live but never expecting it to happen. We moved nearer the stage as the crowd filled up around us. It was by this point that the heaviness of my pregnant belly started to feel the gentle pull of gravity. A tightening of my skin and feeling my unborn daughter move to the music – or so I thought at the time.

Soundgarden took to the stage. This was really why I made the hour-long Tube ride to the show. Watching Chris Cornell belt out *Superunknown* from start to finish is a moment I hope to remember for life. As the chords to '4th Of July' started to play out, strangers in the crowd were approaching to ask if I might actually give birth on that date.

I laughed it off, blissfully unaware that early labour was already in motion.

As the sunset and Black Sabbath opened the not-quite final set of their careers, I bumped into an ex-colleague who was surprised to see me at the show. She laughed at my friends storing their pints of beer under my bump – no one is going to knock into the pregnant woman.

Sabbath are ultimate professionals, and this being the third time I'd seen them live, they made the day of standing worthwhile. As the fireworks exploded and the crowd dispersed, we moved off on to packed Tube trains, to make our way back home to North London. The plan was to get off at Finsbury Park and take a taxi the rest of the way. By this point, I was exhausted, with a full-term baby kicking away. I needed my home and sleep.

But ours was not the only festival on that day. As we reached our destination, we were unaware that another event was taking place in the North London park. Instead of an easy journey home by taxi, we were met with crowds of partying teenagers and a slow three-mile walk home. With the songs of Sabbath still ringing in our ears, we walked slowly up from Finsbury Park, through Crouch End and up Muswell Hill to get back in the early hours. As my daughter lay heavy against my hips, I was still happy to have spent the day watching some of the most iconic rock and metal bands perform.

My first thought when I woke the next morning was, "Whatever happens, child, do not turn up today. I am exhausted." Yet, that wasn't to be. Within an hour of waking, it was clear my daughter was very much on her way.

The first challenge was asking my mother-in-law to leave, so I could give birth. Something I'm not entirely sure she's forgiven me for yet. Then we had to prepare for the home birth. But contractions were coming thick and fast.

There was always a worry that I'd go into full labour at the gig itself. Our back-up plan had been to get a taxi home. In hindsight, that was stupid: it took a little over an hour for my daughter to arrive in the world. My husband delivered her as four midwives and two ambulances arrived at our home, a little too late to help.

Even now, as I tell my daughter what I was doing the day before she was born, I remind her to take the opportunities when they come. You never know when it's the last chance to see your favourite band play their iconic album in full. You never know when the last show truly is. They may play again, or tragedy might strike.

It's for this reason that the British Summer Time gig is the strongest memory for me. I could have easily not gone, put my feet up at home and given birth the next day feeling refreshed and ready. But I much prefer knowing that I went into having taken the chance to be moved by great musicians. Even if I didn't know then, it would be the last time I'd ever see some of them perform.

CYPRESS HILL
VENUE UNKNOWN, SAN DIEGO
FEBRUARY 1996
DENISE BURKE, HAIRDRESSER EXTRAORDINAIRE & DAVID BURKE, M.D. OF BIFF BANG POW WEB DEVELOPMENT

"Spread your arms and legs, mam!", the first words said to us in the parking lot of the venue, downtown San Diego.

"Goodness, that's the best offer she's had all week." Silence. I wouldn't say the doorman glared at me from his 6ft 7in vantage point, more fixed me with a look of contempt mixed with pity at my ill-advised stab at humour!

After enduring a search that almost made my eyes water, and as neither I nor my beautiful then-girlfriend (now even more beautiful wife) Denise had anything of interest secreted about our persons, we were admitted, albeit to some rather odd looks from both security and fellow punters! It was beginning to dawn on us that the core fanbase of Cypress Hill tended not to wear red, white and blue cycling tops (her) or black and gold Fred Perrys coupled with light blue mohair slacks (your humble narrator). Still, no matter; we strode into the venue like Dicky and Lizzy Burton, all British glamour and bad teeth cast asunder in hedonistic California.

On entering the auditorium, we were somewhat stunned to see, or rather smell, that the frisk was obviously not for drugs, as it would have been back home in Blighty at the WAG or Cool Kat or even Funkin' Pussy, but for weapons. This observation was reinforced on site by the large floor-standing bongs the audience were happily hitting on, accompanied by a thick haze of smoke akin to what you'd find in a Regal cinema circa 1975.

Let's step back and put some context around this. What are two pasty English kids doing rocking up to see Cypress Hill so far from home, I hear you cogitating. Well, dear readers, the good lady and I had left our decently paid jobs back in the homeland and, having grown up on a diet of *Kojak*, *Charlies' Angels* and *The Towering Inferno*, decided that what we needed, before we became geriatric has-beens, was to embark on a road trip around the good old US of A. To that end we had beamed down a few weeks earlier into The City of Angels via LAX, which, having never been further than Malaga, was like landing on another planet. We loved LA. Man. We. Loved it.

We went out on The Strip and followed the stars of Belushi, Monroe et al, and man we loved LA! We walked everywhere. We regularly got stopped by cops asking why we were walking, but we just kept on walking. We couldn't stay in LA forever, though (could we? Should we have?).

Hence a few weeks later you find your intrepid travellers heading away from San Fran (a tad disappointing, if I'm being honest; all stained loon pants mingled with faded dreams of free love) and diving headlong back down that beautiful ribbon of a road Highway 1, or PCH, and surfacing in San Diego. Well, all I can say is they don't make burritos like that in Hounslow. $1 of pure heaven in a tortilla! We were getting into the Hispanic mood.

Now, I have always thought those guys and gals looked real sharp and very cool. Maybe not sharp like you or I might check with, but none the less they look good. Hispanic people love their clothes, those Cuban four-pocket shirts, ironed, buttoned up to the collar. They cherish their wheels, too; loads of chrome, loads of love – you get the vibe. The good lady and I were deep into early Nineties hip hop at the time and best of all were Cypress Hill. We'd been listening to their eponymous debut album since 1991 and when Black Sunday hit the decks in '93, we just ate that up! It mixed well with early acid jazz, it sampled Motown and funk, Dusty, Curtis and Stevie. I don't want to be a museum piece; Modernism isn't about the past, it's about now – and back then, they were now. It worked on every level.

Check the scene. You find us lounging one afternoon at our motel (I did actually think I was Hutch, not Starsky!), scanning the small ads, and lo, a very small ad indeed did say to us, "Tonight Only – Cypress Hill performing a warm-up show pre their national tour… pay on the door". Oh my God, The Pharcyde are supporting! I may just have died and gone to hip hop heaven.

Fast forward.

After much deliberation on what to wear, does my hair look good, are my sideburns too long (me, not Denise, cheeky!), we set off in the Ford Taurus to downtown San Diego – well, a large semi-deserted industrial estate, inhabited on this occasion by a motley assortment of 'gangbangers' (I do find that a rather confusing descriptive term) and more mainstream fans who although dressed fairly conservatively, still looked somewhat different to us!

Having now caught up you join us back in the venue, with the Pharcyde assaulting our senses. We'd been digging them since hearing their debut album *Bizarre Ride II The Pharcyde* (1992), a crazy mix of hip hop and psychedelia which, looking back at the times, makes perfect sense, but then it all felt new and different. A top support, but the main act were heading our way and let me tell you, people, the crowd were up and ready. Blunts at the double, they hit the stage hard!

Now, while all the feverish toking and general head nodding was occurring, I had noticed a large, slow-moving gent eyeballing myself and the good lady. He appeared to me a strange mix of Cheech Marin and Private Joe Walker from *Dad's Army*. He had the look of a Hispanic gangbanger, but he was wearing what looked like a 1940s Harris Tweed overcoat. He smiled, I smiled, he glided over.

"Hola amigo."

"All right mate," I squeaked, sounding like a nervous Dick Van Dyke.

Glassy eyed and grinning broadly, he opened his overcoat and, there inside, pinned in nice neat rows from armpit to floor, were bags of what appeared, to my untrained eye, to be dried worms.

"Why is he selling us bags of worms, love?" said Denise, sweetly. "They're magic mushrooms, you knob!"

"You want to buy some 'shrooms amigo? They're good shit, man!"

Now, I'm no preacher of abstinence and certainly no killjoy, however two things occurred to me. One, we were on our own in this place and two, looking at the state Walker was clearly in, if I imbibed said 'shrooms I may simply keel over and expire on the spot. It felt too far from Feltham to be carried out, toes curled up on a bad trip. We declined his kind offer, which he accepted with good grace and he floated away to ply his trade with other, more hardened heads.

However, either due to his altered state or possibly poor map reading abilities, rather than moving away from us he went round and round in ever decreasing circles, asking us and our near neighbours again and again if we wanted these 'shrooms. I don't believe he ever moved more than twenty feet from us, but every time he saw us it was, for him, the first time.

Eyes front, Cypress Hill are doing what they do. The crowd are up and so are we! B-Real giving it large about East Side, West Side and we were in the zone. At "Hands up, West Side!" the place went mental. "Hands up East Side!"… now, our home across the pond at that time was Oxford, and we were proud to come from East Oxford, home of Supergrass, The Candyskins etc. So, being English and having both grown up on the North Bank, Highbury, we love a good chant.

"East Side, East Side" …

Silence. We were the only ones shouting for the East Sid… realising too late we were on the West Coast, like virgin fans wearing away colours in the home pub, for the first time we were worried. Our lone chanting had attracted much attention. Our neighbours looked over at us, me resplendent in bowling shoes and Tootal scarf, madam in DM shoes and Levi's, and I swear I saw pity in their eyes. Laughing, they turned back to the stage and began barracking the band about Ice Cube and other East Coast/West Coast rivalries. It kicked off, as I suppose we always knew it would. It wasn't Brighton '64 or Great Yarmouth '80, but it was boisterous and 'lively', and it can't be denied it was a great buzz up there, if you know what I mean! As we and the rest of the crowd were bundled out by the 6ft 7in security detail, Cypress Hill were still playing, I believe 'Pigs' off the first album.

Jumping into the Taurus and squealing away like Cagney and Lacey, we knew even then that one day our story of the secret Cypress Hill gig would need to be told. What we didn't know was our next gig – Kermit Ruffins at The Little People's Place in New Orleans – would be even more fun.

Keep the faith, kiddos!

We were clued in to The Andy Williams Show, a must-see on a Monday night. On this particular evening, Mum let us stay up a little bit longer than usual, as a new group was going to be on the show. She'd been clued in by her Afro-Caribbean work mates, at the Nestlé factory in Hayes, Middlesex. That night changed my life, literally. I saw five boys who looked like me. I wanted to be one of them. After seeing The Jackson 5, I stopped cutting my hair and with my mum's permission, and within the budget, started choosing my own clothes.

Jackson
Five
5 ARE COMING
Appearing at:
Monday 30th October
Royal Variety Performance
Also Available
Released on October 27th
Jackson Five ... Lookin' Through The Windows TMG833
and Released on November 10th.
EMI

Jackson 5
And Supporting Artists
SUNDAY 12th NOVEMBER
1 SHOW: 7·00pm
Empire Pool, Wembley

THE JACKSON 5
EMPIRE POOL, WEMBLEY, LONDON
12 NOVEMBER 1972
CLINTON CAMBRIDGE, DRESSER

Not long after we moved to East Avenue, where my mum still lives, and I met a kindred spirit in Robert Reed. We became friends because we were always subs for Sandgate Minors FC and never got much of a game. So, Monday nights became an unofficial music night. We would buy records from Rowley's, where Robert's sister, Lorraine, had a part-time job.

Living in Hayes, we were very near Heathrow airport, and we cycled up on our bikes to the Queens Building, an office building next to Terminal 2, to see The Jackson 5 and The Osmonds fly in. Now, as an older person, I understand Beatlemania, Rollermania and any 'mania' for subsequent boy bands because when we arrived at Heathrow, it was electric. Thousands upon thousands of people, mainly girls, were there, screaming and shouting for their idols.

Rob and I both became Jackson 5 nuts! Between us, we bought every bit of music the group produced, and I mean everything! As a gift, a few years ago, someone bought me the complete Jackson 5 cartoon series on video, which I treasure, even though I can no longer play it (since I no longer have a VHS) – it takes me right back to Saturday mornings as a youngster.

I don't envy anyone but have to admit at being extremely jealous of Rob back then, because he sneakily found out he was getting the Jackson 5 Christmas album as one of his gifts. Rob's parents were very tolerant, as we would blast Jackson 5 records from his bedroom the entire time we were there, and they never said a word.

Then, one afternoon during the week at Rob's house, his dad took us into the living room and said to us, "How would you like to go to see the Jackson 5? But Clinton, you have to ask your Mum is if it's okay for you to go first." If I could recreate a moment of euphoria, apart from my children being born, that would be it!

When the time came, Rob's dad took us on two buses to The Empire Pool in Wembley (today it's known as Wembley Arena), and while he went for a drink in the pub, we went into the venue. I can clearly remember the support act being a group called The Sisters Love, because my mum had some of their records at home.

If I'm being honest, you couldn't hear much. But it didn't matter – we had their records! The buzz I got was incredible; the Jacksons just had to move a finger and the girls screamed. I remember them playing their version of 'Papa Was A Rolling Stone' as well as my favourite song, 'The Love You Save'. Rob and I couldn't stop grinning.

As you can see, I still have the ticket stub, and that is something I will always treasure. Seeing those five boys, looking like us up on stage, was an epiphany for two thirteen-year-old boys.

An added bonus was I noticed that girls started to pay me more attention; they couldn't get Michael, Marlon, Jermain, Jackie or Tito, but there was me, Barry, Lawrence and Roland with the biggest afros, until Angus came along and out-afro'd us all!

The concert was over in the blink of an eye, but that feeling has stayed with me for fifty years. Years later I got to meet Tito Jackson, who signed the T-shirt I had held on to since my teenage years.

And do you know what? Hearing The Jackson 5 still makes me think of the odours emitting from the large factory that dominated the Hayes area, where you knew it was going to rain just by the smell of the coffee wafting across the town.

Gilt-edged memories.

SEX PISTOLS
100 CLUB, LONDON
31 AUGUST 1976
STEVE 'TUFTY' CARVER
RETIRED PUNK ROCKER

Summer 1976.

I was bored, my life had descended into going down the pub, drinking lots of beer and playing cards or darts (dominoes was waiting in the wings). I had started to notice a certain type of older gentleman, dressed in brown suit (with flared trousers) and tie, supping brown ale, pale ale, light ale or bitter. Was this my future, I wondered?

My boredom was only alleviated by the occasional gig at Guildford Civic Hall or Hammersmith Odeon (I still refuse to call it Labatt's Apollo), or the long-gone Rainbow Theatre in Finsbury Park. I was a fan of Bowie, Roxy, Mott and Alice, but you had to buy the tickets in June for a concert in bloody October for bands like of that calibre. Some of my mates were getting married. I was only twenty-one; I couldn't see me settling down with a mortgage and a kid just yet. I knew I wanted more.

I was an avid music paper reader, and one Thursday I saw a headline that grabbed me by the bollocks – "Terrorise your fans the Sex Pistols way". Underneath was a photograph of a young band "beating up their audience". I studied it for hours. I just had to see this group.

Right on cue I got a new neighbour, a guy called Paul Weller who'd moved from nearby Stanley Road into the house at the bottom of our garden. That weekend I introduced myself and we hit it off immediately (it turns out he was in a local band). "Have you heard of the Sex Pistols mate? Do you fancy coming to see them on Tuesday?" That Saturday night in the boozer changed my life, forever.

It seems almost insane now, forty-six years later, that we were willing to jump on a train from Woking and head all the way to a club in Oxford Street, London, on a school night, to check out what was essentially an unsigned pub-rock band. I hadn't heard the Pistols play a single note. I was basing my faith on a solitary black and white photograph and gut instinct.

Down the steep stairs into the 100 Club, where bands play on a small stage in a cellar. Strangely, the place smelled of Chinese food, due to a takeaway hatch at the end of the bar. The back of the stage was adorned with flyers for upcoming gigs: Acker Bilk,

Kenny Ball, and other assorted jazz bands. But one look at the punters assured me that the assembled throng were not here to hear Ken Colyer or Ronnie Scott. The audience this night were young – all under twenty-five. Most of the girls had cropped, coloured hair, some of the more extreme fans were (un)dressed in stockings/rubber/fetish clobber, many with homemade graffiti-covered ripped T-shirts. I noticed two members of the support band, Jones and Strummer of The Clash (I had seen a pic in the music paper *Sounds*) posing and looking uber-cool in paint-splattered urban guerrilla street-chic.

Then I saw Johnny Rotten. He was wearing a jacket that looked like it had been rejected by a backstreet Oxfam charity shop, but now rescued and recycled. It was dripping with chains, paper clips, bulldog clips, safety pins and crucifixes. His legs seemed to be strapped together in some sort of makeshift bondage. His bright orange hair appeared to have been attacked and hacked with a razor blade (maybe the one hanging from his earlobe!) into a strange, post-apocalyptic mutation of a Ziggy Stardust 'do. I can honestly say I had never seen anyone who looked anything like that. He looked like nothing on Earth.

The band sauntered through the audience and climbed onstage (there was no backstage dressing room at the 100 Club back then). Johnny removed his jacket, and I could now see he was wearing a complete SEX bondage suit, (SEX, the infamous shop on the King's Road, Chelsea owned by Vivienne and Malcolm) and his arms covered in cigarette burns, which were also restricted!

His posture was slightly hunched. His complexion pallid. He blew his nose into a clean white handkerchief and glared into the crowd, surveying the faces with a mixture of suspicion and contempt.

"GET OFF YOUR ARSES!!!"

Straight into 'Anarchy In The UK'.

I wasn't sure quite what to expect, but the Sex Pistols sound was exactly what I imagined, hoped, wanted. It was explosive, threatening, aggressive, violent. A gurgling bloody mess of noise.

The fans responded immediately; the place became one heaving, sweaty mass. Pushing and shoving, bouncing and (pogo) dancing. I couldn't take my eyes off Rotten. Whatever the 'X factor' is, this guy had it in spades – twisting and turning, spinning and marching, sneering and scowling, hanging off his microphone stand and continuously scanning the audience with his demented laser stare.

OK! No one could accuse the singer of sounding like Plácido Domingo or Pavarotti. Screeching, screaming, growling and whooping, his voice was primal, tortured, guttural. Arsenal's answer to Iggy Pop swapping smack and Valium for cheap lager and speed.

"...DESTROY...!!!"

The song finished. I was hooked. Suddenly everything else seemed a hundred years out of date.

"If you can put up with THAT, you can put up with ANTHING!", John mocked.

Some of the songs they played were immediately recognisable: The Monkees' '(I'm Not Your) Steppin' Stone,' the Small Faces' 'Whatcha Gonna Do About It' ("I want you to know that I HATE you, baby"), The Who's 'Substitute' ("I see right through your WANKER'S mac"), and the set was splattered with original songs: 'Pretty Vacant', 'Problems', 'Liar', 'Submission', 'Satellite' and 'Seventeen', and a quartet of negative numbers: 'NO Fun', 'NO Feelings', 'Don't Give Me NO Lip Child' and 'NO Future', or 'God Sa100 ve The Queen' as it became.

It was glorious. I was stunned by the intensity of the band, the anger and the energy, the filth and the fury. I got the distinct impression that they genuinely didn't care if you liked them or not.

"I am not here for your amusement; you are here for mine."

These four snotty-nosed *punks* from Shepherds Bush and Finsbury Park weren't playing FOR YOU, they were playing AT YOU! A big, bad, beautiful (ugly) noise. I remember thinking I am seeing history being made, right here, right now. I had a new favourite band, and I had only seen them once! (I hadn't witnessed The Jam yet).

With the feedback ringing in our ears and sweat running down our backs, we left the club. I picked up a xeroxed newsletter – *Pistols in (Chelmsford) Prison*, it screamed. I also bought an *Anarchy In The UK* newspaper (blimey, these guys are organised!).

On the journey home we talked non-stop about what we had just experienced. Although it's fair to say a couple of my mates (there were four of us there that night, RIP Dave and Tony) preferred The Clash, the next day I honestly would have swapped my entire (redundant) record collection for a Sex Pistols LP (still a year away), and I grabbed a pair of scissors and started chopping at my hair. I was quite pleased with the result, but Paul remarked that it was all "tufty", resulting in a nickname that has stuck with me for forty-five years!

We became *those punks from Woking*. Between us we wrote a fanzine, but being a bunch of lazy sods, we didn't bother to print or publish the damn thing (wish I had a copy). And within a month we were back in Soho for the 100 Club Punk Rock Festival. And yes, I know if everyone who claims to be at the 100 Club that day were telling the truth you could fill Shea Stadium, but I swear, The Woking Contingent were there.

And if you don't believe me, ask Mr Weller. One day, I will tell you how his band got on...

THE STONE ROSES
HEATON PARK, MANCHESTER
29 JUNE 2012
ROBERT CHAMBERS,
EDITOR OF PANINARO MAGAZINE

For me, football and music have always been inexplicably interlinked. Both have played a major part in my life, more or less running side by side, taking me on some fantastic adventures. Some football matches are like the best gigs, and some gigs resemble the atmosphere at some of the best games I've been to. Both as close to a religious experience as this non-believer will get.

Paul Weller once said, "When I was growing up, the cultural reference points that defined your character were music, clothes and football." As a 15-year-old, I was obsessed with Weller and The Jam. A little bit wet behind the ears, I had yet to learn about the holy trinity of Music, Football and Fashion. On Saturday 9 June 1990 that all changed.

Back then I was about to fly out to the United States to play in a football tournament. Among some of the older boys there was chat of disappointment. Some of them were missing the gig of the year less than a mile from Celtic Park, where we were boarding a bus that would take us to Glasgow airport. This was all new to me. I had never been out of the UK. I had never been to a gig. The Stone Roses had just performed at Spike Island and were now in town playing Glasgow Green that day. At this point I knew fuck all about the Roses. I was getting my musical kicks in my bedroom, listening to my older brother's vinyl records. Like I said, I was obsessed with Weller and The Jam. However, it was 1990, and I felt I needed a band of my own.

The cassette tape I bought of the Stone Roses' eponymous debut album became the soundtrack of that summer in the States. By the time I got back to Glasgow, everything changed. My mind wasn't really on becoming a footballer. I was following something, a paid-up member of the Stone Roses FC. I was in. The music, the Jackson Pollock-inspired artwork, the 1968 Paris Riots. I was consuming it all.

Then click. Music. Football. Fashion.

Weirdly, I missed a gig from a band I didn't even know. But till this day, that gig at Glasgow Green is the one gig I wish I'd attended.

Thirty years came and went. Thatcher got binned. Tony Blair became her greatest achievement. Manchester United won their first title in twenty-six years. Oasis and Britpop rose and fell away. The Roses disappeared up their own arse. Brown had his solo hits. Squire fronted The Seahorses and Mani joined Primal Scream. All in all, their legend lived on.

I was like the rest of us and never thought we would get the chance to see them perform live. Then one day, out the blue, Brown and Squire kissed and made up and The Stone Fucking Roses were back on.

Tickets! How do I get my hands on a ticket?

The Roses announced a weekend gig at Heaton Park in Manchester. Every cunt I knew was out to get tickets. I was making deals with everyone. As it happens, I did have to sell my soul.

And then. Fuck. Cunt. Bastard. Lady Luck wasn't shining on me that day. Tickets sold out in a matter of minutes, and I had not managed to score. Still, the gig was nearly a year away; I had faith in the beautiful universe.

Probably my favourite gig of all time was seeing an ageing Rolling Stones at Hyde Park, or the time my girlfriend and I saw Iggy Pop in the desert at Joshua Tree. Or the time I popped half a pill and saw Primal Scream doing *Screamadelica* at the best venue in the world, Glasgow Barrowlands. All amazing in their own right.

However. Walking to Heaton Park that Saturday night with a group of mates. The hairs on my arm having an erection. The buzz. The sense of togetherness that a sea of people was creating. Then the first few chords of Mani's bass. This shit was real. It was happening. Thirty years on, Reni was still a master of his craft.

A magical night. Oh. Yeh. I got tickets. I ended up with a few.

I was back again on the Sunday night. This time with my girlfriend and my mate Gerry. Gerry had a few quid on Italy to win the Euros. That night they were playing Spain, probably at that time the best team on the planet. As we passed one of the guys from the Inspiral Carpets, we decided to visit the local bookies and throw some more money on Italy. I forget what we stood to win. Gerry was in for a penny, in for a pound. He had turned up at Heaton Park with 100 eccies, I think everything went on the Azzuri.

Brown. Mani. Squire. Reni. They were everything I wanted in a band. We buried ourselves in the crowd and enjoyed the music. What a night. A quick check on the match, 2-0 Italy. Fuckin Yess!!!

To this day I swear my eyes saw 2-0 Italy. We celebrated and celebrated. Hooking up with the rest of the gang in the small hours we found out the actual score. Spain 4, Italy 0.

After that, the Roses continued their tour, adding another comeback a year or so later. Everything went flat. There was no new music. No Second Coming. It was done. In the bin. Still the ticket I wish I had will always be for Glasgow Green 1990, but Heaton Park was a glimpse of what could have been, even if Iniesta and Xavi tried to spoil it.

JARVIS COCKER
PATTERNS, BRIGHTON
26 MARCH 2018
LUCIENNE COLE, ARTIST

On the morning of 26 March 2018, my phone went 'ping'.

"Jarvis would like to invite you to a gig he's doing in Brighton tonight. Let me know if you want to go."

!!

My boyfriend was away. My mate Liz, also a bit of a Jarvis devotee, was too busy with work. A person I hadn't seen for ages, who lived in Brighton and would've jumped at the chance, turned out had just moved to Dorset. Oh, and I had a bad back. What to do?

My boyfriend rang me.

"Have you booked a train ticket yet? Do it! You've got to go, Luce! You'll kick yourself if you don't."

I did it – with enough time to mooch round a couple of record shops and buy a birthday present to myself (a Maxine Brown Kent LP I didn't have and should've bought years before when I'd seen it in a market in Huddersfield, and an unusual Latin soul 45). Oh yes, did I mention it was my birthday in three days? So, you know, it felt like a gift.

I hung out at the old slot machines on the marina opposite the venue, waiting for them to open the doors because quite frankly I couldn't stand in a queue for too long on account of the fact my back was killing me.

Patterns turned out to be a small, dark basement. Perfect. I got myself a beer and sat down on the bench seats along the back wall, watching as people quickly filled up the place with so much anticipation. The atmosphere was great, not quite knowing what to expect.

I'll tell you now I couldn't stay sitting down for long. I figured if I kept moving my back might hold out and, by golly, from the moment they started I almost forgot about my bad back completely!

Jarvis was right THERE. Literally. There was just this weird sort of wire fence thing that came up to your middle between him and us – people were right up against it. At one point he climbed up on it, crouching, with one arm reaching up to touch the ceiling as support.

If you've ever seen Jarvis live, you'll know how much charisma this man has, but it's never ever overblown, if you get what I mean. It's just *there.* He puts every inch of himself into his performance. From the moment he steps out, he creates such intimacy and warmth as well as excitement, and takes you through every emotional ride. He's such a wonderful raconteur and very funny, open and insightful. This particular show, he told us, was one of several small gigs for fans where he was trying out some new stuff with a new bunch of (excellent) musicians that might become a record. It felt quite a privilege and special to be there. He went on to talk about the new songs, about getting older and what was happening in the world.

And what relevance! I think he's always been someone with great motivation, passion and relevance. And MOVES. This man has all the right moves. I was particularly taken with the magnificence of his opening song 'I Am Pharoah'– great timing and statuesque poses, just brilliant.

Fifth on the set list was 'Must I Evolve',

A really exciting song – the way it builds – incredibly clever in so many ways, in its construction musically and lyrically and in what its saying. Could you get any more pertinent in such a brilliant way? Listen to it.

On to 'Running The World', the last song before the encore and the only point where I took out my phone to take a quick video. This was at the height of all the Trump shit, and Jarvis said, "You know, we made this song a while ago but unfortunately it's even more relevant". Everyone in that small basement was chanting at the top of their lungs.

Every song got me: 'You're In My Eyes', a disco song – sad but beautiful; I wanted to whisper back "No, you're never too old to dance under the light of a disco ball."

'Swanky Modes' – OOH-AH…! Like an old Pulp song, this had so much edge – darkness, sex, narrative – and a cutting, catchy line that keeps sticking in your head once you've heard it in his low tone. Then Jarvis asked if anyone knew Camden? A few shouts from the audience. I used to drag my sister to shlep over to Camden from South London till I was allowed to go on my own to the market on a Saturday. I don't know if I remember Swanky Modes* – it was maybe a little bit before my time – but I found out later that it was Esme (Young) from the *The Great British Sewing Bee* telly programme and her mate's shop.

Anyway, at one time I worked at a vintage clothes shop in Camden called Episode. One day, while I was out on my half-hour lunch break, Jarvis came in the shop and bought a shirt. The very shirts I had earlier had to take out of their original cracking plastic packing and painstakingly pull out the rusty pins that had been keeping them neatly in place. On the front cover of his debut solo LP, Jarvis is wearing that shirt.

I digress – back to the gig…

Sadly, I had to leave before the encore finished to catch the last train back to London, knowing I wasn't capable of running with a bad back. On the train I was full of so much emotion and adrenalin. I always carry a small notebook or sketchbook with me, and I wrote a sort of letter about all the times I'd nearly met Jarvis.

A couple of months ago, I went to an 'In Conversation' event between Jarvis and a wonderful writer friend of mine. My friend Yuko came with me and after the talk she naturally wanted to buy Jarvis' new book *Good Pop, Bad Pop*, and we queued up to get it signed. (Yes, of course I'd already got a pre-ordered signed copy, which I'd read cover to cover). We were the last people in the queue and when we got to the front Jarvis looked at me and said, "Hello Lucienne".

**Swanky Modes was a British fashion brand that opened in Camden Market in 1972.*

KYLIE
LONDON ARENA
MAY 1990
BECKY CORNWELL, OFFICE ADMINISTRATOR

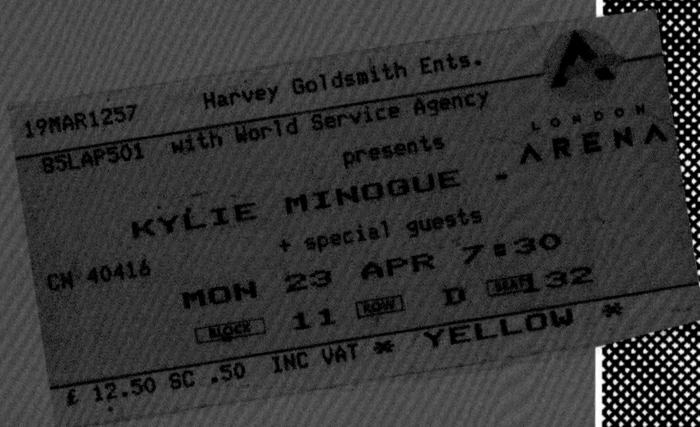

Music plays a huge part in helping form my memories. If I remember a song that was on at the time, I stand a better chance of remembering the experience, especially if the songs in question are played frequently.

When I was young, my parents, my brother and I would embark on a long car journey to visit my paternal grandparents, who lived down south on Hayling Island, a sleepy seaside town that very few people seemed aware of whenever I mentioned it. We made the trip several times a year, usually later at night to avoid the traffic. We'd have the car packed full, complete with duvet and pillow, as our parents hoped we'd fall asleep for some of the journey. The seasons changed but the music on those trips largely stayed the same. We had a cassette player at first, but as the years went on and compact disc players became the new popular music format, my dad upgraded the car radio to include one (it made skipping songs so much quicker!). Thinking about it, he may well have upgraded or changed the car – he liked to wheel and deal in those days.

The songs featured during those car journeys became an unofficial "driving to Grandma seaside soundtrack", featuring a collection of Mum and Dad's favourite tracks from over the years: Dire Straits' 'Money for Nothing', 'Night Shift' by The Commodores, Tina Turner's 'What's Love Got To Do With It', Madonna's 'Papa Don't Preach' and Phil Collins' 'In The Air Tonight' (my dad would get pretty pissed off if any of us spoke as the drums were about to break!).

I was ten years old when I went to my first concert at the London Arena in May 1990, to see Kylie Minogue on her Enjoy Yourself Tour. It featured an appearance by Jason Donovan, who sang his part in 'Especially For You', both of them fresh from *Neighbours* fame when the show had massive viewing figures in the UK and was shown twice a day during the week. My mum would set up the ironing board and get to work in front of the TV for the lunchtime edition, which was followed by *Sons and Daughters*, another popular Australian soap at the time (I only remember the theme tune). I would watch the 5.35 p.m. edition of Neighbours after school with my tea. Scott and Charlene were favourites, and so it was quite apt that I'd see them at my first concert.

Back then, going to London felt special and you'd usually dress up a bit. We were a few rows from the front, but I didn't know how rare that was at the time! Plus, the tickets were less than £15 each! *Birds of a Feather* was then a hit BBC TV show, so it was quite a thrill to spot Linda Robson (who played Tracy) sitting on the floor with her (I assumed) daughter and friends near the merchandise stall, as the queue for the ladies' toilets snaked through the busy corridor. This may have been when I picked up my first useful gig tip from my mum, one I have since adopted for most busy events. Not being a fan of long queues, she whisked us straight into the men's toilets, which were of course empty but a 'hold your nose and hover' kind of affair.

I don't remember much of Kylie on stage; it was all a little blurry. But I do remember the huge crowd, the blinding lights, butterflies of excitement in my tummy at the new experience, probably a little sensory overload thrown in. Singing along to the familiar songs, the waft of surrounding perfumes or aftershave adding a scent to the memory and of course the rush and sharp increase in volume when Jason Donovan made his much anticipated but brief appearance.

New York Dolls

NEW YORK DOLLS
RAINBOW ROOM, BIBA, KENSINGTON, LONDON
26 NOVEMBER 1973
RHODA DAKAR, SINGER

It was the autumn term at school in 1973. Ziggy had played his last ever show at the Marquee Club in Soho for *The 1980 Floor Show*, a US TV special.* I managed to get in the venue for a couple of the recording sessions, where I met Jayne (then Wayne) County, Cherry Vanilla and Leee Black Childers. These were Warholians, Nuyoricans and achingly cool to me, a fourteen-year-old South Londoner. So, when the hyperbolised New York Dolls descended on my city, I was going to be there!

The New York Dolls were on the *Old Grey Whistle Test*, BBC Two's flagship live music show, and were (in)famously described by presenter Whispering Bob (Harris) as 'mock rock'. Even I've since managed to rib him about that jibe. The Dolls weren't mock rock at all; they were glam proto-punk. Musically, they prepared the way for the revolutionary sound that appeared three years later. In fact, it was so obvious that punk impresario Malcolm McLaren even went on to manage them!

Me and my mate Benny Bish (she of the song 'From Benny Bish To Toothless Anne') went to witness what was clearly going to be an event, staged at the Rainbow Room, the venue on the top floor of the huge Biba department store on Kensington High Street. Biba was ultra-cool and well established as a hangout on Saturday afternoons. There were a couple of window displays, but half of them just had huge sofas for us kids to lounge on. I was only fourteen and Benny was a year younger, but this was long before teenagers had to be accompanied everywhere. Dressed up in my mum's post-war Forties-style evening dress, the one I wore in The Special AKA's 'Alcohol' video, a fur jacket and my Biba heels, I had no sense of being 'too young' for anything. I didn't have to sneak out, as going to gigs was considered normal behaviour in our house. My mum had met my dad in his nightclub back in the day, after all!

We bagged a table and watched the audience arrive. It was one of those gigs people would talk about in the future in hushed tones. We certainly felt we were at the cutting edge. Brian Eno, freshly departed from Roxy Music, was there. I was a huge fan and asked for an autograph. He tutted and was so bad tempered, I vowed I'd never behave like that when I was famous! Also in the crowd was 'Jesus', the hippie gig-goer who liked to rid himself of clothing and dance with his eyes shut. Fortunately, this habit (the first half, at least) was curtailed temporarily for the winter.

I remember the stage wasn't very high, so when the show started, we had to push our way to the front in order to drink it all in. I already had the album, so was familiar with some of the songs, but I was transfixed by the sight of the Dolls. It wasn't the 'navvies in heels and make-up' that had become so commonplace on *Top of the Pops*. And though I remember each and every one of the band, Johnny Thunders made the biggest impression on me. There was a nonchalance about his prowess on the guitar that was so different from the likes of Mick Ronson, whom I already idolised. I came to understand that this had more to do with what heroin addiction looked like. And though I couldn't really say what it was that drew me in, they had me, and I followed them and Johnny Thunders in his next band, The Heartbreakers, for many years after.

Towards the end of the gig, David Johansen threw out stickers. I collected as many as I could and put them on schoolbooks and, most importantly, my favourite black patent clutch bag, where they stayed for a good couple of years! I lost a scarf my mum had given me. It was stolen, to be honest, but I tried to look for it. Every item of clothing was what we now call 'vintage' and irreplaceable. Plus, I was a schoolkid, with only pocket money to spend. Anyway, the search meant we missed our last train and had to get a taxi. We'd barely heard of night buses back then. It was fine at first, as Benny lived near Waterloo, but the cabbie only took me to Brixton under duress. He didn't want to leave me "out here in Australia". I guess that meant south of the river, but he wasn't happy!

I got home later than expected. There were questions, but I'd managed to get a cab, which was seen as a win. It was all a massive win from where I stood!

On The Sunny Side Of The Street
Verve
ELLA & BASIE
Verve's Collectors Classics

ELLA FITZGERALD/THE COUNT BASIE BIG BAND
HAMMERSMITH ODEON, LONDON
DATE UNKNOWN
DEREK DEABILL, JAZZ NUT

I was really excited at the thought of these two legends playing together but tickets weren't advertised, and they were difficult to get hold of. So, in my lunch hour from work, I went along to Harold Davidson, the promoter's office, which was above the clothes shop Austin Reed in Regent Street. I asked the girl in reception if she could let me have two tickets. She asked me to sit down and wait while she went into an office to speak to somebody and returned with two tickets, which I paid for there and then.

We went along to the concert, and our tickets were six rows from the front. It was everything we had hoped it would be. Ella Fitzgerald was in fine voice and The Count Basie Band were just fantastic. The show started with Count Basie gently tinkling the ivories and suddenly the whole band came in, which made a terrific sound. I can't remember the name of the tune they played. And it continued in that sort of form, then Ella came on and did her turn, which was equally as breathtaking. What a night!

SEX PISTOLS
SHEPHERD'S BUSH EMPIRE, LONDON
17 JULY 1996
STUART DEABILL, AUTHOR

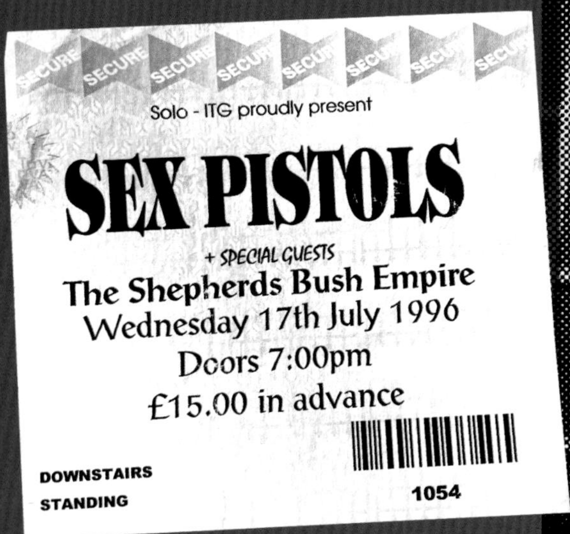

Sex Pistols – the name screams terror, excitement, lust, danger and non-conformity. Well, that's how it felt back in 1976. I was ten years old and like most, first heard about the band after their 'shocking' appearance on *Today*, the regional evening news show for London. The Filth And The Fury! The Decline of Western Civilisation! Were The Pistols Loaded? And so on. For me, going into school the next day it was the talk of the playground at Greenwood Middle – "Did you see those funny blokes that said 'fucking' and 'dirty bastard'? Hahahahaha!" Pre-teen giggles and then back to playing fourteen-a-side football in itchy green wool V-necks, grey semi-flared school trousers and Clark's Commandos. But by the time music entered my consciousness, the Pistols had gone, and I thought The Great Rock And Roll Swindle was gospel. Thanks Malcolm. Bullshit swallowed.

Twenty years on and the Pistols are back! I never thought they would ever reform in a million years. It wasn't a major thing back then for bands to get back together. Nowadays you can almost predict a band splitting and coming back within four years for another payday. A big gig at Finsbury Park was announced, to be held bang in the middle of Euro 96. That summer, a wave of euphoria washed through the nation, as England played with flair and confidence not seen in my lifetime and British guitar bands were ruling the charts. I thought about going to Finsbury Park, but I swerved for the size and the pantomime of it all. Johnny Rotten/John Lydon had surpassed his original awkward persona and enjoyed playing the villain for the press, which was never boring but didn't really work for me as an adult. Or so I thought.

However, a follow-up gig was announced for 16 July at Shepherd's Bush Empire and my regular gig-going pal Al bought four tickets and asked if me and pal Simon Kortlang fancied it. The Empire is one of my favourite venues and it appealed, as it wasn't going to be wall-to wall-crusty old punks from across the country pissed on snakebite. "Yeah, I'm in son – pay you on the night. If you're lucky!"

As usual, when going to a gig at the famous old theatre, we met in the pub next door, the old Bush Hotel (now an O'Neill's chain pub, last I looked). As we enjoyed a pint or four in the warm glow of a beautiful summer evening, a car pulled up in between the venue and pub and was ushered through the side entrance. Inside was bassist Glen Matlock and we all gave him the thumbs up, which he returned. He was quickly followed by Steve Jones, and Al's Metropolitan Police workmate, 'Welsh' Simon, banged on the car, shouting "Jonesy, Jonesy!" in his broad Cardiff tongue, which Jonesy ignored. By this point the entrances had started to bring some of the pub dwellers over to where we were standing and a couple of minutes later a third car approached at speed. I said to Kortlang, this must be Rotten. As we peered through the dark glass, we could just make out Johnny, with shaved sides and an amazing Day-Glo thatch of hair. There was a throng of around twenty-five to thirty peering into the car shouting at him, when Johnny rolled down the window, smiled and stuck two fingers up to us all. Fucking brilliant – exactly what you want from the spiky old spunker! And y'know, it set the tone for the gig.

We finished our pints, now suitably buzzed up, walked into the auditorium and jostled for more lager at the bar. We finally got our drinks (two pints each) and took our position to the right of the stage to gain a decent vantage point, without getting an elbow in the mush. The atmosphere was a cross between high spirits and knife edge, and thankfully it wasn't overrun with the comedy punks with their Camden Town 'pose for pics' Mohicans.

Sometimes you can just walk into a room and know you're going to have a good night, but the mix of a band that had reached a mythic status reserved for the likes of The Beatles combined with a tangible air of tension, adrenaline and excessive alcohol intake sent emotions into a rarefied air!

Against the backdrop of a front page from the *Daily Mirror*, and the music dipping to signal showtime, the band entered stage left to cacophonous, aggressive cheers and lager flying through the air. I was as keyed up for this as I would have been any major Chelsea game, living for the moment, being in the present.

Johnny's first words, "Keep your beers to yourselves, you sorry sad sacks." And then the opening notes of Sex Pistols' most brutal and nihilistic song, 'Bodies', filled the theatre with a menace I'd yet to hear before (or since). I don't think my feet touched the ground for what seemed like minutes. It blew my mind. That was it, I was gone, punk rock – we mean it maaaan.

Seventy minutes of sweat, beer, adrenaline, spittle – which was dealt with brilliantly when some landed Rotten's way, first during 'No Feelings', when he singled out blokes gobbing at him and threatened to pull the gig if it carried on. "Two bob cunts!" – "Silly fucking arseholes." – "Pull that wanker out, security!" and so on. It was direct action – "Do not mug yourselves!" You didn't get that with a Blur gig. It seemed to stir up an even more intense atmosphere within the room, which lifted the gig to another level. Also, for me to hear those songs I grew up with through a massive PA, played with the intensity they had in 1977, denied me any reservations I had. Right place, right time, right location.

As the band finished with a cover of The Stooges' 'No Fun', Jonesy was by this point topless, apart from his guitar strap, which was emblazoned with the word 'SLAG'. Glen and Paul were dripping with sweat, as was the majority of the 2,000 punters in the four-tiered theatre. As the song came to a climactic end, John told the audience, "Good fucking night! Because we love you and never make the mistake of thinking different."

I came out with a big grin to see Welsh Simon shouting expletives while rolling round the floor on his back on some of the bootleg posters and T-shirts the merch guys outside were trying to punt. Having a mad black Taff copper rolling across your snide tour posters isn't what you need when trying to nick a living. But boy, did we laugh!

And no Johnny, we really wasn't cheated.

THE CLASH
NOTRE DAME HALL, LONDON
6 JULY 1979
GEOFF DEANE, MUSICIAN/WRITER

As we all know, many, many millions of Londoners were fortunate enough to see the Sex Pistols play live in the early days. I have personally met at least 700,000 who were at the Screen On The Green gig.

Sadly, I was not one of them.

Hands-up time: I was a bit sniffy about punk at the beginning. I had my own shit going on. Grown-out wedge, skinny-fit suit, Let It Rock painted tie, Warhol glasses and deadstock grey winklepickers from Levitts down the Lane. I'd put in a lot of effort. Especially with those bastard shoes, which were a size and a half too small for me. They looked good but I moved like a man with the worst case of Farmer Giles in medical history. Still, the notion of chucking out my wardrobe and trading in my record collection for some 'new movement' seemed ridiculous.

I came from East London, where punk was slow to make an impression. The first two punks I ever saw in the locale were at the Lacy Lady, a soul club in Ilford. Dyed and cropped barnets, bin liners, multiple safety pins in their ears. To confuse matters they were dancing – and dancing well – to 'Hard Work' by American jazz sax player John Handy. Love a bit of subcultures bumping heads in the dark.

The Spooky Lady, another club, over in Hackney Wick, had started putting bands on and myself and David Jaymes had gone there to see the Geordie band Penetration. The only other punters were two girls who seemed to have got most of their fashion tips from old St. Trinian's movies. As an attempted nod to the times, one had written 'SHIT' in black marker pen on her forehead and the other 'FUCK' on her cheek. The band were okay, if not life-changing. We left before the end and didn't say goodnight to Shithead or Fuckface.

We had Small Wonder then, of course, a record shop and indie label in Hoe Street, Walthamstow, run by a diamond of a geezer, Pete Stennett – a beanie-hatted hippie with Peel-like eclectic musical taste buds. Pete put out a lot of records by new bands, including The Cure, Angelic Upstarts, and The Cravats. But until he eventually came to sign my own outfit, the Leyton Buzzards, none of them were local.

So, what converted me to the cause? That honour would go to The Damned. I'm talking the original line-up with Brian James. I saw them at the Hope & Anchor and they blew me away. I'd seen Rod, Bowie, Roxy, Lou Reed, Mott and the Dolls live. But this was different: frenetic three-chord mayhem played loud and fast in a small venue to a young crowd going mental. What a night. Even the walls were sweating. By the time they left the stage all I wanted to do was start my own band.

Fast forward a few years and the Buzzards were up and running and nicking a living, travelling around the country in an old van we'd bought off a greengrocer for 150 sovs. Although hardly an archetypal punk record, 'Saturday Night Beneath The Plastic Palm Trees' had got us a lot of positive attention, and life was pretty good. Even if I did spend a lot of it squashed between a Marshall stack and a drum kit in a vehicle that pen and inked of old fruit and veg.

On this day – 6 July 1979 – we weren't playing. Instead, the boys were on a beano to see The Clash play a 'secret gig' at Notre Dame Hall. You can find the same venue still there now, revamped and renamed as the Leicester Square Theatre.

Retrospectively there was no better time to see The Clash. With the first barnstorming album and a slightly disappointing follow-up under their collective belt, the mighty London Calling was about to drop. And in a venue that only held about 400. As we piled into the van and headed up West, the excitement – and lager – was palpable.

At this point I must introduce you to another player in the story – Kevin Steptoe, the Buzzards' powerhouse drummer, and the loveliest bloke you could ever hope to meet. Decent to the bone, funny and the heartbeat of the group. Every band should have a Kevin. But there was another aspect to the man, which made him never less than intriguing company. Like a lot of my mates, Kev was a Roman Candle, hailing from a very nice, very straight, working-class Catholic family. Being in any band, and especially being in a band like ours, was an anathema to Kev's upbringing. Which rendered him somewhat conflicted. And the better things went for us, and the more fun he had, the more conflicted he became.

An example.

After spending the night with a girl he met on tour, Kev was so angry with himself the next morning, he blacked his own eye with a peach of a right hook, which somehow, he never saw coming.

Religion eh. You gotta love it.

Kev's regular party piece after a few light ales was to take all his clothes off. And if you're looking for a less subtle metaphor for a man casting off the shackles of repression, I wish you the very best of luck.

On top of all this, Kev was habitually boracic. None of us had much wedge in those days but Kev's well always seemed to run dry first. As the van spluttered past Centre Point en route to the gig, he tried hitting me and Dave up for a loan of twenty quid. Dave, never one to miss a trick, told Kev he'd front him the score if he'd get out the van naked and go for a paddle in the water feature outside the landmark building. Now this was in the heart of the West End on a blazing hot summer's day with the streets full of people. In seconds, Kev was out of his kit, out the van, and frolicking in the water like a toddler on his first trip to the seafront. At which point Dave drove off.

I'm not sure exactly how long we left him there. We definitely parked up and went for a pint. But here's the thing. When we did eventually return, Kev was sat on the side, still naked as the day he was born, with his feet happily splish-splashing in the water. And no one was taking a blind bit of notice. No Old Bill, no offended women shouting the odds, not so much as a solitary Japanese tourist taking a souvenir snap. I couldn't explain it then, and I still cannot now.

The gig itself was electric. The band was bang on it and played everything you wanted to hear. 'Clash City Rockers', 'Hammersmith Palais', 'Complete Control', 'What's My Name', 'Stay Free', 'London Calling', 'Safe European Home', 'Rudie Can't Fail', 'Capital Radio', 'Janie Jones', 'I Fought The Law' … one belter after another. We all got split up, but it didn't matter. The Clash had demanded my complete attention and they'd got it. My eyes never left the stage.

Near the end of the set, during 'London's Burning', something at the front of the crowd seemed to catch Strummer's attention and momentarily distract him. I automatically followed his eyeline. There, at Joe's feet, pogoing for all he was worth, was Kev. I have no idea where his clothes were but once again, they were not on his body. As the singer spat out lyrics about Sten guns in Knightsbridge, it was all he could do to avoid making eye contact with an 'ampton from Leyton.

And Kevin had never looked happier.

These days I understand Kev is an integrated circuit design and semi-conductor executive and vice president of a hugely successful company in the United States. I very much doubt he ever talks about his days as a Buzzard, or the time we saw The Clash play Notre Dame Hall.

But I know he remembers. And I'd wager it's as fondly as I do.

SEX PISTOLS
THE GARDEN, PENZANCE
1 SEPTEMBER 1977
NICK DUCKETT, OWNER OF RHYTHM AND
BLUES RECORDS

Rumours about Sex Pistols gigs were rife during the summer of 1977 and, afraid of public disorder, local councils up and down the country enforced bylaws to prevent them from appearing on their patch. Hoping to dodge such measures, manager Malcolm McLaren decided to bill them as SPOTS (Sex Pistols on Tour Secretly).

I knew Liz at Cowbell management agency, who called me on the morning of 1 September, saying that the Pistols would be playing in Penzance that evening. We got the 2 p.m. train together from Reading and six hours later we were in that far away Cornish town, looking for something to eat. We met up with a couple of people who had trekked down by car and then followed the trail of scruffy punks to the Winter Gardens, which was advertising an appearance by a 'Top International British Group Plus Disco' for the princely sum of £1. (They had played the previous night in Plymouth as The Hamsters).

We paid at the door and headed to the bar, where there were about 100 punky West Country folk, but since it was still summer holiday season, there was also a smattering of middle-aged holidaymakers. Two Scottish matrons dressed in tweed sat in front of us, discussing who they were most hoping to see: Bobby Davro or Freddie & The Dreamers.

The show turned out to be one the finest gigs I've ever attended. A snarling Rotten taunted the audience with his trademark abuse, but his complaints about the constant stream of gob coming from the crowd fell on deaf ears. Sid Vicious mainly had his back to the crowd but he turned out to be a far more competent bass player than his reputation had led anyone to believe. Jones and Cook were on form, driving the band through all the favourites: 'Anarchy In The UK', 'God Save The Queen', 'No Fun' and the rest. No surprises.

The surprise for me came forty-five years after, when I looked on the internet and discovered that there was actual live footage of this very show. Filmmaker Julian Temple had been there: "The performance was shot using one camera and shows the extraordinary, captivating quality of the band at the time. There was shock in the room, it was hypnotising, contagious, and unfolded right in front of you. The Pistols arrived in Penzance unannounced, and the audience couldn't believe what they were getting."

The place wasn't exactly packed to the rafters and when the show ended, the group mingled with the crowd. The future Jah Wobble was working as the band's roadie, and he was wandering around, trying unsuccessfully to flog a pair of Johnny Rotten's underpants for 50p. It's been reported since that he and Rotten laid their future plans for Public Image Ltd after the gig that night.

The highlight of the evening for us was when Sid posed for a photo with us licking a giant ice cream cone. Unfortunately, though, the Winter Gardens bouncer rushed over, grabbed the camera and pulled out the film. Par for the course in the Seventies. Sid then struck up a conversation with an old tramp outside the back door by the bins, and my abiding memory is of him and the tramp walking away arm in arm towards the seafront under the moonlight.

We didn't really have any plan as to what to do next. It was gone 12, and there was nothing left open in Penzance, so after I ripped down a poster from outside the Winter Gardens, we all piled into my mate's car and headed for the motorway for an all-night trip back home.

Halfway there, we stopped at a service station for coffee. The place was deserted, apart from Steve Jones and Paul Cook! We tried to get information out of them about where they were playing next but they claimed not to know. Apparently, Malcolm didn't trust them not to blab, so he only told them on the morning of the gig where they'd be playing that night.

I thought the Penzance gig was worthy of documentation, so I wrote it up, sent it to the *NME* and it got into the next issue. I wish I still had a copy.

PETE DOHERTY & CARL BARÂT WITH DIRTY PRETTY STRINGS
HACKNEY EMPIRE, LONDON
5 SEPTEMBER 2019
JOE DWYER, TEACHER

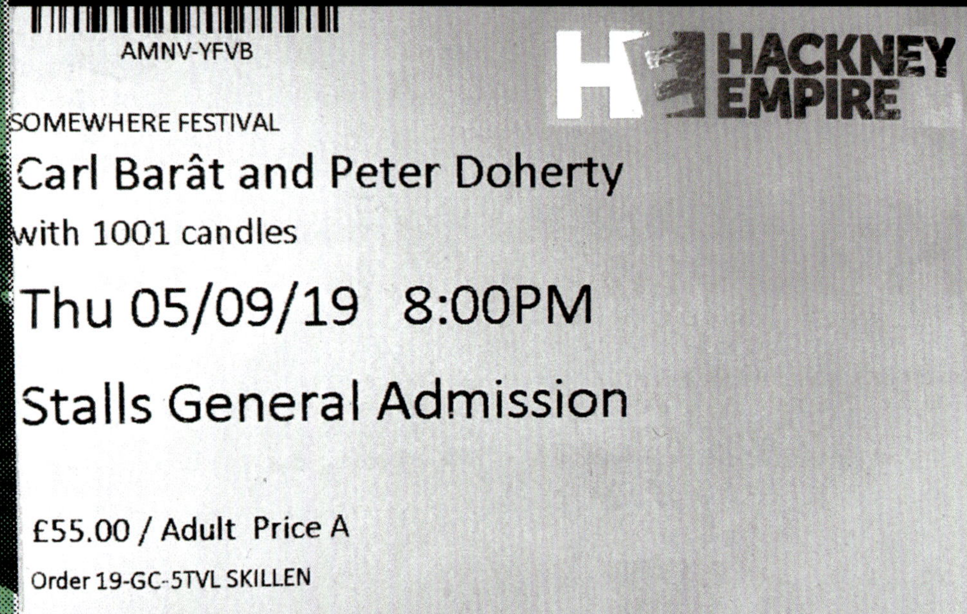

AMNV-YFVB

HACKNEY EMPIRE

SOMEWHERE FESTIVAL

Carl Barât and Peter Doherty

with 1001 candles

Thu 05/09/19 8:00PM

Stalls General Admission

£55.00 / Adult Price A

Order 19-GC-5TVL SKILLEN

"What became of the likely lads?" I think to myself, as I'm sifting through shoe boxes full of old gig tickets, football tickets, fanzines, badges and an array of other 'worthless' crap that paints a picture of the last fifteen years of my life. I struggle with nostalgia. I'm interested in where people are going as opposed to where they have been and yet, as I sit here, I can't help but be transported back to various times and places – times and places where anything seemed possible – and I'm struck by this overwhelming feeling of the past. Memories of friends, lovers, dreamers; of people I shared brief moments of hedonism with – whose names I never knew or can no longer recall – whose faces are etched indefinitely into my mind's eye.

Choosing one ticket to tell a story about was no easy feat; there are scores of stories to be told. But I settled on Carl Barât & Peter Doherty with Dirty Pretty Strings and 1001 candles at London's Hackney Empire.

"Fifty-five quid for a fucking acoustic gig! They're taking the piss, ain't they?" we all agreed, sitting in the pub beforehand. Undeterred, we manage a few more pints and, despite being dragged to the most pretentious pub Hackney has to offer (quite an achievement, I suppose?), the four of us are starting to feel less aggrieved and that pre-gig excitement is kicking in. We finish our drinks and head in – stage time is 8.15, which gives us just enough time to get in and get a drink before the boys in the band take to the stage.

Hackney Empire, for those who haven't been fortunate enough to visit, is one of the finest remaining venues this fair city has to offer. In fact, looking around at the grandeur and décor we're enveloped in, one could be forgiven for thinking we were living the romanticised version of Albion that Doherty and Barat have written and sung about so extensively.

The lights dim and two shadows appear at the back of the stage, flickering in the candlelight. This is a show for the fans, so there is great delight when they open up with 'Seven Deadly Sins', an old B-side to the single 'Time For Heroes' (2003), in its original carnation rather than the reworked version on 2015's *Anthems For Doomed Youth*. Without pausing for breath, they fly straight into 'The Delaney' and 'Boys In The Band' before introducing the Dirty Pretty Strings, who play on the beautiful 'You're My Waterloo' and 'For Lovers'. For those of us in the audience, arcadia's dream had not fallen through; the Albion sailed on course, with Barât and Doherty at the helm.

Maybe it was the candlelight and the accompanying strings, or maybe this was genuinely less shambolic and chaotic than previous (and subsequent) Libertines gigs. This was two performers perfectly in tune with their adoring fans, who sang every word back at them. A band and their audience who had grown up together; this felt like a celebration of maturity, not only for the band and their string quartet, but also the fans, who were in fine voice yet well behaved. That was until the bar ran out of lager around the end of the first set. By the time the first chord of 'Time For Heroes' started the second set, there were pints of wine held aloft in the air – and a more unruly second act followed...

'The Good Old Days', 'Tell The King' and 'The Boy Looked At Johnny' all feature in the first half of a raucous second act, before Barât departs, leaving Doherty on stage accompanied only by 1001 candles. The audience wait with bated breath, in no doubt that Babyshambles' 'Albion' is seconds away. The lyrics of the song paint a picture that is a far cry from Thomas Cole's *Dream of Arcadia*, yet there is something hauntingly beautiful about the words chosen by the last of the great English poets. It's a strange phenomenon, but nothing quite gets a crowd going like mentioning the part of the world you are performing at mid-song, and Doherty doesn't disappoint, including Hackney in the list of forgotten towns and cities he recites in the build-up to the chorus' crescendo, which is greeted by cheers from the crowd.

Then Barât returns to the stage as Doherty departs, they share a hug, and he launches straight into 'Let It Rain', a track from his debut album with The Jackals. Undoubtedly, it's a great song, but it seems like he's fighting an uphill battle after Peter's 'Albion'.

As the end draws close and the pints of wine begin running on empty, anthems 'Music When the Lights Go Out' and 'What A Waster' have the crowd singing back with gusto, before the pair finish with fan favourite 'Don't Look Back Into The Sun' – and we didn't, we went straight back to the pub to celebrate a momentous moment in years of following The Libertines, vowing to make the last Tube home.

I fumble around, getting my key in the door, before stumbling up the stairs and crawling into bed. My then girlfriend (now wife) wakes up and, still half asleep, asks me how it was. "Life affirming," comes my sincere, if not slightly pissed response. She sighs, rolls over and goes back to sleep.

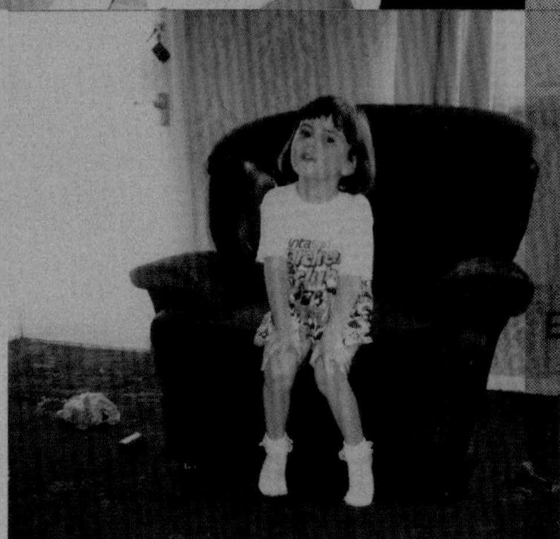

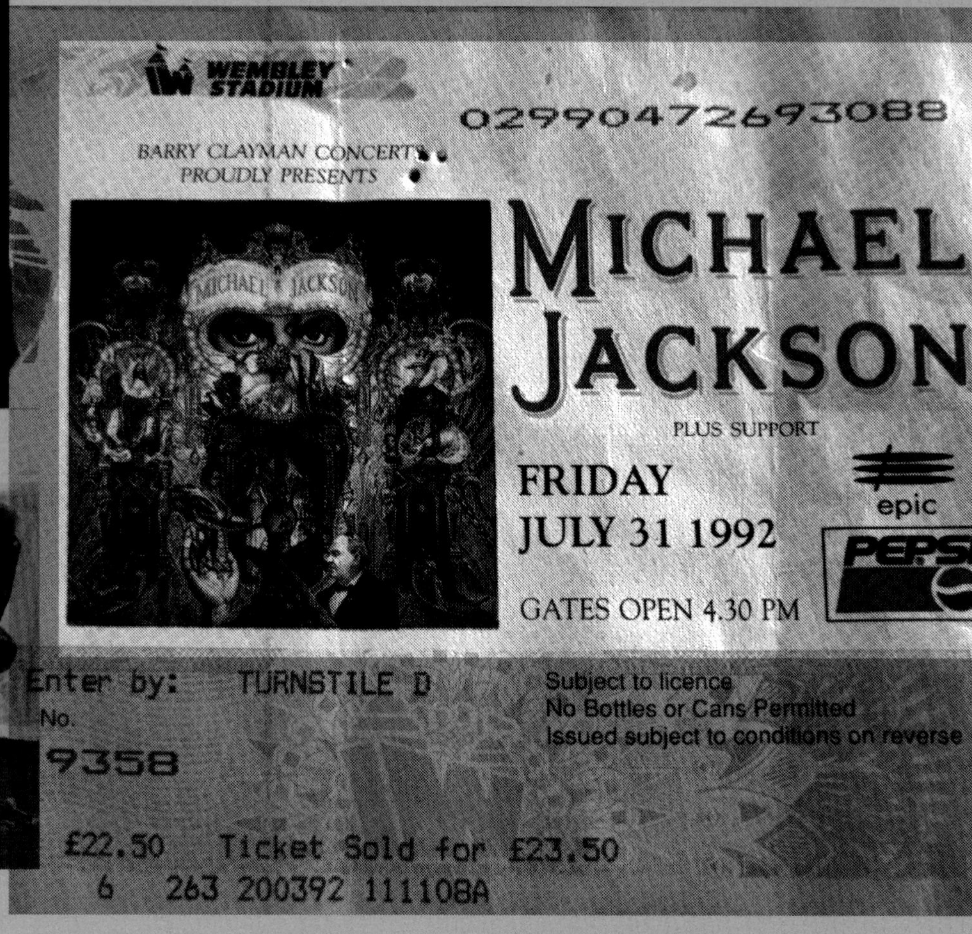
WEMBLEY STADIUM
02990472693088
BARRY CLAYMAN CONCERTS
PROUDLY PRESENTS
MICHAEL JACKSON
PLUS SUPPORT
FRIDAY
JULY 31 1992
GATES OPEN 4.30 PM
epic
PEPSI
Enter by: TURNSTILE D
No.
9358
Subject to licence
No Bottles or Cans Permitted
Issued subject to conditions on reverse
£22.50 Ticket Sold for £23.50
6 263 200392 111108A

MICHAEL JACKSON
WEMBLEY STADIUM, LONDON
31 JULY 1992
KIM EDWARDS, LOCAL GOVERNMENT OFFICER

Back in 1988 Michael Jackson was arguably the biggest star on the planet, following on from the success of *Off The Wall* in 1979, *Thriller* in 1983 and the ground-breaking video that accompanied the title track for the equally successful Bad in 1987.

On Saturday 23 July 1988, my friend Heather and I travelled from Walthamstow to Wembley to see Michael on his Bad world tour, leaving behind my friend's very upset Michael Jackson-mad two-year-old daughter Leoni. The concert was amazing, and when I next saw Leoni I told her all about the day. I then made a promise that the next time Michael returned to London, and she was old enough to be allowed in, I would take her.

Fast forward three years and the Dangerous album was released, with the concert tour announced for the following summer. Leoni was six going on seven by the time of the show, and thankfully now old enough to go. Back in those days there were no online ticket sales; you either went to the venue, a record store or an agency to buy your tickets. The tickets were going on sale on a Saturday morning, but all plans for getting up early to join the queue were scuppered by a typical Friday night after work in Central London. Drinks began in The Albert pub in Victoria, which ended with a group of us going to a party somewhere in South London, the wrong side of the river for an East End girl.

Still partying at 1 a.m., I realised that getting home wasn't an option, so I crashed round a workmate's house and woke up with a start at 7 a.m., realising I should have been on my way to the Virgin Megastore in Oxford Street to buy tickets. A quick turnaround after some much-needed tea and toast to soak up the previous day's alcohol, and I made it to the store, with a banging hangover.

Several hours later and after a few visits to the next-door fast-food restaurant for more tea and sustenance (thanks to people holding my place in the queue), I'd managed to secure the tickets. It crossed my mind several times to say they had sold out and to go home and recover, but each time I closed my eyes, Leoni's face would appear. How could I do that to a six-year-old?

I came back and broke the news to a very happy child, who must have thought a six-month wait to go was a lifetime away, but she could drive her mum mad with all the "when?" and "how long?" questions, while filling the time playing the albums and videos until the big day arrived.

Fast forward several months to Friday 31 July 1992, and now there are three of us, Heather, Leoni and me, making the journey from Walthamstow to Wembley. When we arrived, we made our way to the pitch to ensure we had a great view, only to be told that Leoni was too young to stand on the pitch and we had to find seats in the main stand.

As the moment came for the concert to begin, we realised that a six-year-old might not get to see much, so I picked her up and then Michael shot out of the stage from what appeared to be a giant catapult and, in that moment, I saw the smile of the happiest six-year-old in the world.

Thirty years on and with Michael's name making it into the news for not always good reasons, I often think back to that day and the happiness it brought to the thousands of people there, but especially to a Michael Jackson-mad Leoni, now 36, and who I'm still in regular contact with.

DR. LONNIE SMITH TRIO
RONNIE SCOTT'S, LONDON
13 MARCH 2015
PETE EVANS, DJ

In these days of electronic communications, I can't remember the last time I had an actual paper ticket for a musical evening, a train journey or even a dental appointment! The performances I've attended are wonderful memories but although I collect records, concert stubs have never been something I've hung on to. Having said that, I'm quite likely to write out lists of artists past and present whose performances have thrilled me over the years. I can remember seeing Kai Winding and Don Lusher with the Pat Smythe Trio in Manchester at the Royal Exchange Theatre back in 1980 as though it was yesterday!

I've chosen a relatively recent date for this book for a couple of reasons, and my memory of this Friday 13 February night in 2015 is very precious to me. Nothing unlucky about it!

This was a chance for a get-together with my oldest pal – my dear friend and jazz mentor John May, who was an artist of some repute and a former colleague of mine from the earliest days of my teaching career, when I arrived wet behind the ears at Willesden High School in 1982. Back then I was firmly into jazz fusion and buying records by Jeff Lorber, Dave Valentin and Bob James. It was John who opened me up to the wonderful world of modern jazz and hard bop, and I marvelled at his collection of mono deep-groove original LP pressings.

These were halcyon days, listening to Gilles Peterson's Mad On Jazz on Radio London, dashing in the car to Honest Jon's Records after school to sift through the racks and soaking up the unique and vibrant young London jazz scene of the time. Something special was evolving and for a few years it felt like I was connected to it in a very tangible way.

My lifelong obsession had begun, and it was after a trip to Mole Jazz in Gray's Inn Road and the purchase of Freddie Roach's Soul Book LP on Transatlantic that I started to embrace the organ jazz of the Sixties. I hooked up with and befriended Jason Jules and followed DJs Andy McConnell and Baz Fe Jazz around the West End, eventually bringing boxes of my LPs to DJ with them at the Wag on Wardour Street, negotiating my entry past Winston on the door on Monday evenings. It didn't matter in those days that I was teaching all day Tuesday after arriving home in Finchley at 4.30 a.m. – I was young then!

Baz was big news and would go on to tour in with IDJ and The Jazz Defektors, playing the kinds of records I was buying all the time. I remember the thrill of putting the needle on the wax and seeing young London hipsters grooving to Blue Note tracks like Donald Byrd's 'Pentecostal Feeling', Jackie McLean's 'Greasy' and Lou Donaldson's 'Rev. Moses'. This was off the scale! Tommy Chase with his quartet was an uncompromising force on a scene that finally connected the jazz tradition with clubland in terms of dance. It had all been fusion and Latin prior to this.

Having seen many of my Hammond heroes live in concert over the years, I was conscious of a glaring omission from my list – Lonnie Smith. I'd seen Jimmy McGriff and Jimmy Smith at Barrowlands in Glasgow. I'd seen Charles Earland both in Leeds, at The Yardbird Suite, and at the Jazz Café in Camden Town, where, over the years, I'd also been treated to and witnessed first-hand the grooves supplied by Brother Jack McDuff, Big John Patton and Reuben Wilson.

So, when the opportunity to catch Dr. Lonnie Smith arose in 2015, I had to bite the bullet and buy into the corporate world of Ronnie Scott's!

John was turning eighty and I wanted to enjoy a special celebration with him to mark this milestone. For his seventieth he'd been on a trip to New York with his son Daniel and seen Bobby Hutcherson with Kenny Barron at the Lincoln Center. John had also donated a painting of the USS Intrepid to the Intrepid Sea, Air & Space Museum in Manhattan, something which he took great pride in as he was obsessed with US military planes. Incidentally, the painting, Aboard Intrepid, still hangs in the museum to this day.

Anyway, I booked the tickets and a night at the Z hotel in Soho's Moor Street. John and I met at St Pancras station after Friday evening train journeys from St Albans and Sheffield, then proceeded to Soho with a spring in our step. After checking into our rooms, we walked up a staircase to the terrace, where we had a uniquely different but wonderful rooftop view of this cramped but vibrant and exciting place. As the evening progressed, we decided it was time for some pre-prandial drinks and it was a couple of pints of McMullens in the Spice of Life in Cambridge Circus before heading off to queue on Frith Street opposite Pizza Express! Along with many others, we were patiently anticipating an evening of swinging music supplied by a living legend, someone whose records were never far from our turntables.

As we entered at 10.30, all it took was a quick scan of my phone and we were escorted to our table by one of the staff, as Mac Rebennack, better known as his stage name Dr. John, was tentatively making his way from the stage, complete with iconic walking stick and minder, having been the headline act for the first house of the evening.

Then very soon after that, it was time for a bottle of red, a perusal of the menu and an order of food – it was showtime! You could feel the excitement in the room as that tension and sense of electricity descended upon the place. The singer-songwriter Omar was sitting at the next table with his entourage of family and friends, and there was a feeling that the great and the good wanted to see and hear this performance. It seems strange, but it was one of those occasions when you felt genuine sympathy for those unfortunate souls who hadn't managed to get in.

Dr. Lonnie didn't disappoint; he was full of joy and the place responded. Describing his set seems superfluous really; it was exactly what we expected and more. This was no greatest hits package, it was all new songs, but rooted in the great tradition of those records I'd grown to love so much.

After Lonnie departed, it was time for the Late Late Show, and I was confident we would be ready to call it a day as the clock was approaching 1 a.m. But John was having none of it, and his decision was justified! We stayed for drummer Mark Fletcher and his jazz rock, Billy Cobham-inspired band Fletch's Brew, who played till 3.30 a.m. We were also knocked out by a young British trumpeter who was on top form – namely Freddie Gavita, an artist whose career I have subsequently followed with interest and have seen in Sheffield more recently. His compositions are first-rate, and his improvisations have something of the Morgan about them (Lee, not Piers!).

As the final number concluded and we realised how late it was, John and I left the club, feeling that sense of fulfilment you get when you've seen something worthwhile but also because it's jazz – unique! We wandered back to the hotel as the cleaners and dustbin men were in full flow, tackling the detritus of a Soho Friday night with typical deadpan stoicism. A rickshaw driver asked us, with a bit too much enthusiasm for that time of night, if we needed a ride. "No!" John shouted back. "We're off to bed!" And with that resounding statement, we walked down Old Compton Street, the buzz of music still in our ears…

:Sadly, since this evening Dr. John, Dr. Lonnie and my dear friend John have all passed away. I'm so glad I made the decision to travel down to London for this celebration of life, friendship and, of course, music.

LED ZEPPELIN
THE O2, LONDON
10 DECEMBER 2007
STEVE FURST, COMEDIAN/ACTOR

The list of artists I've seen is pretty impressive, from the Stones to Tony Bennett to Soft Cell to The Smiths to The Jam to Motörhead (my first ever 'proper' gig in 1981). As my tastes have morphed, so too has the list of artists I've experienced in a live arena. But there was always one that eluded me. Actually, make that two. The first was Cardiacs; I came to them too late and then came the sad, untimely demise of front man and co-founder Tim Smith. The other was Led Zeppelin, and because of the untimely demise of their legendary drummer John 'Bonzo' Bonham in 1980, this was never likely to happen. Plant, Page and Jones vowed they would never play or tour together and that promise went seriously unchallenged for over twenty-five years. Until 2007.

That year, rumours were rife that there would be a tribute concert held for Ahmet Ertegun, the man behind Atlantic Records. It was he who, alongside their fearsome manager Peter Grant, transformed Led Zeppelin from a dynamite blues-based four-piece from England into something approaching deification on a worldwide scale. There were rumblings that the remaining three members, all of whom were still playing, recording and touring in some form or another, would take to the stage, with Jason Bonham filling in for his deceased father. Zep always felt like a tight-knit family affair, so it was only right that Bonham Jr would fill his dad's shoes.

Speculation was laid to rest as the band held a press conference on 12 September 2007. The one-off gig was happening, on 26 November. It would be a charitable affair at a flat rate of £125 per ticket, which would be made available through a lottery system. One name, two tickets. No more.

This was a hot ticket. Actually, 'hot' doesn't really do justice to the incandescently insane furnace-like demand for a seat at this show. To put it into perspective, the gig made the 2009 Guinness Book of World Records for 'Highest Demand for Tickets For One Music Concert'. How many requests were processed? Nearly 20 MILLION. For a venue that holds 20,000. Although on this occasion only 16,000 would be sold, meaning just 8,000 names would be selected for their allotted two tickets. You don't have to be Stephen Hawking to work out that the odds were insanely stacked against us, and that 99 point whatever per

cent of applicants were going to be VERY disappointed. Ah well. Any strings I could pull, avenues I could explore, to get on some sort of guest list? Ha ha ha. HA HA HA.

Much happened that autumn. I had split from my then wife and had taken a job in pantomime for December and January at the Barbican in London. I was living in Hastings but was staying back in London most of the time for rehearsals, which were due to take place in November with performances beginning on 1 December.

On 1 November, more Zep news was announced; Jimmy Page had fractured his finger and the gig would be postponed until 10 December. A certain number of tickets would be made available again due to many ticket holders now being unable to attend the rescheduled date. Well, that wasn't any of my concern. Besides, I was super busy now, even having to fly to the United States to film a batch of those ubiquitous Orange mobile phone ads in the middle of rehearsals.

Then, one morning before leaving for work I received a text. I was a lucky recipient of two of the newly released tickets. What?? How? I hadn't entered myself into the second and even more insanely over-subscribed lottery. I called my wife. It was her. She'd signed me up on the website and forgotten to tell me. But it paid off. Elation! But then I was instantaneously crushed, as the realisation that I was about to begin a December pantomime run and the gig fell on Monday 10th. Monday the 10th?? Wait. Wait one second. We had about three days off before Christmas … and one of those was MONDAY 10 DECEMBER. IT WAS A NIGHT OFF. I WAS GOING TO SEE LED FUCKING ZEPPELIN.

Due to heightened security, you couldn't just turn up and collect your tickets like a normal gig. Of course not, that would be too easy. You had to make the inevitably long trek to the O2 the weekend before the gig and queue up with ID to get your tickets and wristbands. I should state that my wife wasn't a Zep fan and had no intention of going, so I called one of my dearest friends, Adam, knowing he couldn't and wouldn't say no.

I remember there being a very long wait at the venue. There were lines of excited people, and also many upset people, who eventually found themselves at the front of the line only to be told their 'tickets' were bogus, illegal, made up and ultimately worthless. So many fans had paid hugely inflated amounts to unscrupulous ticket agents, who saw this one-off hugely in-demand concert as an easy way to make money. Was my text and information also bogus? The closer we got to the front of the line the more worried I became. Then the moment arrived. Everything was kosher. Adam and I were given the tickets and the wristbands were ceremoniously fastened to our wrists, and at that moment I felt an almost overwhelming sense of emotion. Tears filled my eyes. I was going to see one of the greatest bands ever. Tomorrow night.

The seats weren't half bad. We were up quite high but close to the stage. Almost in line with the front of the stage. We were well oiled by the time we arrived, and we'd filled up hip flasks with Jack Daniel's so we wouldn't be forced to leave the auditorium for ANY length of time.

It is almost impossible to break down the 16-song gig that followed, to describe it in a reasoned, impartially objective way. From the moment the band took the stage I was transported into another dimension. Literally. We were so intoxicated with the noise coupled with the highly charged atmosphere, which accelerated us through those two hours at blistering speed.

For those who couldn't wait to re-live the magic, a slew of grainy, poorly shot early camera phone footage appeared online. Thankfully a DVD capturing the entire gig was eventually released. I actually know Dick Carruthers, who directed the concert DVD*, and he did a frankly brilliant job. I've watched it many times over the years since … from the opening bars of 'Good Times Bad Times' through monumental tracks like 'Black Dog', 'No Quarter', 'Stairway To Heaven', to the epic 'Kashmir' and into the two encores of 'Whole Lotta Love' and 'Rock And Roll'. It is a masterclass in understated brilliance. And there is something extra magical with the band knowing that this was it; there wouldn't be a world tour to follow, no excruciating publicity interviews and press conferences to endure. There is added delight in having Jason Bonham more than ably sitting in his father's seat but also maintaining the look of a genuine fanboy, who delights in sharing cheeky grins with each of member the band throughout the set. There's a moment at the end of the second encore, 'Rock And Roll', when he plays a short solo, with Page, Plant and Jones watching him all with beaming smiles. It says it all.

And I was there. I still can't believe I was there. But I was. Right there. The odds were terrible, and even more truly ridiculous for the rescheduled date. But I was there. And it was magnificent and magical.

There are rumours they might tour again. Really? I've heard those rumours before. But I don't care. Because, did I mention? I SAW LED ZEPPELIN LIVE!

It's called Celebration Day, released in 2012, if you fancy purchasing it.

SUNDAY BEST PRESENTS
CURATED BY JOSIE & ROB DA BANK
BESTIVAL
4→7 SEPT 2014
ROBIN HILL · ISLE OF WIGHT
ANNOUNCING HEADLINERS ...
OUT KAST
+ NEXT WAVE OF ACTS COMING SOON
BESTIVAL.NET · #BESTIVAL14

OUTKAST
BESTIVAL, ISLE OF WIGHT
5 SEPTEMBER 2014
QUINCE GARCIA, CREATIVE DIRECTOR OF ROADWORKS MEDIA/EDUCATOR

It was 2014 and I made my way to the Isle of Wight to be part of something I knew would uplift and delight my well-being, for the many troubled years that were on the way. Nevertheless, it provided with a twinkle of optimism, and the sort of laughter I believe would get me through. But no, this was not a visit to the island's notorious prison to see my old friend who was doing 15 stretch at the time. Rather, this was an occasion for less familiar inhabitants, outside my usual circle.

After taking myself to Waterloo, I boarded a train to Portsmouth and from there a boat to the island. I found out fast – and still to this day I find it difficult to believe – that there are dwellers who have never left that island. My recovery from a life of crime played out too, as I began creating stories of kidnapping, murders and pilferage.

Thankfully, I was able to function healthily by focusing on the thought that I was meeting up with fun people who were taking part in the festival. I met the amazing Helen Davenport and her daughter Sherrel, who were building costumes and relying on me to take photographs of their participation in Bestival. I'd been very reluctant to come, and they'd initially struggled to persuade me to join them out there – until, that is, they mentioned that Outkast would be performing. Umm, who? YES! Andre 3000 and Big Boi were my musical heroes, and I quickly changed my mind and began thinking about creating an identity with the name 'Quince Garcia' (oh yes, that happens to be me!) and drawing out the money that would get me there. I ensured Helen over the phone that I would be there and, yes, I would be bringing my camera along too.

Back on the Isle of Wight, and I was controlling my anxiety with hot dogs, cheeseburgers, crispy fries and a stream of Pimm's cocktails. Then the day passed with me capturing some of Helen's out-of-this-world costumes, me wearing one of the incredible masks she'd created.

I'd had a night to remember, one where I ignored my dodgy-filled stomach. Instead, I focused on the stars that shone brighter and held the gratitude for the twaddle that was still keeping me alive.

The sun rose, then the morning followed, with jam and buttered toast and a polystyrene cup of tea magically appearing, to begin a day that made me feel like I was sharing it with druids and monks. Edging closer and closer to the evening that I was here to serve.

Then the moment arrived where I could prepare to see Outkast on the main stage and witness a performance I knew would bring me a story, with the hope that one day, somebody who is geeky enough would be interested to know about. The cynics and pessimists would say, "Eight and a half years too late, Quince, bore off, see ya with ya 'Hey Ya'." Well, thankfully I've got a small number of friends doing peculiar things, with intriguing ideas, and I know I could potentially fall in line. So, I am reassured by my own sense – I'm in very good company.

Big Boi had his over-the-top hockey and streetwear combo, defining his own look. Andre 3000 was wearing a white wig, white Rays and a grey jumpsuit that had written across it 'My Dad had Cool Albums.' The dream had come through, as my own passage of time reopened to discover an affinity that lies within, and I encountered many memories of looking through my own dad's albums, which were a mix of reggae, soul and funk from the late Sixties, Seventies and early Eighties.

The contrast between the two artists who formed Outkast has always interested me and their demonstration of accepting each other was art to me. Then to hear how that belief is replicated in the sound they produce – this is why I'm a huge fan. Yep, all the classics came out, from 'Ms. Jackson', 'So Fresh, So Clean' and 'Hey Ya' to an obscure favourite of mine, 'Prototype'. I was swinging my hips to the high-energy, high-tempo music that had everyone on the feet. The stage was set with lights and visuals to keep you drawn into their performance. Later, after the show had ended, I nearly fell asleep next to Helen when I accidentally crawled into her tent, but thankfully her snoring was loud enough to startle me and make me realise I was in the wrong place.

That was my flash-in-the-pan moment of a festival, which produced something that I can now share with so many others. Placing in my heart for the world to now recognise.

BILL HALEY & HIS COMETS
THE ROYALTY, SOUTHGATE, LONDON
8 MARCH 1979
RAY GELATO, SAXOPHONIST

I've always been interested in music because of my dad. He was big rock'n'roll fan, and he loved Chuck Berry, Fats Domino and Bill Haley. He's from New Jersey but settled over here in the 1950s, when he was over as part of the US Air Force. When I was a kid we had an old-fashioned mahogany record player, which had a lovely smell, and which was full of vinyl. Loads of music of the day, stuff like Sammy Davis and Dean Martin, along with all the rock'n'roll greats.

When I was in my early to mid-teens, I used to sneak into the Teddy Boy clubs and then the rockabilly clubs of the early Eighties, where the DJs dug deeper than the standard rock'n'roll offerings and played great R&B songs. There, I heard tunes by Louis Jordan, Wynonie Harris and Joe Turner, so my ear slowly turned more towards that direction.

My dad's influence came not through *telling* me about the music, but by *playing* it, when he used to put the records on and dance around the house. My picking up of the saxophone in my late teens comes from hearing the tenor sax solos on Little Richard and Fats Domino records, which I played along with and learnt that way. They really caught my ear. The solos I heard on those great records were so well constructed – they only had twelve bars to work within, so they had to be.

As a young teen, I also loved watching *Top of The Pops*. That was where I first saw Roy Wood and Wizzard, who often had two saxes in the line-up, baritone and tenor. Another big influence of mine.

The first record I bought was a cheapo Chuck Berry greatest hits on vinyl that had all the big records on it – 'Maybelline', and all that – which I got with my own money from Woolworths. Thankfully these were the original Chuck recordings and not those terrible re-recordings they used to put out.

My dad first saw Bill Haley live when he started out, in the high schools back in the States, where he was playing a more country and western/bluegrass style of music. This was way before he had all the hits, and he built his audience through those gigs. He had a sort of R&B hit with 'Crazy Man Crazy' before he did the rock'n'roll. I loved the sax solos and that big beat dancing sound that Haley created, so I was very much a fan of his.

Bill was a fairly regular visitor to the UK, but then he announced his retirement when his original sax player died. At that time, Bill was still only in his mid-fifties and I thought I'd never see him, but somehow he changed his mind, and he returned with a big European tour. You couldn't get tickets, mate, there was big demand, but I managed to finally get a couple.

The build-up to the gig went on for months. We all wanted to see this iconic figure in the flesh. It was to be his first gig in three years, and fittingly it was at The Royalty in Southgate, a big rock'n'roll club.

Finally, the day arrived. The atmosphere on the night was fantastic, with the crowd dressed up to the nines. The place was full of the old-school Teds in their drapes, then us at the rockabilly end of it in caps and box jackets, and the nutters in donkey jackets and steel toe-cap boots, calling themselves hillbillies. It was a mad old scene in 1979.

A lot of the other original rock'n'rollers had by this point fully embraced the Seventies, so you'd see Little Richard and Chuck Berry in flowery shirts and flares, and they'd end up playing twenty-minute versions of their hits. But Bill was great, as he'd hardly changed. I loved his image, with the mad kiss curl, the bow tie and the tux, and his Gibson guitar. He looked pretty good, if a little heavier.

His vocals were exactly the same as they were back in the Fifties, too, and he was using the same arrangements, so it was like listening to the records, with that mad high voice. Tunes on the set list that night included 'The Saints' Rock 'N Roll', 'Rip It Up', 'See You Later, Alligator' and 'Rock-A-Beatin'-Boogie'. Looking back, he probably only sang seven or eight numbers himself and farmed the rest out to the band, which was made up of a couple of British Comets, which we really didn't mind because they still sounded pretty good. I guess it might have been better to have the original band, but I loved it.

I was still at school at the time, so I bunked off the next day, because we got absolutely hammered that night. But it was a knockout, and we were high for days after.

Bill died a couple of years later, in 1981, on the Texas–Mexico border. His last years were quite sad; a couple of his business ventures had failed, hotels and that, and he died a chronic alcoholic.

Still, he will always remain an iconic figure. He didn't invent rock'n'roll (no one did; it was a conglomeration of all sorts of different stuff), but Bill kicked it all off with '(We're Gonna) Rock Around The Clock' in 1956 and the 1955 film *Blackboard Jungle*. He was the first popular rock'n'roll star, predecessor to the likes of Chuck Berry and Elvis Presley. Some would say he stole it all from black American artists, but so did everybody at the time, and people also stole off him, because he had very much a country-influenced sound, which he cleverly mixed with rhythm and blues to create his own big beat sound. People should talk about him more because he was a pioneer. He is really only maligned because he didn't look like Elvis (he wasn't a handsome guy; he looked more like a farmer or something, I guess).

But you know, I prefer Bill to Elvis. Elvis was the better singer, but overall I preferred the Haley package. Bill was a hero of mine and, when asked to contribute to this book, I thought of this gig immediately, because it reminded me of growing up hearing my dad's records and learning to play the saxophone along to them.

adidas
adidasunderground

THE STONE ROSES
VILLAGE UNDERGROUND, HOXTON, LONDON
6 AUGUST 2012
JOHNNY HARRIS, ACTOR

I could write a long list of unforgettable gigs. Paul Weller in New York City. Ocean Colour Scene and The Specials at Gunnersbury Park … that was an incredible night. But the one that really blew my heart open was when The Stone Roses reformed and played a tiny secret gig in Hoxton's Village Underground in 2012.

Shane Meadows had just directed me in This Is England '86 a year or so before, and we'd all heard that he was now holed up somewhere with the Stone Roses! It was massive news that the band had reformed … and Shane was now hidden away with them somewhere in the countryside, capturing the whole thing for what would eventually become his documentary on the band, Made Of Stone (2013).

That first album was the one! 'Fool's Gold' was like nothing I'd ever heard before. Up until that point, all of the music I'd really been into had always come from the generations before – The Clash, The Beatles, The Stones etc. But once that album landed in 1989 … from that moment onwards, it felt like my generation had a soundtrack and a scene all of our own. I never saw the Roses live though, and had given up any hope of that ever happening in my lifetime after they disbanded in 1996.

However, fifteen years later, and I definitely remember there being a whisper of a secret warm-up gig going around. A real buzz, but no one was quite sure of when, or where it was, or even if it was true. Either way, there seemed to be zero chance of buying a ticket. Then my mate and fellow actor Vicky McClure contacted me, saying, "Shane's messaged. He can't say why, but he's told us to keep next Monday night free. He's inviting us somewhere special!" I felt like a kid at Christmas. I must have played the album a thousand times that week.

The night came and it was all confirmed. My ex-wife Maria and I met up with Vicky, her partner, Jonny Owen, and Jo Hartley (from This Is England). We'd been invited to the pre-show party. I'd not been invited to many things like this before and it all started to get a little surreal. I'd look to my left and there was Paul Weller. Look to my right, and there was Jimmy Page, or Mick Jones. The whole place was buzzing.

We then went into the venue, and you could feel the intensity. It was tiny. A few hundred at most, all packed in, and the stage was just yards away. The DJ was playing some great tunes and the excitement was really building. Then a text message came through, saying there had been a row backstage and it had all kicked off – between Ian and Reni, I think. It looked like they weren't going to come out and that the whole thing might fall through. This went on for about an hour and it genuinely seemed like it was all over. I couldn't believe it. I was gutted … and then … all of a sudden, 'Stoned Love' by The Supremes came on loud over the speakers and the whole place erupted. It was like someone had plugged the room into the mains, it was just incredible.

I was stone-cold sober that night. I just remember feeling so completely present as they walked out on stage. It felt like slow motion. I was taking in every single detail and then it just went off in the biggest way. Ian Brown had us in the palm of his hand. I've never known an energy like it. Unbelievable. There was another moment during 'I Am The Resurrection'. Jonny Owen and I were sort of pogoing and sweating and I remember feeling like I was floating in mid-air and thinking, "This is the greatest night of my fucking life! I don't ever want to forget this moment … and I never will!" It was powerful stuff.

I remember Maria and I walked all the way home together that night, from Hoxton to Elephant and Castle. We just didn't want the night to end. Walking and walking, over the river, trying to take in what had just happened. It kind of signified something for me, that gig. It felt like certain things had come full circle in my life. I couldn't quite believe I was there … and so were they. Very surreal. Just a glorious, glorious night.

I'll never forget it.

THE JAM
WEMBLEY ARENA, LONDON
1 DECEMBER 1982
MORGAN HOWELL, ARTIST

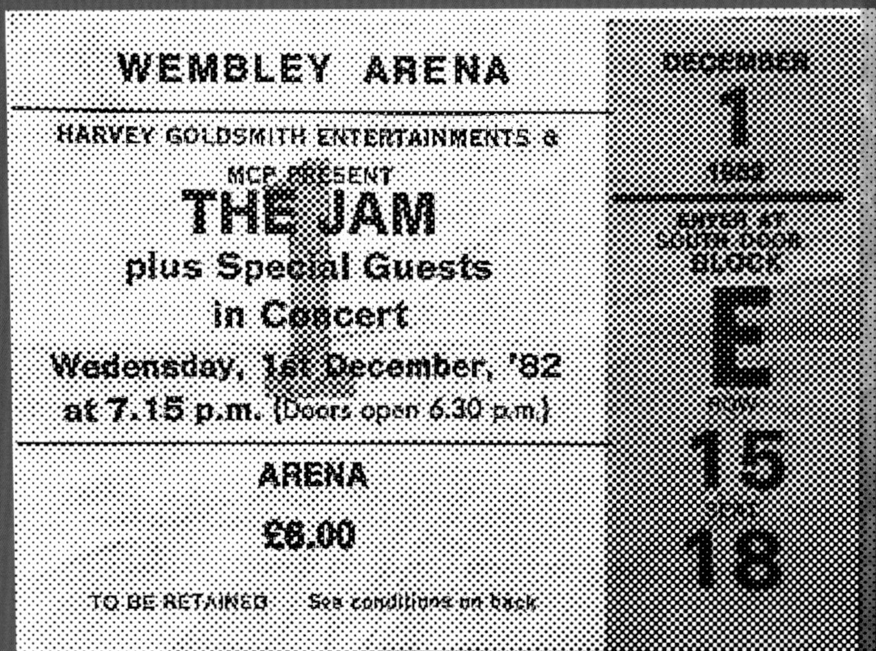
WEMBLEY ARENA

HARVEY GOLDSMITH ENTERTAINMENTS &
MCP PRESENT
THE JAM
plus Special Guests
in Concert
Wednesday, 1st December, '82
at 7.15 p.m. (Doors open 6.30 p.m.)

ARENA
£6.00

TO BE RETAINED See conditions on back

DECEMBER
1
1982
ENTER AT
SOUTH DOOR
BLOCK
E
ROW
15
18

It's not easy remembering events forty years on. I do know that I'd left Verulam Boys School in the summer of 1982 at the tender age of sixteen. I'd learnt a bit of attitude, how to dress sharply in my dad's Barker shoes and an Oxfam suit, but not much else in all truth.

By 8 July I'd met Jacquie, who would be going back to Loreto College in September to pass all her A-levels. I had hopelessly fallen for her when she accepted a chip from me on St Albans Market, where Dad had his smart stall on Saturdays selling his watercolours. Working on the market was great for meeting girls. And learning a thing or two about presentation. At sixteen, the only thing I could do well was paint and draw. And today a little art direction, too. That long summer had me traipsing around the art colleges with my portfolio, choosing the right course. I'd had a chance, albeit a slither, to go to art school in the States, but I just couldn't leave her. We're still sharing chips forty years later.

Art school was a shocker. I'd been the best artist at school by miles, and I knew it. I'd even won the school prize. But here I wasn't. There were others who outshone me, and it was tough at first. It was the only thing I could do, for Christ's sake. Apart from the band that is. That started when we were thirteen or so. A three-piece, a bit like The Jam, with me on guitar, centre stage, the singer; Sean on bass; and my best mate Sid on drums. I thought we were great. We were awful. (Except Sean who was, and still is, a great player). Back then Weller was everything to me. It seemed somehow achievable to be someone like him. He made it look so effortless and I reckoned, if I concentrated hard, I could probably write songs like that too.

So here I was, in the crowd but on my own at Wembley Arena on 1 December 1982. My new art school mates weren't into The Jam, so I'd gone on my tod. It was the end of their Beat Surrender Tour. Now I don't remember if we knew at the time that these were the last Jam gigs. I could look it up but that would be cheating.

My god, all those amazing songs: 'It's Too Bad', 'Boy About Town', 'That's Entertainment' (and yes, I can still recite all the words), 'Mr. Clean', '...Malice', 'But I'm Different Now' and The Kinks' 'David Watts'. What was I thinking? I'll tell you exactly what I was thinking: I could never do this. I could never write these songs. I could never mean this much to all these people. I'll stick to what I know. I went to the bar for some warm lager and met one of the Modettes from art college. Very lovely, but she was no Jacquie.

In truth, I don't remember much else about the night. No phones being held up, that's for sure. Gigs were so much simpler then. No flash lighting or screens. It seems obvious to say but you just had the music and the crowd. And on that night, for a change, not many skinheads about, so I don't remember the fear that often accompanied going to gigs in those early days.

The Jam had been my band and in them I saw everything I had wanted to be at that tender age. That night marked the end of all that. Waiting at the station a massively rowdy crowd only had one song to sing, and we did – "The distant echo, of faraway voices boarding faraway trains."

Fast forward to 2018 and I'm exhibiting my work at the Q Awards. Paul Weller was there presenting a Lifetime Achievement Award to The Kinks. This is relevant because when Paul was just ten, he'd bought The Kinks' 'Wonderboy' 45 on Pye Records, the first single purchased with his own coin. It was also John Lennon's favourite Kinks song. I had been asked to help celebrate the fiftieth anniversary of *The Kinks Are the Village Green Preservation Society* with one of my pieces. Somehow, I managed to persuade the record company, BMG, and Ray Davies to commission me to paint a giant facsimile picture of this 7-inch single for a special celebratory exhibition (painting supersize images of classic singles is what I do). On the night, Rick Buckler was there. First time I'd seen him since Wembley Arena way back in 1982. For me, the work represents a very special moment, when the baton was handed from one great British songsmith to another. All three surviving Kinks signed it.

Outside the Q Awards, Paul was in the Roundhouse car park, pulling on a smoke. He beckoned me over for a chat and asked after Lynval and Horace from The Specials. I'm glad I stuck to what I know.

LIAM GALLAGHER/THE CHARLATANS
ETIHAD STADIUM, MANCHESTER
1 JUNE 2022
TOM HOY, BROADCASTER

Normally people know me as either a radio presenter, modernist style enthusiast or just that blonde guy with glasses who thinks he's Michael Caine!

Through my work, I'm very lucky enough to have met lots of different people within music and fashion that lead very interesting lives. My good friend Wilko, who does lots of work for Liam Gallagher, texted me one day and asked if I'd like to join him and help him out in the photography pit at Liam's sold-out night at Manchester City FC's Etihad Stadium. I won't lie, this did come as a surprise to me. I'd done a little bit of photography in the past, but I wasn't about to turn down this opportunity! It couldn't be too hard. Could it?

I've been in Manchester now for about eight years. Everyone who lives here knows that this is a city that takes two things very seriously: music and football (all right, and maybe the rain too). My knowledge of football is quite limited; I enjoy the odd international game, but I mostly know bits and bobs about West Ham that I got from my East-ender Grandad growing up.

I'd never been to the Etihad before. I knew it was big, but it wasn't until I got there that day that I realised the scale of the place. The area surrounding the stadium is bigger than the stadium itself – it's a football village, with bars, merch stands, food vendors and big screens. It all felt very American. As you can probably tell from my ramblings that make me sound as if I've just been transported from the 1850s to the present day, I don't spend a lot of time at football stadiums!

Liam had two support artists that day. The first was Goat Girl, a post-punk band from South London. They're very much part of the new generation of post-punk surfacing at the moment. The second support were fellow Manchester legends The Charlatans.

Goat Girl were great – a friend had seen them before and gave me the heads-up. Aesthetics are something that have always been important to me and they are a cool-looking band, so much so that at first I couldn't tell who the lead singer was – they all looked great.

Next up, The Charlatans. Although I wouldn't say I'm massively familiar with all of their songs, I've always really respected Tim Burgess and what he stands for, and his support for the music scene as a whole. He also reminds me of a piece of Warhol pop art, with his blunt haircut and art school-like sensibilities. He's a cool guy.

After making our way back out the stadium between acts, we had a chance for a quick cup of tea, then we got the call. Walking back into the stadium, the anticipatory atmosphere had cranked up another level. I'd met Liam before and I'd seen him perform too, and whatever you think about him, no one quite holds an audience like he does. His music has now been handed down to a new generation of fans who, even though they weren't alive in the Nineties when Oasis ruled the world, hold his songs close to their hearts. The songs mean something to them, and you can tell.

A sea of bucket hats, parkas and City blue filled the stadium. Flares filled the air. I made my way into the photography pit, and straight away I saw a fan holding a flag that read, "from Argentina to Manchester, for your maracas!" I waved at the guy and captured the image. I think the picture shows just how much Liam's fans love him, the fact they'd travel to the other side of the globe just to see him play in his hometown.

Then, the stage went dark and the walk-on music started, the crowd erupted to the sound of 'Fuckin' In The Bushes'. A VT showed LG throughout the years, captions would display reading, "Godlike", "Celestial", "Rasta", highlighting Liam's sense of humour and the iconic status he has achieved.

Then, the man himself walked on, wearing a floral overhead smock, tambourine in hand, to a hometown audience that welcomed him like a king.

The music started and we were thrown straight into the deep end of the Nineties with the Oasis classic 'Hello'. The ground vibrated with the feeling of thousands of fans jumping up and down. And all I could think was, "How the hell am I here?"

As much as I was taking loads of pictures of LG, I was taking pictures of the crowd too. I could only imagine how it felt to be Liam on stage, gazing upon this sea of fans.

Next up on the set list was 'Rock 'N' Roll Star'. By now I'd settled in, and I was right beneath Liam in the pit, seizing every opportunity I could to get a good image. I lined up the viewfinder and then saw Liam had come right to the edge of the stage, waving tambourine above his head, and straight away I thought, "This is going to make a great picture!" Someone then tapped me on the knee – who was that? Was I too close and being moved on? I looked around and no one had tapped me ... the tambourine had! Liam had attempted to throw it off stage into the crowd and missed, hitting me instead! Another photographer picked it up and threw it into the crowd.

I wouldn't say this was my favourite gig of all time, but it was certainly one of the most memorable for me. It was my first time working in the photography pit and a completely new way of seeing a gig. I felt like a fly that had landed on a microphone stand, soaking up the atmosphere – something that you wouldn't normally get to do. I loved every minute!

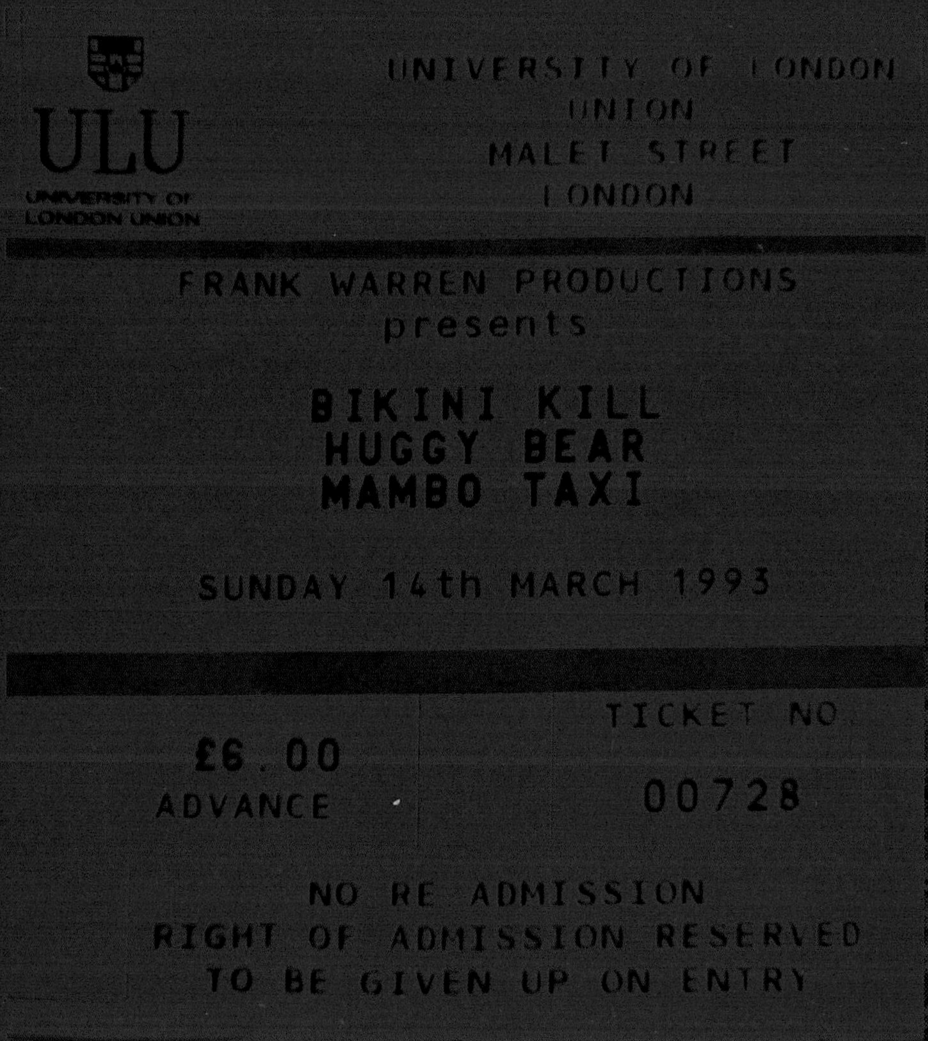
ULU
UNIVERSITY OF LONDON UNION

UNIVERSITY OF LONDON
UNION
MALET STREET
LONDON

FRANK WARREN PRODUCTIONS
presents

BIKINI KILL
HUGGY BEAR
MAMBO TAXI

SUNDAY 14th MARCH 1993

£6.00
ADVANCE

TICKET NO.
00728

NO RE ADMISSION
RIGHT OF ADMISSION RESERVED
TO BE GIVEN UP ON ENTRY

BIKINI KILL/HUGGY BEAR/MAMBO TAXI
ULU, LONDON
14 MARCH 1993
PHILIP ILSON, ARTISTIC DIRECTOR,
LONDON SHORT FILM FESTIVAL

Musically, I was obsessed with what was coming out of the American alternative scene in the late Eighties. I hoovered up anything released on SST, Dischord and Blast First and saw early London gigs from Dinosaur Jr., Meat Puppets and the Pixies. Everything changed with the release of Nirvana's platinum-selling album *Nevermind* in 1991, and although I was a fan, the newly named grunge scene started to hold little interest. Simultaneously, our own indie underground embraced a tweeness in the Eighties, encapsulated by release of the C86 cassette and bands such as The Vaselines, Shop Assistants, Talulah Gosh and The Pastels. Over in Olympia, Washington state, bands releasing on Kill Rock Stars and K Records took on an element of that 'twee' aesthetic.

Many US bands breaking through had female members, including those bigger names such as Sonic Youth, the Pixies and Throwing Muses, and K and Kill Rock Stars were releasing lo-fi releases by female-centric bands including Mecca Normal, Bratmobile, The Make-Up, and Bikini Kill. The 1991 International Pop Underground Festival in Olympia brought together many of these acts, with their DIY, lo-fi and fanzine culture. The political aspects of DIY culture had the grass roots support of feminism, and many female band members began to meet to discuss sexism and misogyny in the music business, even within their own scene, the results of which they published in fanzines such as *riot grrl* and *Girl Power* to sell at gigs. Bikini Kill became the unofficial mouthpiece for this confrontational underground feminist punk movement through singer Kathleen Hanna's passionate on-stage rants and her rebel call of "Girls to the front!".

My first introduction to the riot grrrl scene was a *Melody Maker* cover story in October 1992, after which I made many trips to Rough Trade to pick up 7-inch singles and compilation albums of bands whose names are forever lost. There was now an emerging UK scene, most notoriously Brighton-based Huggy Bear, who started an actual riot on the Channel 4 late-night magazine show *The Word* when they were booked to perform live and were later ejected from the studio by security.

Bikini Kill first came to the UK in 1993 when they released a split album with Huggy Bear on Kill Rock Stars, which resulted in them touring together. On 14 March, I went alone to ULU in Central London to see this show. The student union was a regular on the gig circuit for smaller and medium-size bands, and I had been many times before and walked upstairs to the bar. The fanzines were on sale, there now being a significant homegrown following of the riot grrrl movement. PJ Harvey, dressed in mid-length denim shorts and giant DM 'bovver' boots, was sat on the floor against the wall, engrossed in reading one. She was still a significantly underground artist with just two lo-fi albums of her own out at this time, not yet crossed over, and I think I was one of the few to recognise her.

First band on that night was Mambo Taxi, part of the London lo-fi scene based around Wiiija Records, which also included the indie-punk bands Cornershop and Voodoo Queens.

I was wary of the confrontational aspect of Bikini Kill, so I watched the show from the small circle area in the ULU venue. I was surprised how much talking Kathleen Hanna did between songs, but she was, and is, an impassioned performer with a lot to say around sexual and gender politics. Even though the gig had a strong political stance, musically it was raw and exciting, with Hanna flitting between angry polemic and a tweeness that harked back to that C86 aesthetic.

That gig, and indeed the rest of the tour, were documented by filmmaker Lucy Thane in her film *It Changed My Life: Bikini Kill in the UK*, which I bought on VHS at a later gig. I got to know Lucy well ten years later through my own work in the film industry. However, riot grrrl fizzled out soon after, though in retrospect this was largely down to many artists and musicians refusing to talk to the mainstream press due to being misrepresented as "men-hating lesbians" (sic). The 1996 short documentary *Dirty Girls* was a negative look at alternative culture among those high-schoolers who didn't conform.

Bikini Kill split up in 1997 and Hanna had much greater commercial success in one of her next band projects, Le Tigre. The all-female punk bands Sleater-Kinney and Hole had both emerged from the scene to create more polished and commercial rock music, to much acclaim.

Since then, the riot grrl movement has experienced a resurgence, returning to the public consciousness via Sara Marcus' 2010 book *Girls To The Front*, the 2013 documentary feature on Kathleen Hanna *The Punk Singer*, and the 2021 Netflix feature Moxie about a teenage girl discovering her mum's *riot grrl* fanzines and memorabilia in a suitcase under the bed. Bikini Kill have also reformed, playing two sold-out nights at the 5,000-capacity Brixton Academy in 2021, which was great.

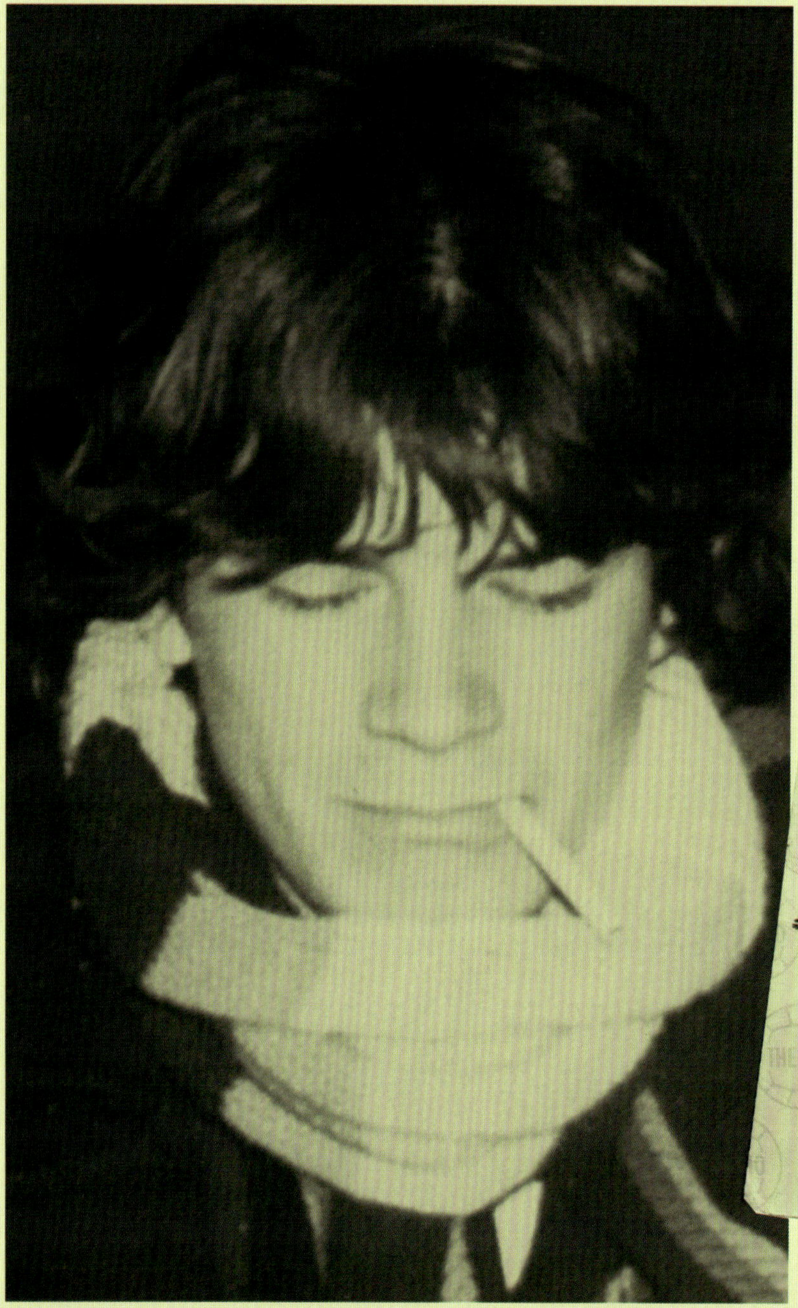

THE WHO
CHARLTON FOOTBALL GROUND, LONDON
31 MAY 1976
JOHN INGLEDEW, PHOTOGRAPHER

We knew their records were terrible, inane and idiotic – 'My Coo Ca Choo', 'Wig Wam Bam' and "Ho-chi-ka-ka-ho Co-Co". This childish nonsense was the weekly fare of *Top of the Pops*. The performers were prancing, glittery and satin-clad, teetering on ridiculous platform shoes. It was not for us. It was the mid-Seventies, we were fifteen, and instead of this weak pop we craved to discover and taste much stronger, more potent stuff.

I lived in Orpington, a commuter town south-east of London. Here there'd been occasional glimpses of more exciting things; older lads at our school had been spotted walking round with mysterious looking LPs tucked under their arms, packaged in card-board sleeves, stamped crudely with band names as if done with a John Bull home-printing kit. Through the grapevine we discovered these were bootleg records, secretly taped by smuggling recording equipment into live concerts then pressed as LPs, by pirates!

How on earth could we get our hands on such thrilling-sounding booty? We now knew there was no point in asking for them at WH Smith's Record Department or the Spinning Disc, the high street's only other record shop, as bootlegs could only be procured on the black market – and there wasn't one of those in Orpington.

The Who Live At Leeds seemed to be being carried around more than others, though I was confused by the title, thinking it meant that the band lived in the West Yorkshire city. A copy was eventually borrowed from a mate's older cousin, and we gathered to listen. This seemed like the hard stuff at last: illicit, and intoxicating. We were hooked.

We applied for tickets the week the news appeared that The Who were going to play live concerts. The ad for the three-date tour featured a map of Britain, on which cartoon haracters of the band cavorted, a colossal football bouncing out of the page with the names of all those appearing. The significance of the ball was that the concerts were to be held in football stadiums, with one at Charlton's ground just twelve miles from Orpington, a short ride on the train. Perfect.

I can't remember which of my mates sent off our postal orders, but the tickets were four quid each, every penny of a whole month's pocket money. Sacrifices had had to be made and issues of Score were missed and packets of TOPPS football cards went unpurchased.

When they arrived, the tickets were beautiful. Shiny with black text, a large 'WHO' logo with a repeated pattern of blue footballs in the background. Mine was number 022047. I'd never been to an event with 22,046 other people and wondered what it would be like. It said 'THE WHO and their friends' – great to know it was to be a friendly affair and also thrilled to see the concert time for all the bands was from 2 p.m. to 10 p.m. This was brilliant news, as I hadn't yet asked my mum and dad whether I could go, and these were respectable, parent-pleasing concert times – practically a guarantee that I would be back on the train home by eleven, at that point the time at which I had to be back from parties. The concert was also a few days after my sixteenth birthday, and this was to be used in persuading them I was now easily old enough to be allowed to go with my mates to my first ever rock concert.

The deal was negotiated and, having promised not to drink alcohol, smoke cigarettes and be in by eleven, I was going to see The Who.

I bought the booze from Graham Turley, nicknamed Turl. Funds were low due to the ticket costs though drink was vital as we were going with girls who would need to be impressed. Turl was the answer. He was in my year at school and had a bit of a business going making homemade wine in his parent's basement. 'Turl's Wine' was 50p a bottle and had quite successfully fuelled our parties when the local off-licences had proved reluctant to serve us anything other than tins of shandy.

On 31 May 1976, with a couple of bottles of Turl's '75 vintage white in a duffle bag and ten No.6 cigarettes in the pocket of my Levi's jacket, I set off to meet my mates Alex, Simon and Fraser at the station. The girls coming were called Patsy and … I can't remember the name of the other. But beautiful Patsy Watson I can still picture now. She'd just started going out with Simon.

What a day. The reporters from the music papers *NME* and *Melody Maker* praised the concert, saying it had been brilliant and The Who superb – in fact, by far the greatest band in the whole world. What concert had these journos been at? Impossible that it had been the one we'd witnessed – violence, a decrepit death-trap venue, the misery and the horror, the horror!

I'd been a bit worried by the zero at the front of my ticket number 022047 – did that mean they were going to sell 100,000 tickets? It certainly looked like they had as we queued for hours to get through the turnstiles.

Inside it was already packed to bursting, touts had sold tens of thousands of fake tickets, and some, like young Suggs from Madness, for whom this was also his first live concert, had simply climbed over the wall of the ground with his mates.

It's difficult to believe now but crushes and crowd surges were laughed off as being part of the pageant of being in any big football ground in the Seventies, and that day in Charlton's ground it was no different. We could have died.

Another distinctly Seventies phenomenon was the extremely high prevalence of casual violence. If you think people are touchy now, then to catch the wrong bloke's eye, even look in their general direction, brush past or, heaven forbid, be within yards of his girlfriend meant impossible-to-diffuse explosions of anger and a smack in the mouth. The perpetra-tors of such violence were known as being 'hard', and it was plain to see this concert had a high hard bloke count.

By mid-afternoon heavy rain was falling and any lingering high spirits had been doused. The crush meant the hard types had their excuse to bloody strangers, and fists flew all around us. We were trapped, impossible to escape in the packed crowd. It was nasty, frightening, an ugly, menacing atmosphere, and that was before the glass bottles started raining down. There were five whole hours to kill, or be killed in, before the band were due on stage.

They came on late, waiting until darkness so their weedy lasers would show up in the sky. The stage was soaked and singer Roger Daltrey at once slipped and went flat on his arse. They played their hits, Pete Townshend talked a bit, drummer Keith Moon looked chubby, bassist John Entwistle bored, the crowds sang along, the hard blokes punched strangers. It was bloody loud. After an hour and a bit, the show was done, ten minutes of cheering and clapping unable to persuade the band to return. And that was it.

Following the concert, for no apparent reason the police forced us and many thousands of others to wait for two hours in the terraced backstreets outside the ground. Where had they been earlier when they should have been arresting all the ticket touts, hard blokes and wall-jumping Nutty Boys?

We were damp, bedraggled, dog-tired, ears loudly ringing, last trains long departed and with a dozen-mile tramp home ahead of us and furious parents awaiting our return. Who were the clueless bozos that had put on this shamble of shit? This was supposed to be entertainment, I felt mugged, mugged off, a mug. Drenched and rinsed.

After the Charlton debacle the organiser's had a genius idea to make good with the many thousands of fans with genuine tickets who'd been locked out when the gates were shut due to the massive overcrowding. He'd bus them up for free to the next date of the tour, at Cardiff City's stadium, thereby causing massive overcrowding again.

In the end, parents were phoned and as dawn broke our sorry party were picked up somewhere near Bromley. Lesson learnt; we won't get fooled again.

This three-date UK tour was clearly a cynical smash-and-grab to make The Who lots of quick cash. Charlton had presumably been picked as the London venue because of its cheapness and possession of a dodgy safety certificate, allegedly.

We'd also now grasped that music journalists will always write that a big band are amazing live, as to avoid doing so would mean kissing goodbye to their Access All Areas passes to the next tour, and they'd be out in the rain with the rest of us punters.

I never again paid hard-earned postal orders to see a band that have reached the stadium-playing stage of their career. Soccer grounds are for football and that's the only thing I've watched in them in the forty-five years since. We should have known The Who were played out by 1976; they'd been at it well over a decade and every member had already shown their disinterest in the band by releasing at least one piss-poor solo album. I'd expected more than just hearing the hits and a sing-along. There'd been nothing special or unique, and I thought it pathetic not to play us an encore after what we'd had to endure! Who doesn't play encores when the crowd are baying for one? This showed what they felt for their fans – deep contempt. We'd seen The Who just going through the motions – apparently barely speaking to each other at the time, their only real means of connection to the crowd being to play as loudly as possible. They were yesterday's men.

Of course, this isn't what I told my mates at school, which was that it was amazing and I'd undoubtedly seen the greatest band on earth.

A couple of years later I was at art school in London, exactly the right time and place to see the brilliant punk, new wave and Two-Tone bands emerge. The music was raw, vibrant, remarkable. This was my generation, so much better than those Sixties has-beens.

Simon and Patsy split up shortly after we'd been to Charlton. Though I was desperate to ask her out I knew it could never work; no relationship could possibly survive what we'd all experienced that day. The horror, the horror!

THE
WHO
THE SENSATIONAL
ALEX HARVEY BAND
LITTLE FEAT • OUTLAWS
STREETWALKERS
WHO PUT THE BOOT IN
AT CHARLTON ATHLETIC FOOTBALL CLUB LONDON 31st MAY
CELTIC FOOTBALL CLUB GLASGOW 5th JUNE
SWANSEA CITY FOOTBALL CLUB SWANSEA 12th JUNE

BILL HALEY & HIS COMETS
DOMINION THEATRE, LONDON
FEBRUARY 1957
ANDREW LOOG OLDHAM, THE GUVNOR

My mum had a 'sideboard style' record player, stacked with 78s by Frank Sinatra, Nat King Cole and Johnnie Ray. With a record player at home, music began to play an increasingly influential role in my life. I bought fan magazines, to learn all I could about Mr Ray, whose chart-topping single, 'Cry,' had won him the devotion of British fans. His concerts at the London Palladium led to mass female hysteria. To me, Johnny Ray took music to another level, with his sexual presence, and despite his sexual preference he was a popular star with women.

In April 1955 I bought my first record, a single by Perez Prado called 'Cherry Pink And Apple Blossom White', and when I played it, I was transported to glamorous movie sets featuring femme fatales and white dinner jacket-wearing could-be-villains.

Johnny Ray was booked to play the London Palladium in spring 1955 and I was among the hundreds gathered outside, and then I hung around until he appeared later to sign autographs.

Then, I became all shook up by the excitement that American singer Bill Haley was generating in the UK. 'Rock Around The Clock' was causing a sensation among British teenagers, already hooked on rock'n'roll. I bought the record, played it endlessly, and teased my hair into a Haley-inspired kiss-curl.

Bill then came to town in February 1957, to play the Dominion Theatre on Tottenham Court Road. I was twelve and I had a ticket, which cost ten shillings and sixpence. I went by myself, which was fine, since most others wouldn't have understood my pre-show ritual in the men's room, perfecting my kiss-curl.

The Dominion is a magnificent theatre and its stalls slope towards the object of the evening's awe like an audio-visual wedding train. I sat among 2,000 Teds, ready to rock in their powder grey drape jackets and brothel creepers, with their girls all bleached and quiffed, every inch the pearly queens.

Teds were magnificent specimens, with an attitude way out above any station. They were the first teenagers to stand up, let it rip and be counted. Beatniks didn't count: they sat around drinking coffee and smoking Gauloises, while Teds draped and ducks-arsed themselves into a national outrage that made headlines. They spent their newly disposable incomes taking the piss. I loved the sight of a Ted on a high street a whole lot better than the first American rock'n'roller I got to see live.

Haley was a nightmare. After an hour and a half of Vic Lewis & His Orchestra, we then got a paltry thirty-five minutes from this fat, kiss-curled housewife from the middle of America, the uncle you never wanted, Bill Haley. He looked like a short-order cook from Oklahoma City.

Haley had also featured in two rock flicks the previous summer of 1956, Rock Around the Clock and Don't Knock the Rock. Audiences on both sides of the Atlantic danced in the aisles, ripped up the seats, and gave rock'n'roll a reputation to live up to. I saw the films in the sterile Haverstock Hill Odeon, with twenty other patrons, who tutted and shifted in their seats while I quietly tore a gash in mine.

Confronted by the mediocrity that was Haley, I thought for a moment that rock'n'roll was over. But recalling the then of Johnnie Ray and the now of Buddy Holly and Little Richard saved the day.

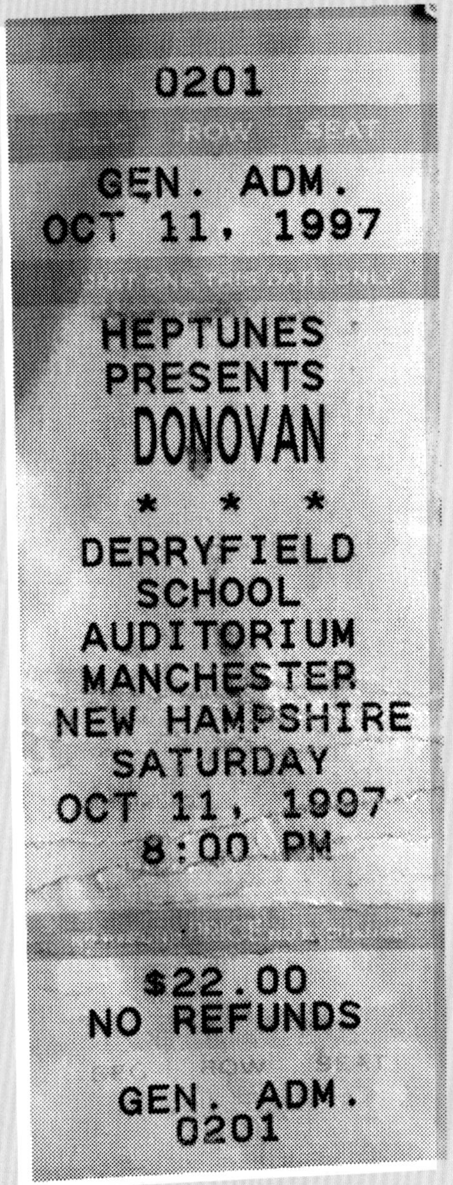

DONOVAN
DERRYFIELD SCHOOL AUDITORIUM, NEW HAMPSHIRE
11 OCTOBER 1997
CHRIS MAKRIS, TEACHER

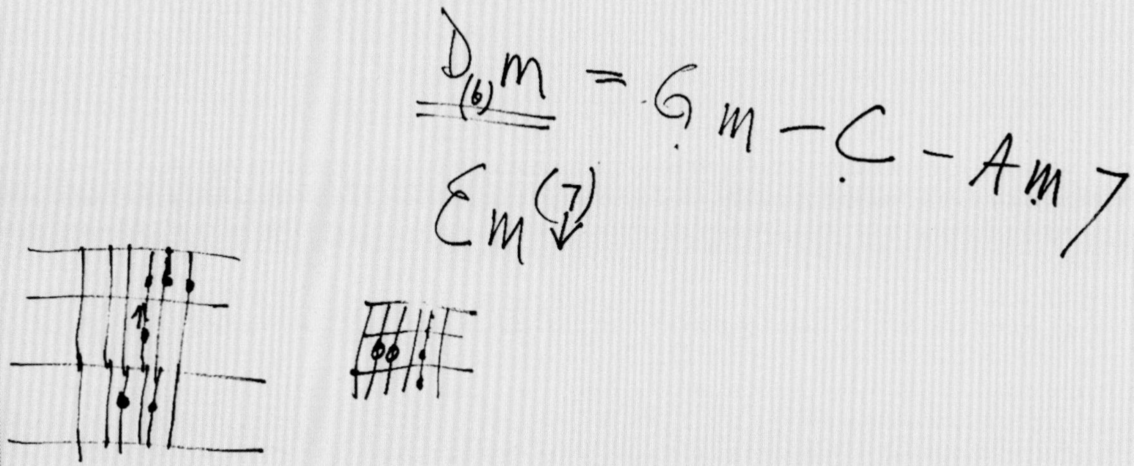

In 1964, at the age of ten, one of my best friends was AM radio. It was a lifeline. I now refer to these early days as my first experience with remote learning. My teachers? Beatles, Beach Boys, Rolling Stones, Supremes, Kinks, Mamas & Papas, Lovin' Spoonful ... too many to mention.

Their songs lifted me up. I connected with music on such a deep level. Since then, it's always been a huge part of me, helping shape the person I am today. I've noticed that, as many people have grown older, music has slowly faded out of their lives. It's become something to 'turn down' because it's too loud or a distraction. I still say turn it up.

When I see people today wearing earbuds, in a variety of settings, I chuckle and think back to that ten-year-old boy. Listening to music sixty years ago wasn't swiping a tiny computer to choose a particular song while walking down the street, watching television or having a meal. It meant constantly turning the dial on a device that wasn't always portable, hoping to catch a favourite song. There was significant investment and focus involved. Very little if any multitasking. More often than not, I'd hit the jackpot but quickly realise I'd missed everything but the tail-end of a favourite tune. The search would immediately begin again. I was smitten, and devoted to sounds coming from England. This would develop into a lifelong appreciation of the people and culture of that remarkable country. In fact, what I heard on the radio eventually led to me becoming a university exchange student in West Sussex and multiple trips over four decades to London, establishing meaningful and enduring friendships there.

Among the many musicians who made a positive impression on me was Donovan Leitch. He wrote and performed beautiful songs that, for me, were more than a few notches above the norm. His deeper LP cuts like 'Sand And Foam', 'Young Girl Blues', 'Sunny Goodge Street', 'Isle Of Islay' and so on were even better than his hits. Digging deeper into his catalogue, I found and appreciated his jazzier side as well as his earlier pure folk period. He was highly respected. When he came on the scene, he was dubbed the British Dylan. I love the scene in D.A. Pennebaker's 1967 documentary film *Don't Look Back*, when Donovan visits Dylan's hotel room. The respect on Bob's face is clear as he watches and listens to Donovan play. Also, worth mentioning is that in addition to contributing "sky of blue, sea of green" to *Yellow Submarine*, he wrote songs alongside the Fabs while all were on retreat in Rishikesh, India. I digress.

Jump ahead to 11 October 1997. I saw Donovan perform at a private school in New Hampshire to a small group of people (maybe fifty) in a very intimate theatre. Got there early and planted myself in a seat front row centre, just a few short feet from the small stage. One song and related story after another. After his performance I managed to talk my way backstage and found myself face to face with the man. Just Don and me. He was totally cool, friendly and ready for conversation. My years spent in independent study of all things related to pop music were paying off in a big way. We spoke of a few things, most of which have now been long forgotten, but I clearly remember part of it very fondly.

I'd always been taken by his song 'Lord Of The Reedy River'; it's a hauntingly beautiful tune that was picked to open Mary Hopkin's first LP. In addition to Mary's voice, Don and McCartney accompany her on acoustics.

Being somewhat of a guitar player I had tried to learn the guitar part from listening to the record but could never completely figure it out. Since the atmosphere was so relaxed, I jumped in the deep end and asked him for some help. He took the time to show me, additionally ripping a large piece of paper from a nearby sketch pad to write down the chord sequence and tabs.

A private guitar lesson from one of the good ones.

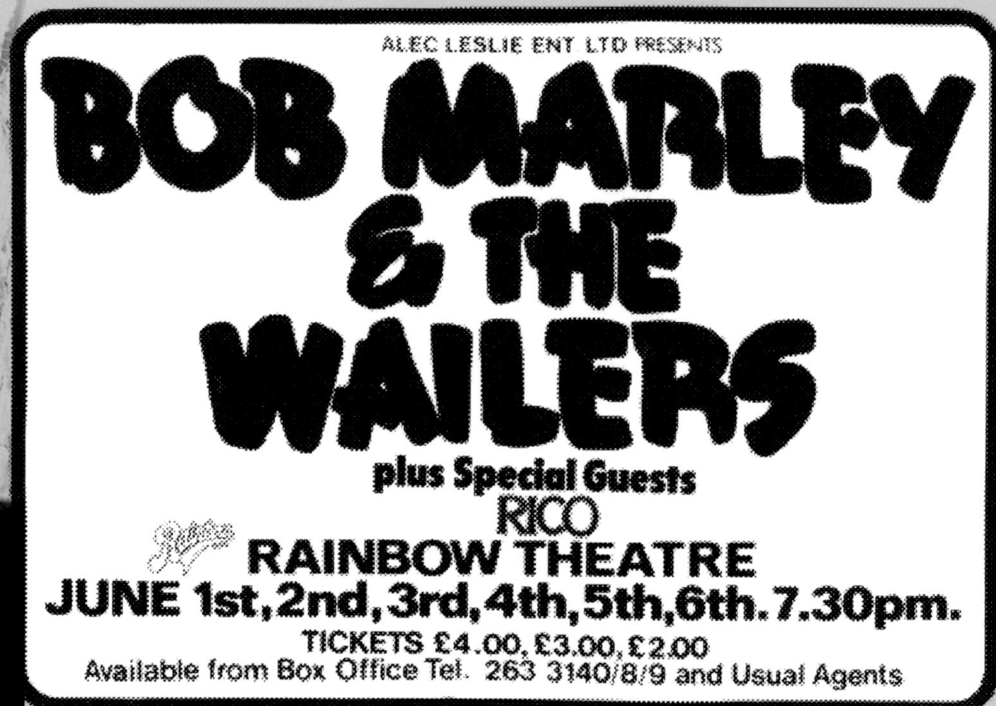
ALEC LESLIE ENT. LTD PRESENTS
BOB MARLEY & THE WAILERS
plus Special Guests
RICO
RAINBOW THEATRE
JUNE 1st, 2nd, 3rd, 4th, 5th, 6th. 7.30pm.
TICKETS £4.00, £3.00, £2.00
Available from Box Office Tel. 263 3140/8/9 and Usual Agents

BOB MARLEY & THE WAILERS
THE RAINBOW THEATRE, FINSBURY PARK, LONDON
JUNE 1977
GERED MANKOWITZ, PHOTOGRAPHER

I first got interested in music in the late Fifties. The first single I bought was 'Diana' by Paul Anka in 1958 and the first single that really hit home was Elvis' 'Jailhouse Rock'. 'Stay' by Maurice Williams & The Zodiacs was the single that set me on the road to find Motown and Stax, and eventually to soul and R&B.

I discovered photography around the same sort of time as I discovered music, when I was thirteen or fourteen. I developed a serious interest in quite quickly and I got an apprenticeship at Camera Press, a big photo agency, when I was just fifteen, and it took off from there.

The Bob Marley gig came at an extraordinary time for my wife Julia and myself, because we had just had our first child the previous year, so Jessie would have been about eight or nine months old and this would have been one of the first concerts we went to, together, after she was born, which was a huge thing in our lives.

Rock Against Racism had also been born in 1976, and there was this incredible upsurge of support, sympathy, interest and care, you know, for the issues relating to racism and particularly in music and the music business, which had come together for the movement.

Marley was an incredibly important global artist, who somehow embodied so much of what we all admired in black music back then. Having been drawn to black music from the early Sixties, including going to the first Tamla Motown show in 1965 in London at the Odeon Hammersmith, we were huge fans of Motown and Stax, and now reggae was so much of that moment in the 1970s.

I was quite aware of Bob from the beginning, because I did a lot with Island Records and Chris Blackwell [Island Records founder] was someone I considered a good friend. I'd been working with Chris since the Millie Small days and 'My Boy Lollipop', and I photographed Jackie Edwards, The Spencer Davis Group and later Traffic. I was conscious of the Jamaican roots of it all, and of Marley from the moment he emerged on the scene.

The Hammersmith Odeon, the Royal Albert Hall and the Rainbow were the foremost venues in London at the time. The Rainbow was particularly loved, although a pretty awkward place to get to. But it was a beautiful building, so the whole thing was a very special night on so many levels.

That night it was packed with Rastafarians, and an enormous percentage of black Londoners I guess, plus a lot of the music business was there, as it had always been very much a music business venue.

We went with a gang of friends who revolved around our studio, which was based in Great Windmill Street in Soho at that time, and we were all part of Rock Against Racism. We were all very much on the same page – anti-racist, anti-fascist, anti-NF [National Front] – and those nights became a rallying point, so being there on the night seemed important.

The atmosphere was fantastic, and the audience didn't stop moving, the vibe was just bopping, everybody was grooving. Honestly, the dope was so thick in the air that everyone was high because even if you weren't smoking, you were engulfed by it.

This was really paying homage to Marley and his music. I mean, he had a great band, with the backing singers all dressed in marvellous Rastafarian green head dresses. It was just fantastic. He played all his great hits and had slightly different sets each night. I honestly can't remember individual tracks, but it was a great night. I'm sure there was a lot of police around the building, because there always were, but I don't remember any static or issues. It was just a lovely, beautiful experience.

THE ROLLING STONES
BILLY PRESTON/THE METERS
EARLS COURT, LONDON
MAY 1976
WENDY MAY, DJ

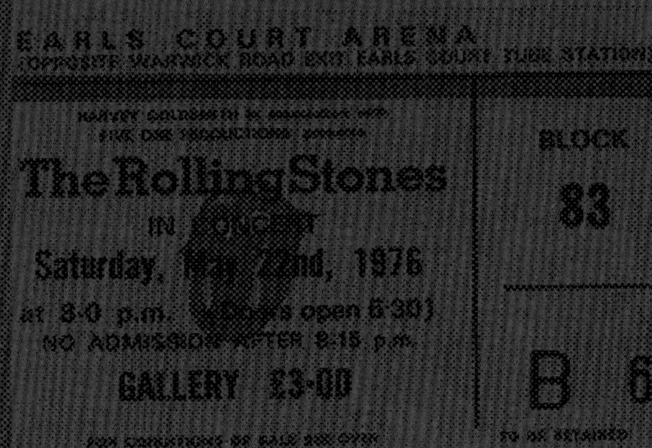

From as way back as I can remember, music has been in my life. I'm the youngest of loads of brothers and sisters, so I was surrounded by the rock'n'roll my brothers were listening to, from the likes of Buddy Holly to Tommy Steele. Then later I shared a bedroom with my sister Tina and she had a Dansette in our room, and from as early as I can remember I was always dancing and showing off in front of the others. She used to play her singles – mainly Motown and ska.

The first thing that felt like was mine was The Monkees. I was a big Mickey Dolenz fan, 'Circus Boy', y'know. I was quite late to buying records myself because my brothers and sisters had loads and my sister Jenny had a reel-to-reel, so I used to listen to that. I bought some singles from a record shop in Clapham on the Doctor Bird label when I was fourteen, and I played them on Tina's Dansette, as I didn't have a record player of my own till I left home at sixteen.

Once I left home, the first album I bought was The Pretty Things' *S. F. Sorrow*, from Beano's in Croydon, which was quite a jump from The Monkees!

As for this gig, I wouldn't say the Stones are one of my favourite bands, though I love the early stuff, but I'd gone right off them, when *Black And Blue* came out. I was going out with Dave Allen, who went on to produce The Human League and The Cure. He was five years older than me and we were living in a squat in Kingston at the start of the hot summer of 1976. I have no idea how we got the tickets, because they were like £3 to £5, which would have been quite a lot of money, and apparently it was completely oversubscribed. Not sure if we bunked in or what? Knowing us, we probably did.

I really wanted to see The Meters, because I was going to see pub rock bands, and I'd heard of them through those bands who were doing Dr. John songs and playing the New Orleans sound. They were supporting the Stones, so that was why we were there. I wasn't really going to big gigs then; I was seeing Graham Parker & The Rumour at ULU Tech, Ducks Deluxe and Bees Make Honey, bands like that. So, it was a bit different seeing gigs at a great big venue.

I grew up in Earls Court, so knew the exhibition centre really well from some of my earliest memories. My mum used to take us to the Ideal Home Exhibition, where we'd drool all over the things we couldn't afford to buy, like all working-class families did – that sort of aspiration for things we'd never have in our own home. The exhibition centre going was a real loss to London, I think, though the sound wasn't great there.

My main memory of the gig was that I was ejected! I got chucked out for dancing! We started moving when The Meters came on. Being eighteen, I always danced – nothing would stop me dancing. Anyway, I stood up and this woman behind me kicked me in the back of the legs and said something like, "Oi, I haven't paid good money to watch you gyrating your arse about in front of me!" and I said something, being the annoying teenager I was, that she was at one of the most danceable events in your life and you are going to just sit there? (Of course, I love a seat at a gig now!) The next thing I know, I was having an argument with this woman and this security person turned up and we got chucked out, during The Meters' set. But then, we got back in again. My memory's vague, but I've spoken to Dave and, yeh, we got back in through a toilet window.

As we got in, Billy Preston was playing. He looked fantastic and he lifted up the whole vibe. I felt really young in there; everybody else seemed so much older than me, and all happy to sit down in front of the so-called best rock'n'roll band in the world.

So we saw half The Meters, a bit of Billy Preston and half of the Stones once settled again. Of course, what was really annoying was that, by two-thirds through the Stones set, everyone was up and dancing! The Stones weren't my favourite thing of the night, definitely not. No, that was seeing The Meters, who years later became The Neville Brothers. They got the support on that tour when Mick Jagger had seen them at a party Paul McCartney had put on in California in early 1975, and Jagger absolutely loved them, so he invited them on their US tour the same year.

But The Meters didn't have a singer, and so they did a few dates without one before realising they really would need one to compete with Mick Jagger. So that's how Cyril Neville ended up in the band, and that was the line-up they brought over to the UK and which we saw that night.

As for me starting DJing, I guess the best bits of what I was hearing from my brothers and sisters, like the blues from me brother Arthur and the Motown and ska from my sisters, fed into that, but for me it was going to work in a record shop when I was eighteen, and then everything opened up. I was exposed to everything then. Punk was kicking in, of course.

I had a huge record collection by this point. When the skiffle group the Boothill Foot Tappers split up, their former agent, Ollie, who was now managing the Town and Country Club and putting all the bands on there, asked me to come DJ. He knew I had all those records and that I could throw a good party. We got all and sundry down and we had a great night, called it The Locomotion and started doing it regularly.

Eddie Piller summed it when he said there were other soul clubs, like the 6T'S all-nighters at the 100 Club and things like Sneakers over in Shepherds Bush, but they were mainly Northern Soul and R&B, so you wouldn't hear The Clash, Dexys Midnight Runners, The Smiths even, which I occasionally mixed with the James Brown beat, Joe Ely and 'Groovin' With Mr. Bloe'. My night definitely wasn't elitist.

I think the thing about me, compared with many DJs on that scene, was that records and live music was my thing. I never used to go to clubs, places like The Blitz. Wasn't for me. I would just go to see bands and if they had a DJ before and after the gig, that was great. Gigs at the Electric Ballroom were like that, somewhere you could stay late and carry on drinking and dancing. Loved that.

THE WHO/ROD STEWART & THE FACES/MOTT THE HOOPLE/DJ JEFF DEXTER
THE OVAL CRICKET GROUND, LONDON
18 SEPTEMBER 1971
MICHAEL MCCANN, PRINT WORKER

I seem to remember it was a fundraising gig, at a time when there was a real chance of the Oval going bankrupt. One of the fellas who put on the Isle of Wight gig in 1969 was looking for a venue to stage a concert in aid of Bangladesh. Surrey Cricket Club, looking to raise some funds, offered up the Oval.

I joined a queue for tickets at something like 6.30 a.m. and got in with my £2 ticket at about 8 a.m., and found myself not far from the front of the stage, sitting next to a fella who had come from Newcastle, whereas I lived a twenty-minute walk away. I remember it being a lovely sunny day. I've read since that there was something like 40,000 there. I had my Zenith camera with me, as photography was a hobby, and I was pleased I was close enough to get some good shots.

Security was controlled by the Hells Angels, so I intended to keep my nut down and behave, only I suddenly heard someone shouting, "Michael McCann! Up here!", and I looked and spotted a snapper I knew who worked on the *Evening Standard*. How he spotted me among that lot, I'll never know, but he did, and I have the photo he took of me in the crowd, with a thumbs-up salute sent his way. Anyway, he later found me and gave me his press pass, telling me to behave and not get pissed if I used it. Well, within ten minutes, I was up on the side of the stage taking my photos, some that I have still got. A right result.

A little fella then came out to MC the gig at about 11 a.m., dressed in cricket whites complete with pads, and I found out later that it was the legendary DJ Jeff Dexter. I remember Quintessence, Mott The Hoople and then Rod bounded on stage, understated as ever in a leopard-skin suit, which he later auctioned for the fundraiser. On stage with him were the legendary Faces: the two Ronnies, Wood and Lane with Ian McLagan and Kenney Jones, and they raced through their hits, like 'Maybe I'm Amazed', and that certainly got the crowd going. Rod had also kicked a load of footballs into the crowd, and they were soon whizzing about all over the place. Such a brilliant, good-time band.

After a bit of time setting up some gear, Jeff Dexter says, "All the way from Shepherds Bush…" and out come The Who. Moonie nicked a cricket bat Jeff was waving about and used it as a drumstick for their first number, 'I Can't Explain', and then lobbed it into the crowd! At the end of their show, the stage was full of broken instruments as Pete and Keith ran riot as per usual. The crowd was going potty and asking for an encore, but they had no chance. It was running over time as well, and I seem to remember the Old Bill getting edgy and looking to move everyone on.

£15,000 went to the Bangladesh fund and £3,000 to Surrey Cricket Club. There'd been more people at the concert than they'd had the entire cricket season.

A magic day.

THE CONCERT HALL

Billy Bragg

Thursday 14 December 2006

19:30

£16.00

Stalls

ST

Ticket B 6

BILLY BRAGG
READING TOWN HALL
14 DECEMBER 2006
ELAINE MCGINTY, MUSICIAN/WRITER/COMMUNITY ORGANISER

I was sitting in A-level theatre studies, 'Oppose the Criminal Justice Bill' stickers all over my files, side eyes to the confident drama students from St Georges Hill, the haven of Sixties pop stars and, lately, oligarchs, it would be a long time before I knew of the land The Diggers claimed for egalitarian endeavour, of 'The World Turned Upside Down' and the Bard of Barking my East Ham cousins talked about in the early Eighties. Then, playing 'The Internationale', 'Red Flag' and the Bard's version of Blake's 'Jerusalem' loudly in our flat, to the annoyance of the upstairs neighbour's boyfriend, who wore camouflage to do the gardening (didn't work, I could still see him).

And suddenly I was forty, and all the things we said we'd fight against were still appening. And I still hadn't seen him live.

Reading Town Hall. My sister, brother-in-law and I and a seated affair. Wallis Bird supported, engaging she was, we enjoyed her set. Billy Bragg came on, with a guitar and a cup of tea. (I don't do that first name thing. Even as a teenager I wrote a letter responding to Paul Weller's request for young singers – 'Dear Mr. Weller…'. What? How rock'n'roll! I never posted it, too shy. Can't do the 'last name only' thing that blokes in pubs who like facts do – "The thing with Bragg is…".)

Billy Bragg, the raconteur who weaves the kindness of the ordinary into songs of hope and change. Hope not hate. We felt a long way from it, and from the Rock Against Racism and Red Wedge that seemed only yesterday. All the hope then. I think his involvement in the event this time was sparked by the election of BNP councillors in Barking. He said people of Barking aren't racist, those with agendas to pick over economic misery, and somehow those who hope and believe in inclusion must make their voices louder.

As expected, he was playing to the converted, but a shout – "Why don't you go back to Barking then!" fell like a damp squib. He'd engaged the crowd in his belief in the good hearts of his hometown, so they shushed and tutted. The inverse proportion of talent to loud gob is never realised by the geezer who even in a seated music show has to puff his chest.

To hear songs of the collective, 'There Is Power In A Union', 'The World Turned Upside Down', 'Waiting For The Great Leap Forwards' and feel the solidarity gives hope to those feeling like fish swimming upstream, oddities in the Conservative suburbs. We flock to find like-minded people who know the words to songs that exhort us to remember the heritage we could have in a society that sees common treasury for all.

I wondered why people thought Billy Bragg was purely polemic when the beauty of life as we experience it, with all our flaws and vulnerabilities, is one of the things he encapsulates in three minutes so well. 'Levi Stubbs' Tears', 'Tank Park Salute'. My brother-in-law'shandreachedformysister.Hehadlosthisfathersuddenly.Partoftheexperience, communication that only a live gig gives while you reflect on life outside the room. 'The Milkman Of Human Kindness' appeared, and he delivered gold top.

On the way filing out, a woman said to her husband, "Just push past." My sister whispered, "I think they've missed the point…".

DAVID BOWIE
THE 1980 FLOOR TV SHOW, THE MARQUEE CLUB, SOHO, LONDON
20 OCTOBER 1973
JULIE MILTON, ARTIST

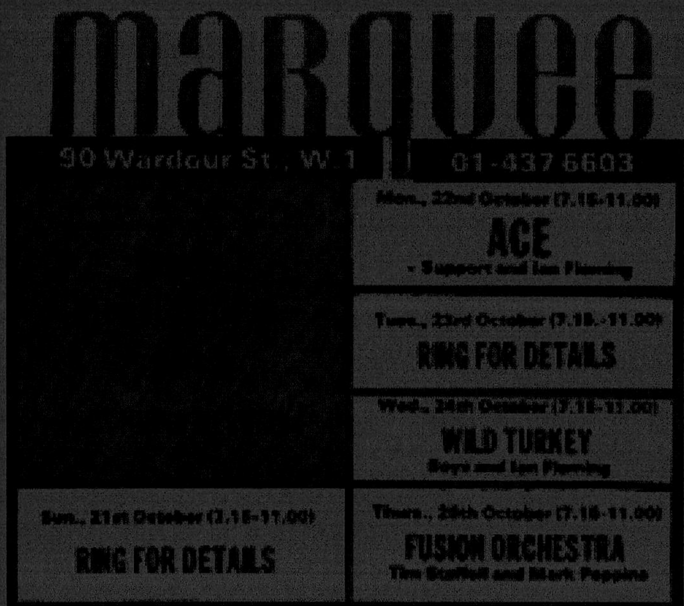

I had originally been drawn to David Bowie for his music and lyrics via Peter Noone's version of 'Oh! You Pretty Things'. The song was so out of kilter with the Herman's Hermits frontman's usual middle of the road output that my interest was immediately piqued. Anyone that can fit the words '*Homo sapien*' into a song has got something about them.

I later read an interview with Noone, who praised Bowie's songwriting abilities, and so I became keen to learn more, which wasn't easy in the early Seventies, with *NME*, *Sounds* and *Melody Maker* your only real points of reference. I discovered that the original track was on the forthcoming album *Hunky Dory*, but unfortunately, being only thirteen at the time, I was always strapped for cash, so the album didn't appear in my collection until some while later. I did, however, send off my postal order (something like 25p) to join The David Bowie Appreciation Society.

This section of my story has been much written about. On 6 July 1972 Bowie appeared on *Top of the Pops* with 'Starman' and for me from that moment on, everything changed. He looked so different from the rest of the bands at the time – his outlandish clothes, the makeup, and when he pointed into the camera and sang, you felt yourself smile at his confidence, his impudence, as if he were saying I know your parents will be appalled, but you'll think this is great. The final straw in the Milton household was when Bowie casually draped his arm over Mick Ronson's shoulders, at which point I was embarrassed to look at my dad, who was muttering something about "bloody queers"! My mum just sat motionless as if she couldn't quite believe what she'd seen.

There must have been further discussion about 'that' TV appearance at my aunt's coffee morning the following week as she mentioned, with some embarrassment, that her friend used to take Bowie to school at Burnt Ash when he was a child, and "who'd have thought he would turn out like that". Of course, I was delighted with the tenuous link! This was 1972; everything was brown or beige, the world seemed to be full of suits. But not anymore. Now there was colour, vibrancy, hope.

For outsiders, I don't think the effect of that performance can be underestimated. For those of us who didn't quite fit in or lived on the margins and had to manage their lives by being evasive or withdrawing, here was a man who, for whatever reason it matters not, made us feel included with a big thumbs-up. You might say it was a ploy to garner interest, increase sales, shock, but I could not have cared less – he just made me feel better, stronger.

I saw Bowie at the Lewisham Odeon in May 1973. It was an outstanding gig and amazingly we were at the front. It was loud, hot, sweaty and the audience was frenzied. Mick Ronson was utterly superb. I seem to recall Bowie getting his words mixed up on 'The Width Of A Circle' and my being both pleased and disappointed that he was human after all. Little did we know at that time that this tour would culminate on 3 July 1973 at the Hammersmith Odeon.

Fast forward, and I am invited to the recording of *The 1980 Floor Show** at the Marquee Club on 20 October 1973. I couldn't believe my membership of The David Bowie Appreciation Society (remember, 25p) had got me into this event. It felt like a personal thank you for supporting him during his leaner years. This, after all, was Ziggy's final appearance. I'm not entirely sure how I got my dad to both take me and pick me up from Wardour Street. I think he was concerned about me travelling late at night, and I had to be evasive about who I was seeing (I'd seen The Velvet Underground at Imperial College during the same sort of period and had told my mum I was going to see Neil Reid!)

I remember us piling into my dad's red Austin 1100 and being driven through the drizzle and darkness of South London's streets to the drizzle and bright lights of the West End. On arrival, there was a smallish queue outside the Marquee, waiting for the doors to open. With Dad in tow, I was relieved that everything seemed reserved, calm and orderly. The wait to get in was short and the place small and packed.

Wayne County (now Jayne County) was hovering near the entrance. I was now fourteen and this was simply unbelievable, being in a club situation with Bowie, his entourage and guests. Bowie was yet to come on stage, but the rest of the band were doing sound checks, just wandering around; you could literally have gone up and chatted to anyone but, being a kid, I lacked confidence and anyway, what could I possibly have to say of any interest? I think most of the kids stood around staring in disbelief.

The atmosphere was very relaxed, but this was work, and a long day of recording for the musicians and dancers appearing on the TV special, including performances of 'I Can't Explain', 'The Jean Genie', 'Space Oddity' and '1984'. Bowie's costumes were absolutely over the top, but I guess that was the point and I have to say he wore most of them very well. The finale was a duet of 'I Got You Babe' with Marianne Faithfull (an interesting vocal performance). Bowie seemed to be really enjoying himself at this point, possibly pre-empting the crowd's reaction on seeing Marianne's bare backside (her clerically inspired outfit lacked material in this key area) when exiting the stage at the end of the song.

That magical golden invitation was like stardust. It led me, albeit temporarily, into a world of glitz and glamour, of film crews, clapper boards and costumes, of flamboyant people, great musicians and fun. This was so far removed from anything I had ever experienced, or indeed would again.

These were heady times and even at such a young age I recognised that this was a significant event in my life. Notwithstanding David Bowie's brilliance as a musician and songwriter, recognised by all the accolades deservedly received during his lifetime, I will always and simply be grateful to him for being 'other', for being brave, for embracing everyone and inviting all outsiders to just be. He changed my view of the world and opened my eyes to new possibilities.

Still to this day I play his music alone while working as an abstract painter, not only to keep him near but also perhaps in the vague hope a little bit of his stardust might just rub off on me.

**The 1980 Floor Show was a rock musical featuring David Bowie performing as his character Ziggy Stardust for the last time. It was broadcast on NBC on 16 November 1973 as part of the US TV series The Midnight Special.*

CURTIS MAYFIELD
LEICESTER POLYTECHNIC
AUTUMN 1987
TONY MINVIELLE, JAZZ FM BROADCASTER DJ/WRITER

I was in my third year at Leicester Polytechnic, the usual red-brick homage to sixties design, and I'd been pretty lucky to have befriended the then social secretary, Neil Mather, in the first few weeks of my first year and ended up becoming the resident DJ/backstage gopher at the student's union, where we hosted a pretty incredible roster of live acts during my time there. The Smiths, Heaven 17, Kurtis Blow, Afrika Bambataa, Sandie Shaw, Aztec Camera, The Blow Monkeys, Fashion, The Associates, Pride w/ Sade, Simply Red, even Sigue Sigue Sputnik – this was just a handful of the many groups that had the misfortune of having me as their accompanying DJ. It was a role I cherished and revelled in, playing a mixture of soul, indie, dance and pop to keep the 1,500+ students who packed out the venue on a regular basis happy.

Autumn term 1987, Neil informed me that one of the acts he'd booked for later in the term was soul/R&B legend Curtis Mayfield. To say I was excited was an understatement; the shy kid from the projects of Chicago who went on to conquer the world with his socially conscious lyrics and sweet falsetto vocal stylings was my total inspiration. I'd been introduced to his music many years before, while working at Page 43 Records near the Oval in South London as a young teenager. I was influenced by the shops owners, Mick and Simon, who schooled me in the ways of jazz, rock, soul, reggae, country, alternative, Latin and so much more, like two Shaolin masters instructing a young novice – an education I am still grateful for some forty-five years later. I'd also had a vague memory of seeing Curtis performing some of his iconic hits on *The Old Grey Whistle Test* (my musical lifeline) when I was very young.

On the day of the gig, I got into the venue early and went through the archive of records in our student union record storeroom – a collection that went back years – to pick out the ones I needed for the night. I then added these to the ones I'd brought myself from my own collection. I'd picked out all manner of classic artists from the lexicon of soul, jazz and funk, including The Isley Brothers, Leroy Hutson, Marvin Gaye, Jon Lucien, Marlena Shaw, Donald Byrd, and Earth, Wind & Fire, plus a few up-and-coming artists from the period – Sade, Prince, Mtume, Luther Vandross – and the usual student dancefloor fillers from the time, like Blue Rondo, Pigbag and Aztec Camera.

My anticipation for this night was off the scale and I was determined to play all the right nuggets to accompany the incredible show I hoped was coming. I caught a glimpse of the sound check, with Curtis only making a brief appearance to check mics and so on.

At 7.30 p.m. the doors to the student's union were opened and the masses poured in. On-stage time was at 9.30 sharp, and I was hoping to get the dance floor going fairly quickly before Curtis came out. It wasn't too hard a task as a fairly sizeable contingent of the audience was made up of non-students – people who were serious soul fans from Leicester and the surrounding cities of Nottingham, Derby and Northampton. I can't remember whether there was a support act – there may have been, but I don't remember much about them if there was, as all I was focused on was Curtis.

The DJ booth was adjacent to the dressing rooms, with a large window looking out on to the dancefloor and another one situated in the door out into the backstage corridor, where out of the corner of my eye, while cueing up records, I could see various comings and goings from the corridor, but no one discernible as yet.

Then, roughly half an hour before showtime, there was a polite knock at the door – not too hard, not too soft, you know the type. I had my headphones on as I was busy cueing up a record so without looking up, I said, "Come in."

I looked round, while taking off my headphones, and nearly fainted with the shock, as there stood before me wearing a soft burgundy leather jacket, a paisley shirt, dark trousers and those gold rimmed spectacles we'd become so familiar with was the icon Curtis Lee Mayfield. At this point, for me at least, time stood still, and I was rendered speechless until he uttered the words, "Hi, how ya' doin – I'm Curtis. Really loving your tunes."

We then engaged in the most wonderful five-minute conversation in which he looked through my records and imparted that he had played with that artist, and written for another, and was due to do a session with this one in the coming weeks, as he held up another record. I even got him to sign an LP for me. He congratulated me on having some great records and then he was gone.

The set was magical: 'Move On Up', 'Keep On Keeping On', 'We The People Who Are Darker Than Blue', plus 'It's All Right' and others from his Impressions days, including my personal favourite, 'We're A Winner'. The band was on fire. Curtis sang some of the songs with the band and others he just sat on a wooden box on the stage, just him and his guitar. There was at least one encore, maybe two, and then it was over and he was gone.

Fast forward ten years and I'm living in Atlanta, working as a computer programmer during the day, helping out my now lifelong friend Jamal Ahmad on his programme at local jazz radio station WCLK Atlanta at the weekends and writing for acclaimed jazz magazine Straight No Chaser. It's the mid-nineties and the nu-jazz scene was popping on both sides of the Atlantic. I get a phone call from Paul Bradshaw, editor of *Straight No Chaser*, based in London, asking if I'd like to interview Curtis Mayfield as he was based in Atlanta and was well overdue for some rep – he also had a new LP on the way (*New World Order*), which everybody was getting excited about.

Of course, I jumped at the chance, and a week later I was making my way to a small, gated community enclave on the outskirts of Atlanta, where it was rumoured James Brown and Whitney Houston (with Bobby Brown) had abodes. Time had not been kind to Curtis, and he was now a quadriplegic after a stage accident at a gig in upstate New York in 1990, so I was very apprehensive over what I would find when I arrived at his house.

Once at the house I was welcomed by his family and was ushered down to a huge basement room, where I was greeted by the sight of a couple of large-screen TVs, lots of books and records, a couple of settees and a large bed positioned right in the centre. There, lying on the bed, was Curtis, a picture of serenity and wearing the hugest of grins. He later told me that the reason for the grin was because he very rarely got new visitors and also that he had recognised me as the young English man of colour whom he'd met on one of his many tours in Europe, and who knew so much about his music. Amazingly, he even remembered some of the LPs in my record box at the time of our first meeting nearly ten years before.

We spoke of many things while I was with him, including the little-known fact that he'd written speeches for Martin Luther King, Jr. I included most of the salient points of our chat in the article I sent back to the UK for publishing in *Straight No Chaser*, and it's the one I'm most proud of from my intermittent thirty-year journalistic career. It was during that interview that Curtis questioned me about my life and goals in such a way that I decided by the end of it America was not the place for me and my wife to be raising our young family.

It was also during that interview that Curtis gave me a book of his poetry/lyrics (which I have cherished to this day), and imparted much wisdom to me, including this insightful mantra that has always held me in good stead.

"The truth always comes in pieces and to hear the whole truth you have to hear all the pieces."

Curtis Mayfield
1942–1999

ROCK EN SEINE FESTIVAL
PARC DE SAINT-CLOUD, PARIS
22–24 AUGUST 2014
NATALIE MITCHELL, SCRIPTWRITER
PLAYWRIGHT

It was a music festival that first brought Steve Keogh into our lives. Benicàssim 2003. My husband Sam was nineteen years old, a fanatical music lover – young and enthusiastic. Over the course of a few days he made firm friends with Steve, a fast-talking Scouser old enough to be his dad. Hours were spent watching Blur, Echo & The Bunnymen, Super Furry Animals, clambering onto speakers for a better view (and falling off them), sharing pills and pints.

As with a lot of friendships forged in such an environment, Steve fell in and out of Sam's and then my life over the years until he made a proper return in 2011, travelling over from France, where he was now living, to see Pulp play their reunion gig at the Wireless Festival in Hyde Park. The next few years of our friendship were spent going backwards and forwards between London and Paris, our time together always focused on music. Like Sam, Steve was a music obsessive, an original member of the famous Eric's Club in Liverpool (despite still being underage). We'd go to gigs including The Stone Roses and Johnny Marr, ska nights in Deptford, exhibitions in London and Paris (most memorably The Velvet Underground and David Bowie.) Even a night in, playing Monopoly, would somehow revolve around music as the perfect bands to accompany the game would be carefully chosen (invariably The Style Council, since you asked).

In 2014, as Steve's fiftieth birthday approached (or 25 x 2, as he referred to it), he invited a group of us over to Paris for Rock en Seine – a three-day festival held in Parc de Saint-Cloud in the west of Paris. An eclectic mix of bands, it was headlined by Arctic Monkeys, The Prodigy and Queens of the Stone Age. There were so many Scousers going, we renamed it Rock en Skem.

There are so many moments that stand out for me over those three days. Steve wearing a T-shirt bearing the slogan 'Made in 1964'. A classic set by Blondie (the voice may be lower, but the distinctive halo of white-blonde hair and insouciant coolness of Debbie Harry was unmistakeable). An early-career Janelle Monáe with the crowd in the palm of her hand. Watching Portishead as the sun slowly went down. Making friends with a hijab-wearing French family who couldn't speak English, bonded by the language of music and raving in the dark to an electric set by The Prodigy.

As soon as tickets for the 2015 festival went on sale, we snapped them up. We shared suggestions of Airbnb's to book, made plans to extend our stay into a full holiday. Sam and I popped over to France a few weeks later for a last-minute weekend break to stay with Steve. We'd actually planned to go to Manchester, but rail closures meant it was quicker and cheaper to go to Paris. So why wouldn't we? We went shopping, Steve bartering on our behalf in perfect French, spoken in a broad Scouse accent. We visited churches (Steve was Roman Catholic and a passionate lover of religious architecture) and ate a beautiful Thai dinner. I had a heavy cold so went to bed early one night, only to be woken up by the sound of the Benny Hill theme tune and belly laughs from Steve and Sam as they watched football mishap videos on YouTube in between listening to Elvis Costello and Grimes.

We said goodbye, excited to see each other in a few months for Rock en Seine, if not before. Sadly, it wasn't meant to be. A few days later we received the news that Steve was gone. He'd taken his own life.

We replayed that final weekend over and over. The laughs, the chats. Benny Hill. Searching every interaction for clues and answers. But there were none.

Steve was buried in an unmarked grave in Étampes, the town he lived in just outside of Paris. None of his friends were told until after the burial. Our beautiful friend, the person who lit up any room he was in, had no one with him to send him on the next part of his journey. To say goodbye properly. Our hearts hurt.

Initially we were unsure whether to go back to Rock en Seine, the thought of being there without Steve too much to even consider. But we soon agreed he'd be furious with us for not going, so decided to combine our trip with a visit to Étampes in an attempt to find and mark his final resting place.

As with the previous year, the festival was great. Fantastic performances from The Chemical Brothers, FFS, The Libertines and more. But it was underlined by a huge sadness that we were here, and Steve wasn't. During Mark Lanegan we sat on a hill overlooking the park and drank a toast to Steve.

A few days later, in torrential rain, we took the train to Étampes, armed with a small notepad where I'd written out in French questions to ask the local funeral director about the location of Steve's grave. Fortunately, they knew exactly who we were referring to and drew us a map of the cemetery. By an enormous stroke of luck, we also managed to track down Steve's ex-girlfriend, Isabelle, whose mum lived in an apartment backing on to his. Neither of them spoke English, but Isabelle's mum was obsessed with Boy George, and we'd previously bought her a tote bag with his image on. We shouted his name up at her window until she recognised us. They ushered us into the apartment, gave us a change of clothes and fed us a simple lunch of bread and radishes before driving us to the cemetery. As the rain lashed down, we traipsed around with the disintegrating map, the ground turning to mud beneath our feet until we found it. Steve's final resting place. We placed a small plaque with his name on to mark his grave, and lit a candle (pointless in the rain, yes, but it felt important) before telling him all about the amazing three days we'd just had at Rock en Seine.

It's hard to explain Steve to people who weren't lucky enough to meet him. He just had it. The X Factor. He would make you feel like you were the most fascinating person in the room. That an ordinary night playing Monopoly was special and should be remembered. You were always guaranteed a good time when you were with him. Rock en Seine will forever be entwined with Steve in our memories. How lucky we were to know him. How lucky we were that in 2014, we were able to share a perfect weekend of music to celebrate him.

THE JAM
+ SPECIAGUESTS
ROYAL HIGHLAND BITION HALL,
Monday Septem 7.30pm
Tickets £5.0 VAT).
№ 342

THE JAM
ROYAL HIGHLAND EXHIBITION HALL, INGLISTON, EDINBURGH
27 SEPTEMBER 1982
SCOTT MITCHELL, PHOTOGRAPHER

I'd just moved from Jersey to Edinburgh and was living on the west side of the city. There were a lot of mods in the area and even a new scooter club. I kinda fell into it because they looked cool and as someone new to the place, it was a great way to make friends.

Effectively, this was actually my first ever gig – no one really played Jersey other than The Grumbleweeds. I remember it was pissing down and the only way to Ingliston showground was by bus, and every one was full by the time it got to us. So we walked, getting our parkas soaked.

As we were waiting to get in the venue, the wire and concrete fence gave way. No one was hurt but it was still pretty scary. I think then they decided to let us in early, and it was still raining heavily.

We were so happy to be out in the rain but soon the room began to fill with steam off all these wet parkas. The Questions were support, as they came from our part of Edinburgh, though we thought they were shit. They may have actually been quite good.

Then at last The Jam. The place went crazy and pretty much stayed that way the whole gig. I recall Paul was wearing a red silk shirt; Christ, he's always been so cool. On the last song I got hit in the head by something. Turns out it was Rick's drumsticks. Someone faster than me got to them before I realised.

Then the long walk home in more pissing rain. I remember The Exploited (local shit punk band) had said something about the mods at Ingliston. Punks driving by in cars used to throw bottles at people. It was so tribal back then, so you had to watch out.

For a first gig it was something really rather special; I felt so lucky to have seen The Jam. To this day they are still my favourite band. I can't believe I still had the ticket, obviously in a bit of a state after all that rain. Also, that I recall all these little details.

Years later I remember talking to Paul about the show, as well as the Edinburgh Playhouse gig in April 1982, when the seats got ripped up by the crowd.

THE CONCERT FOR NEW YORK CITY AT MADISON SQUARE GARDEN 20 OCTOBER 2001 DOMINIC MOHAN, JOURNALIST/PR

Just thirty-nine days after the 9/11 terror attacks were seared onto our memories forevermore. Ground Zero was still smouldering, the acrid smell of burning across the scarred city a continuous reminder of the horrors that had altered the world forever.

Maybe it seemed a trivial response in some ways. After all, what could a bunch of rock stars hope to achieve as the planet mourned almost 3,000 victims? But Paul McCartney responded in the only way he knew, leafing through his peerless contacts book and rapidly assembling a pre-eminent line-up of pretty much everyone in the business who could hold a tune to honour The Big Apple's emergency workers, the City itself – and the dead. It also felt like a palpable risk.

We were all tired and paranoid. Weeks of devastating rolling news bulletins and nightmare images had taken their toll. Would the Concert For New York City – to be held just three miles north of the World Trade Center at the cavernous Madison Square Garden – itself become a target for a follow-up attack, taking out rock royalty, a president, the city mayor and 20,000 others all in one go? But it was also a vital and necessary act of defiance, an important step in the mourning and healing process for many, two NooYorkFuckin'City fingers up to terrorism. And as *The Sun* newspaper's Showbusiness Editor at the time, I had been invited by Paul to shadow him and document this unique event, what would become an evening of pain and sorrow, of unfathomable highs and lows, when rock'n'roll attempted to embrace a city and its people, to lead them out of the darkness of grief – for a few hours at least.

I was even permitted to watch McCartney rehearse in Manhattan, where he revealed he had written a song called 'Freedom' in response to the attacks – having witnessed them unfold from a plane parked on the tarmac at JFK airport. He said he would premiere the song at the concert and the story ran as an exclusive front page on the day of the show, under the headline 'Macca's Song for Freedom'.

Sleep-deprived and anxiety-ridden, there was a real sense of nervousness as we arrived at the mythical Garden. Outside, that pungent smell and enduring taste lingered in the nose and throat while police helicopters thundered overhead, followed by the most intense security and intimate searches imaginable (unsurprisingly). And then, an Access All Areas pass plonked around my neck. I later discovered this piece of plastic would actually allow me on to the hallowed stage itself. It is something I cherish and still have today.

Inside the arena, what struck me instantly was the number of ashen-faced men and women in uniform, many of them clutching pictures of lost loved ones and colleagues. Some had visible scars and injuries, others were in wheelchairs. It was heart-wrenching, unbearable almost. We all had tears in our eyes. If you didn't, you weren't human.

Bowie opened it with a spine-tingling version of Paul Simon's 'America' as he sat like a cross-legged Buddha, prodding a small electronic keyboard before an understated 'Heroes'. He got the tone just right – as always. Jay-Z, Destiny's Child, Eric Clapton, Kid Rock, Janet Jackson, Billy Joel and James Taylor followed. Jagger shadow-boxed backstage as Keef chatted with Bill Clinton, and police, fire and ambulance workers mingled with rockers who had left their egos at home. There was a real feeling of unity, that we were all mourning as one, but also a sense that fun was still allowed to exist within the darkness.

This was encapsulated perfectly and absolutely nailed by The Who. Their half-hour set, one of the most powerful I have ever been privileged to witness, was Great Britain's love letter to a city that has always held this band dear. If you haven't seen this magical performance, then I urge you to seek it out forthwith. 'Who Are You'. 'Baba O'Riley'. 'Behind Blue Eyes'. 'Won't Get Fooled Again'. Name me a more pulsating thirty minutes of music to be served up in a live context like this extraordinary one. I'll wait. AAA pass in hand, I made a run for it and sneaked on to the side of The Who's stage and what I then observed was an unmatched masterclass – absolute power, fury and love. Pure catharsis. Uniformed men and women wept even more tears as their solar plexuses (or is it plexi?) rattled.

They punched the air with their orders of service, crumpled photographs and scrawled memorial banners aloft. "My dad is your hero", read one, I remember. A frenzied Townshend played until his fingers bled and windmilled with teenage ferocity as a possessed and Moon-like Zak Starkey savaged his colossal drum set. John Entwistle took care of business in what would be his last ever live performance on US soil. In unison, Daltrey and the crowd spat out 'Won't Get Fooled Again' with screaming venom, as images of the Union flag and the Stars and Stripes merged slowly together on a big screen, followed by poignant footage of the Statue of Liberty and of the Twin Towers themselves. Maybe tonight wasn't about the music, but The Who delivered. "We could never follow what you did," bellowed Daltrey, as the band exited stage left.

Mick and Keith knocked out 'Salt Of The Earth' and 'Miss You'. Elton John gave us a remarkable 'Mona Lisas And Mad Hatters'. This was that special relationship between our two nations told in song, an emotional release and rock'n'roll relief from death and sadness. McCartney's turn included 'I'm Down', 'Lonely Road', 'From A Lover To A Friend', 'Yesterday', a mournful 'Let It Be' and the aforementioned unveiling of protest song 'Freedom', when he was joined onstage by dozens of emergency workers.

Those I spoke to afterwards said that the experience had helped to heal and bring some light into their lives, knowing the world had their back and giving them some respite from their grief. Still uniformed, a number of them joined us for a truly bizarre and impromptu afterparty at the nearby Hudson Hotel, where McCartney took to a tiny stage at 4 a.m., joined by Harrison Ford, Jim Carrey, Dan Aykroyd and Sheryl Crow. We stayed up all night, toasting the city that never sleeps and shaking our heads in gawping disbelief at what we had just witnessed.

A moment in time, when members of the pantheon of British rock'n'roll in particular put their arm around the city, and where we all shared something harrowing but also very special. This astonishing evening reminded all of us of the force music can wield in our lives, and how songs can be all-powerful tools when we find ourselves in times of trouble.

JAMES BROWN'S FUNKY PEOPLE
TOWN AND COUNTRY CLUB, KENTISH TOWN, LONDON
20/21 JULY 1988
ED MYLLES, THIRD SECTOR WORKER

Moving from Scotland to London in May 1988, aged twenty-one, put me exactly where I wanted to be for the reasons I wanted to be there. Gigs. Having devoured the music papers religiously since my early teens it was inconceivable that I wouldn't end up in London and therefore entering the mythical venues listed in the weekly inky gig guides.

By chance (maybe) my early flats were all within a two-mile vicinity of the Town and Country Club in Kentish Town, NW5. The T&C was a beautiful art-deco venue of Irish dance hall heritage with ornate corniches, sweeping staircases and upstairs booth-seating lit by chintzy red lampshades. It's been The Forum since 1993, but it still feels too soon for me to call it that. It was at T&C I saw true legends of soul – and other – music. More than once: Curtis Mayfield, Gil Scott-Heron, Bobby Womack as well as Etta James, Junior Walker, Martha Reeves and many, many more.

The most memorable and meaningful were the two gigs in late July '88 by James Brown's Funky People. Not James Brown himself, but the key players, associates and voices that interpreted and delivered his music across the globe.

At this time, 'rare groove' was at its peak in London clubs, led by Norman Jay at Dingwalls and the fledgling Kiss FM. The tunes were largely unknown, sometimes previously unheard, records and demos by Seventies and early Eighties soul, funk, R&B and jazz-funk artistes. Being an economic migrant, I wasn't a record collector and rarely a clubber (except for Wendy May's Locomotion, also at T&C). I did have the first of the essential compilations of James Brown's Funky People, released in 1986 to capitalise on the strength of the rare groove scene. Norman Jay had personally made the transatlantic connection with Ms Vicki Anderson and Mr Bobby Byrd with a phone call to the family home in Cincinnati*:. They apparently had no idea of the popularity of their sounds among the youth of London and the UK (or even of hip hop duo Eric B. & Rakim's heavy sampling of 'I Know You Got Soul' – a massive hit in '88). They were up for some gigs though.

** Vicki and Bobby were married in the mid-Sixties, and remained together until his death in 2007. Byrd discovered James Brown and was heavily involved with many of his hits and the development of soul and funk music, while Vicki is best known for her performances with the James Brown Revue.*

In 1988, the 'Hardest Working Man in Showbusiness', as he was known, was having serious 'issues' and off the road (Brown was eventually sentenced on charges of assault and battery with intent to kill, serving just over half of a six-year sentence). This left members of his band without income. If Brown hadn't been jailed, would this convergence of the disparate JBs have come to pass? Highly unlikely.

That summer, posters and flyers appeared everywhere, it seemed, for two London dates of James Brown's Funky People, promising an all-star line-up of comrades from the 'Godfather of Soul's vital reign. The aforementioned Bobby Byrd, Fred Wesley, Maceo Parker and Pee Wee Ellis, and a tour de force group of vocalists – Ms Vicki Anderson, Lyn Collins, Marva Whitney and Mr Brown's newest vocalist, Martha High – were all due on one stage. This was unbelievable and I was beyond excited. These gigs were hugely anticipated.

Part of the anticipation was, of course, for the night, the event, the performance, the gig itself. But this also felt like a rite of passage; from the excitement of listening and dancing to great soul and funk 'non-mint' records to the thought of being in the same room as the talent that produced game-changers like 'Papa's Got A Brand New Bag', 'Hot Pants', 'Get On The Good Foot' – staples of teenage years. It just seemed ... mad!

On the first night, I made my way upstairs to a front-of-balcony seat/booth, keen to get a good view and soak up the experience. As the venue was filling up, I could see the stage was set tightly for a full band along with the four self-styled Soul Sisters and Bobby Byrd. This was no promo PA, no backing tapes – this was proper funk performed by its pioneers.

A sudden roar and it was 'showtime'. The JBs sauntered on, suited and booted, to wild applause, and The Horny Horns punched into 'Doing It To Death'. We were gonna have a funky good time...

Although this ensemble had never played live together, they illustrated their brilliance as the originators of funk. And it looked like they were loving it as much as we all were. The JBs, off the leash for their time in the spotlight.

What unfolded was a classic revue-style show – the kind anyone would have loved to have seen at any Apollo, Harlem or Glasgow. The JBs started with huge energy, kicked on and just built and built ... and built. 'Gimme Some More', 'Pass The Peas' and Fred Wesley's 'House Party' all featured, as the Horns traded solos, hollered encouragement and did a few steps.

The Soul Sisters each took two or three songs and kept up the pace, punctuated occasionally by slower but no less powerful funk of 'Do Your Thing' and 'Put It On the Line'. Vicki and Lyn were the best known at the time, having released their own great records such as 'Message From The Soul Sisters' and 'Rock Me Again & Again & Again...'. There was also the unexpected introduction of sixteen-year-old Carleen Anderson (daughter of Vicki and Bobby) with an incredible rendition of Deniece Williams' 'Free'. I wondered what was going on, but the response to Carleen's unique soaring, acrobatic voice was immense. Just when you thought there couldn't be more love from the audience.

The crowd, 2,000-strong, were brilliant too – joyful and triumphant at the sight and sound of this once (twice!) in a lifetime event. No tension (which can serve many a gig well), no violence (of course), just a shared emotional rush of exhilaration and euphoria at a show that did not let up.

Bobby Byrd – long-time number two to Soul Brother number one – played his part in a Seventies-style white double-breasted suit (kick flares and wide lapels), red shirt and medallion. Working through an intensive half-hour set featuring 'Sex Machine', 'Try Me', 'I Need Help (I Can't Do It Alone)' and 'Hot Pants', Bobby brought the audience to a crescendo with 'I Know You Got Soul', the tune of the moment. I can't remember if the old chestnut of the 'roof came off' was a cliché then or not. Maybe that was when it was invented.

And then it was done. And we floated out on a high onto Highgate Road, grabbing a complimentary poster on the way. Thinking back, post-gigs we can all recall snapshot details and/or broad impressions that serve as memories. Nearly thirty-five years down the track, it's the authenticity of performance and the pure, shared joy in the room that marks these shows as so special for me. You can get a sense of the gigs on the LP Finally Gettin' Paid. Only eight tracks, but better than nothing.

The success of these shows meant that Messrs Ellis, Wesley and Parker spent many years after gigging in the UK and Europe and taking their jazz and funk to new audiences in settings befitting their mastery. And Carleen Anderson would soon make a permanent move to London to front the Young Disciples.

These nights were a privilege to be at. It was magical.

CONFLICT
THAMES POLYTECHNIC, WOOLWICH, LONDON
19 DECEMBER 1984
CHRIS NEWSON, PUBLISHING AGENT

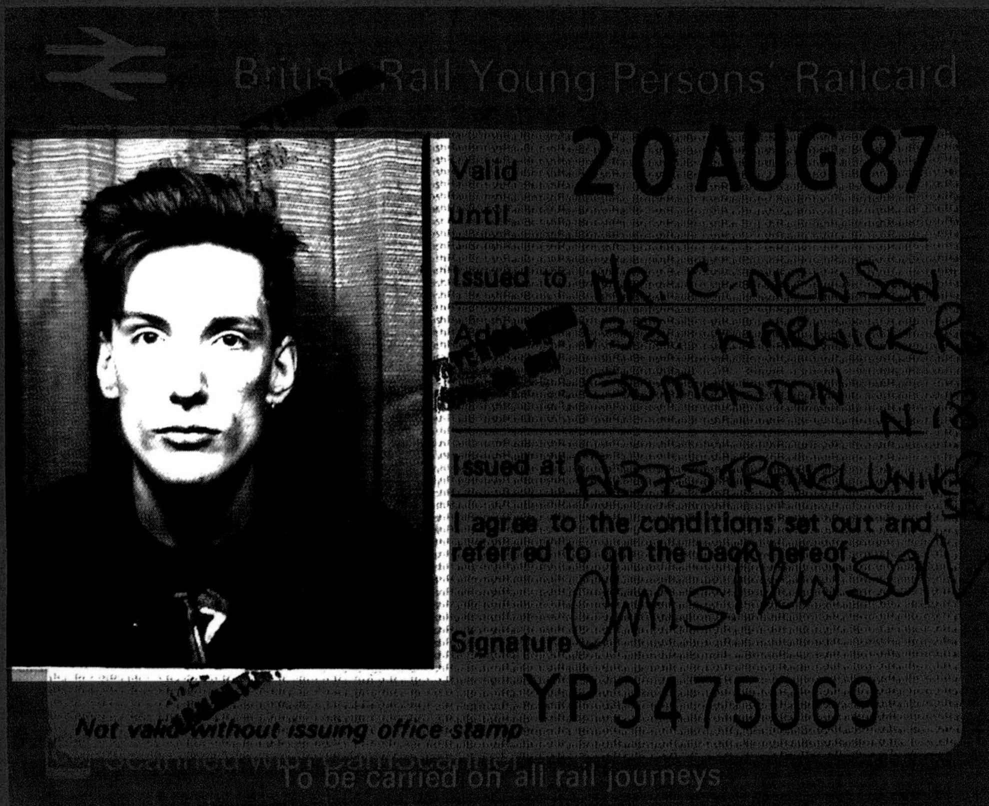

Back in the early Eighties when the world seemed so much simpler and very much angrier, I genuinely felt real change was possible. It would be achieved through the medium of loud, angry and shouty music.

At the vanguard of the forthcoming revolution were Conflict, hailing from Eltham. They had kicked off their career with their bruising *The House That Man Built* EP on Crass Records, followed by perhaps one of anarcho-punk's greatest artefacts, the album *It's Time To See Who's Who*, released on the Crass Records imprint of Corpus Christi in 1984. The artwork defied Crass orthodoxy and carried a full-color gatefold sleeve with no sign of stencil-style fonts. Of course, the lyrics were largely unintelligible but printed in full on the glorious gatefold sleeve that boasted a Hogarth print of citizens forcibly removing the local aristocracy.

I loved Conflict and forgave them all of their sins.

Gigs were rather haphazard and largely organised through sporadic mailing lists. The local postman in Tottenham refused to deliver letters with badly soaped stamps and simply, and rather understandably, chose to chuck them away. Another win chalked up to the system.

A couple of mailing list gig notifications eventually made their way past the postie, and I'd gone along to gigs down at the Thames Poly campus in Woolwich. They had been riotous and very sweaty celebrations of righteous anger, aimed squarely at the everyone from the local butcher through to EMI and, of course, the government of the day. Stalls were always present, distributing leaflets and books – ostensibly from the Animal Liberation Front and the Hunt Saboteurs Association. Both causes very close to my heart at the time. Music was secondary to the message, which was curious, as it was almost impossible to make anything out when played loudly thorough dodgy PAs.

Eventually I persuaded a friend to make the journey from North London for what was to be my last gig attended in Woolwich. My long-suffering and anarcho-punk-hating girlfriend at the time also made the trip. Quite pointedly, she'd observed on numerous occasions that many of those in attendance couldn't (and hadn't) run a bath, let alone run a revolutionary organisation that would right the world's untold wrongs.

The gig was obviously splendid. However, we had to leave ten minutes early, allowing Tom, who looked like the archetypal end-of-tour NWOBHM* roadie, to catch the bus back to Trafalgar Square. From which, if all being well, he'd connect with the night bus back to Tottenham. He'd then catch a few hours' sleep before starting his Sainsbury's shift at 6.30 a.m.

Of course, this was not to be. While walking through Woolwich looking for the bus stop, a souped-up Cortina packed with testosterone-fuelled lads tried running us over. Having successfully jumped out of the way, I perhaps chose the wrong course of action and shouted something questioning their driving abilities. Needless to say, the brakes went on and the Cortina reversed at speed before all four blokes came tearing out. In comedic style, the first idiot's haymaking swing missed but caused me to land heavily on my arse on a pile of bricks. Complaining loudly about my backside hurting, I was helped back to my feet with a mumbled apology by the least aggressive Gary Lager. Tom, however, wasn't faring quite so well. He was being booted up and down Woolwich High Street by Gary's three mates, who had obviously watched one too many coked-up Jean Claude Van Damme movies. The only saving grace was that they were wearing daft slip-on Miami Vice-style footwear, rather than anything manufactured by Doctor Marten.

Tom was still left a bloodied mess: split lips, blackened eyes and damaged ribs. A real state. Quite luckily the bus arrived soon after and let the three of us on – Tom in considerable pain and me complaining about how uncomfortable the seat was, what with a bruised arse and all.

Inevitably half of the Conflict audience were waiting at the next stop. As the exit doors opened, a hundred or so punters jumped on and fully expected the driver to obligingly carry us all back to central London. Instead, he called in a major incident and within five minutes police cars had come to a screaming halt and surrounded the bus. The local cops then began dragging off all and sundry with extreme violence. Tom got a baton round the shoulders and legs for his troubles. Maybe the South London constabulary genuinely hated the NWOBHM, or perhaps they were just being vicious bastards?

We eventually got home around five-ish. I slept all day, while Tom, who looked like he'd been run over by the N90, spent his entire shift in the pissing rain and driving wind rounding up wayward trolleys in Sainsbury's' extensive car park. His shift manager quite rightly didn't want him scaring away the customers.

Postscript

My girlfriend dumped me soon after for being a complete knobhead. Tom is stil the nicest person one could ever wish to meet. And the downfall of capitalism failed to materialise.

I've met up with Colin Conflict (Jerwood) on a few occasions over the last few years. Colin now operates some interesting ventures, makes music and still doesn't eat animals. He's also failed to deliver the first draft of his autobiography that was promised four years ago.

** New wave of British heavy metal.*

NOBLE FEST
FURZEDOWN FARM, HAMPSHIRE
2004–06
EMMA NOBLE, DJ/VOCALIST

Hour after hour, people in their hundreds came walking down the hill carrying crates of beers, and as the light went down, the illuminated trees started to come to life and dance in the smoke. Slowly the woods started to fill up and it wasn't long before we were in full swing.

In the grand scheme of things, it was small, but to us it felt massive – so big to me in fact, my sixteen-year-old self decided the night deserved two outfit changes.

We (the six Noble siblings) had always talked about how good it would be to put on a little music festival in the woods on our family farm. We knew it could work, and between us we'd have enough ideas to make it decent. We knew all the right people that could help us bring it together and we had the perfect space. There was just one thing that stood in our way – Dad.

Dad was always nervous about letting a load of people come to the farm and party, and rightly so. But then he had a couple of big life changes happen to him, which altered his outlook on things, and in 2004 he agreed to let us do it.

He loved his music, so we just had to sell it to him that we'd get the best local bands and musicians involved, which we did. Everyone wanted to be a part of it. Big parties didn't happen all that often in our little town, so the opportunity for local musicians to play on a stage – albeit a makeshift one – and in front of a crowd was an exciting prospect for most.

My brother, Simon, was also promoting in Oxford at the time, so he had lots of great DJ and music contacts from that area, which we utilised to really take things up a notch in terms of the line-up.

We had a real range of music, from covers to originals bands playing soul, funk, rock'n'roll, disco, jazz, hip hop – everyone we booked brought so much energy. People danced hard and partied the night away and there was a real atmosphere of love in the air.

In my head I can picture it all so clearly, but I should probably set the scene for those that weren't there…

We set up a tractor and trailer in the most open part of the woods, which became the stage. We'd up-lit all the big old trees, which looked beautiful and created a magical atmosphere; it almost felt like the trees were looking down, keeping an eye on us.

A life-size T. Rex head we made was protruding out of the rhododendron bushes and looking out over the main dancing area. That alone took weeks to build – we moulded the head shape out of chicken wire, covered it with papier-mâché and then painted on the details. It ended up looking wicked – so good, in fact, we left it up for weeks after.

We had the words 'Saturday Night Fever' projected onto the side of a Portakabin up the other end from where the stage was, and there were tepee tents filled with straw set up on the small island of our pond, which we named 'The Love Island'.

The festival was only intended to last for one night, but it ended up going on for two days' straight because no one wanted it to end – for those two days it felt like the best place on earth. Everyone and anyone you could possibly want to be with was there and in that moment, there was nowhere else any of us would have rather been.

After the success of the first one, we went on to do it for two more years. Every year it got bigger and better. We printed out little square tickets and each one of the brothers and sisters would have a bundle that we would give out to our mates. Of course, word would soon get out that there was a big old party happening down the Noble's farm and loads of extras turned up. But that's what made it exciting. We didn't charged people to come, and all the bands and DJs played for free. This really added to the positive atmosphere of the party. We were one big family.

It's hard to distinguish what happened in which year; all the memories merge into one. But there was one particular year that always makes me laugh, and that was when the police turned up.

They had found the party in the deep depths of the woods and made their way through the crowd and up onto the stage. They were trying to get everyone's attention, most likely to shut us down (as the music could be heard for several miles through the local area). Then suddenly, a local lad (who I won't name) seized the opportunity to join them on stage ... completely stark bollock naked. The police officers looked at him, then back out to the onlooking hysterical and applauding crowd and just walked back off stage and up the path back into the darkness. They realised there was no way of stopping us, and I think they could see it was a bunch of nice people having a good time, so they let us be.

Another year, people were stripping off and sky-training into the pond – I think there were a couple of injuries from that, but nothing too serious thankfully. I look back at that now, knowing the state everyone was in, and think "Christ, we were lucky no one drowned."

After our third year, we decided to call it a day. There were some natural cues to suggest it was time, and looking back now, it was the right thing to do, because we left the legend of 'Noble Fest' on a high and people still talk and reminisce about those legendary parties today some twenty years on.

We were still finding empty bottles in the bushes ten years later – that was another reason we decided it was time to stop. The woods are first and foremost a conservation area, so it was important to us not to overdo it.

But those three parties we put on created memories for our family, friends and strangers who turned up that will stick with us forever. Those that were there will have their own special moments – and those that weren't probably wish they had been!

Thanks to Deryk Noble, Lucy Noble, Bob Noble, Martin Noble, Simon Noble, Tom Noble, Emma Noble and all our mates that helped make it happen and stayed to clear up after!

PLÁCIDO DOMINGO
ROYAL OPERA HOUSE, LONDON
JANUARY 2018
ANTONIO POLLEDRI, OWNER OF BAR ITALIA
AND LITTLE ITALY
FRITH STREET, SOHO, LONDON

I've always had a love of opera, especially from when my school was chosen to be involved in any opera that had children's parts and was due to be performed at the English National Opera at the London Coliseum. I was even lucky enough to appear on stage there as a child, in *La Boheme*, *Tosca* and *Carmen*, and I made my debut in *Cavalleria Pagliacci*. Being of Italian heritage played an immense part in my passion for the genre too, and as children my mum and dad would play different operas at home. I was into pop music as well, but from the age of twelve to fifteen, every birthday I'd get a vinyl box set of a different opera, and I'm proud to say that I still have them today. They were all I ever wanted.

I've been lucky to go Bussetto in Parma, where one of my favourite tenors, Carlo Bergonzi, lived and by chance managed to see him give a masterclass through a drawn curtain. I also went to Puccini's house in Torre del Lago, so I have a massive and genuine passion for the opera. I go about five or six times a year – always a special occasion. Over the years, I've seen Pavarotti sing, when tickets were selling for £2,000 each outside. Pavarotti sang in Tosca this particular evening and took a tumble in his riding boots!

Anyway, one day, I found out that one of my idols, Plácido Domingo, was conducting, not actually singing, in an opera that I'd sung in, Tosca, at the Royal Opera House in January 2018. I naturally bought tickets as soon as I could. On this evening, I coincidentally I ran into my friend Salvatore who runs the front of house at Covent Garden. The performance was mesmerising, the production and the singing. I marvelled at my idol, Plácido, conducting. Il Maestro has sung every major role as a tenor and a baritone and recently played a small part in La Traviata.

When the opera had finished, I was standing there, totally enamoured with it all. As I went to leave, I had a tap on my shoulder from Salvatore. I told him how wonderful the performance had been. He said, "Well, now I have something really wonderful for you," and he invited me and my cousin Eugene Lusardi to go backstage and meet Il Maestro. The chances of us meeting him were minimal and only a very few select people ever get to meet him after a production. So, Salvatore took me and Eugene backstage, and there was Plácido, as well as the cast. Being introduced to Il Maestro was an incredible once-in-a-lifetime event for me – it was something I'll never, forget. We got on very well from the start, and he asked me what my profession was. I told him I'm a restauranteur and he was inquisitive about that and I was very flattered by his interest when I told him it was a family-run business located in Frith Street, Soho since 1949 – Bar Italia and Little Italy next door.

Then the time came to part company and I left having a good feeling about him and hopefully he the felt the same about me. Then, two days later, I had a call from Salvatore telling me that Il Maestro would like to come and eat in our restaurant after a performance in La Traviata. Amazing! But I had to make sure everything was on point. It meant a late night and long day because he wasn't going to get to us until 11.30 p.m. Little Italy can sometimes be a noisy and chaotic place, so I wasn't sure how it was going to work. However, it was midweek, so that was an advantage. On the night, I was there, dressed in a black suit, ready to look after Plácido and his entourage, including his son and about twelve other people. He came in and I whisked him through the mass of noisy customers who were all dancing and drinking. He must have thought, what are you bringing me into?

Obviously opera singers have to careful with their voices and make sure they don't scream and shout, because of the damage they could do, but by the time he got upstairs to the top floor, it was much quieter. I was prepared to look after Plácido and serve him, and once again found him inquisitive about me, my family, our Italian roots and my love of opera, including him remembering I had sung operatic children's parts. The party all then sat down at a long table and he asked where I was going. I told him I was going to look after everything and make sure all got served in good time, and he said, "No, I insist you sit next to me."

I was gobsmacked and honoured to be sitting next to my idol – nobody else, but me. Therefore, I sat and had dinner with him. The mark of the man was that he made me feel comfortable. The chef came out to meet him. Il Maestro wanted spaghetti pomodoro, which was fantastic after a few starters, and everybody else had the same too. He told me many stories about his career, which were incredible. One that stuck in my mind is of the Scottish landlady, who had a glass of gin in her hand when he checked in, and then he noticed the smell of cats all over the place. He was laughing his head off and said he couldn't stay there, so left. Then sporadically at the meal he'd burst into song, all of my favourite arias, singing 'Sotto Vocé', and I will never forget listening to one of the three tenors' singers – my own private concert.

The evening seemed to go so quickly, because when we looked at our watches it was 3.30 a.m. Salvatore had ordered a chauffeur to come and pick Plácido up, but Soho was chaotic at that time of night. So, I ended up outside with him, trying to find his driver. We went across the road and got in the wrong car and he then looked at a rickshaw to get back to The Aldwych, where he was staying. He mentioned his night finished at 4 a.m. and he had firm instructions: he was not to be disturbed by anyone before midday. That's his pattern. Then he starts his daily routine.

As he left, we exchanged numbers, and we keep in touch. He called me personally a year later in 2019 to say he had been given a prestigious award and he could think of nowhere else in London where he'd rather receive it, and celebrate the win, than at Little Italy. Once again, he asked me to join him and we had a dinner together again.

We get in touch every Christmas and Easter without fail, and I am still honoured that he replies to my messages personally. He always wishes me, and all of my family, best wishes. What a gentleman, what a talent and what a friend.

Grazie, caro maestro.

★tkasg.

proudly present

NEON WALTZ

+ Special Guests

Friday 17th April 2015

Westgarth SC

99 Southfield Road, Middlesbrough TS1 3EZ

Tel 01642 242184

Tickets £6 STBF

Doors 7:30pm

Ages 14+ (14-17 yrs with an adult)

www.thekidsaresolidgold.co.uk

00005

NEON WALTZ
WESTGARTH SOCIAL CLUB, MIDDLESBROUGH
17 APRIL 2015
DAVID POTTINGER, TEACHER/BLOGGER

If you're a follower of the 'holy trinity' of clothing, football and music you'll know that these three things often go hand in hand. On the night of this Neon Waltz gig at the legendary 'Westy', it was no different. The Boro had a crucial game away at the glamourous Norwich City, so me and the boys arrived at the venue early doors, knowing they'd have the game on in the bar area where the old boys would sit, chew the fat and play the occasional game of snooker when they could be arsed to get up. What followed was Aitor Karanka's plucky reds seeing out a 0-1 win after scoring early and then sitting back for eighty-odd long minutes of sustained pressure. I'm sorta glad those days are behind us now; my young heart couldn't take it.

After some nail-biting footy, we surged into the small downstairs room, full of ale and anticipation. We were about to witness a band we'd been following for some time since discovering them as a support at another gig earlier in the year. The promoter (The Kids Are Solid Gold) was notorious for plucking some of the best up-and-coming talent from across the country and bringing them to this hallowed venue in the heart of the Boro. Neon Waltz were fucking electric, there's no doubt about that. From the first moment we ever saw these boys we knew they were going to play a big part in our listening patterns over the next few years.

The downstairs room in the Westy was warm, proper warm, and as always packed to the rafters with some of Teesside's gig-going finest. The bar arced along the right-hand side of the room and sat snugly in that corner; it was always a nightmare to get served when there was a good band in town. This problem would bring up the usual groans from my mob of, "Why can't it be in the fucking bigger room upstairs!?" There was always one and thankfully this night it wasn't me.

Pints of Tuborg secured, we set out finding a decent plot to from which to watch the boys. Chatter of the result, what trainers you were copping next and who you had on your coupon faded into the sweat-soaked walls as Neon Waltz took to the cosy, yet domineering, stage. The band asked everyone to take a step forward before bursting into a soaring rendition of 'Bring Me To Light'. Boss! A chaotic, yet dreamy, indie-pop song with a soothing vocal that instantly lights up the room. The energy in the room lifted and even the muso dads propping up the bar were tapping their feet.

The band were tight, and we all couldn't quite believe we were seeing them for the measly sum of six quid! The perks of being sussed, ey! The first tune ended and the whole of the room broke into a raucous applause, which spurred the band straight into 'Folklore', a tune that hits you from the off with its off-beat guitar and drumming patterns almost reminiscent of 2Tone. The tempo in the room lifted again and a bit of pogoing ensued during the instrumental parts, which got a smile from frontman Jordan, who was on serious form that night. There was a collective appreciation in the crowd that night of just how fucking good this band were, and a slight arrogance against those who slept on getting tickets.

A few words from Jordan followed and then the band launched into three stomping tracks off their forthcoming debut album, which, little did we know, was going to take another two years to perfect. A standout moment here was during 'Dreamers' (only a demo at this point), when Jordan had the whole room in the very palm of his hand with a tune no one had heard before. Magic that! The entire room was together in perfect harmony, and it was one of those moments which hits you and says, "It ain't half bad this world, after all!"

The final four tunes ran out at lightning speed and everyone was convinced that this band were the next big thing! 'Bare Wood Aisles' was played second from last and was belted out from the lungs of every man, woman and muso dad in attendance.

Music really was the winner that night, even if I did get Guinness on my sand suede Desert Treks...

HARVEY GOLDSMITH ENTERTAINMENTS IN ASSOCIATION WITH TRINIFOLD MANAGEMENT
PROUDLY PRESENTS
ROGER DALTREY
JOHN ENTWISTLE
PETE TOWNSHEND
THE WHO
perform
QUADROPHENIA
Words and Music by Pete Townshend
FEATURING
BILLY IDOL
LIVE AT
EARLS COURT
FRIDAY 6th DECEMBER 7.30pm
TICKETS: £27.50 & £25.00 (SUBJECT TO BOOKING FEE)
IN PERSON FROM BOX OFFICE
(NO BOOKING FEE TO PERSONAL CALLERS)
BY CREDIT CARD ON:
0171 373 8141 - 0171 420 1000
0171 935 1173 - 0171 344 4444
0171 734 8932
ALSO AVAILABLE FROM
STARGREEN BOX OFFICE, ARGYLL STREET, W.1.
VIRGIN MEGASTORE, OXFORD STREET, W.1.
PLUS SUPPORT
95·8
CAPITAL FM
QUADROPHENIA TICKETLINE 0990 22 55 66

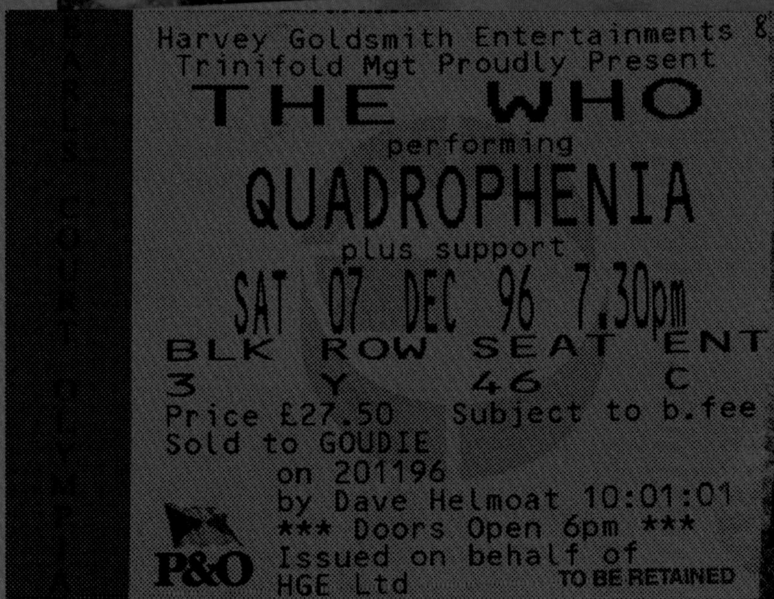
Harvey Goldsmith Entertainments &
Trinifold Mgt Proudly Present
THE WHO
performing
QUADROPHENIA
plus support
SAT 07 DEC 96 7.30pm
BLK ROW SEAT ENT
3 Y 46 C
Price £27.50 Subject to b.fee
Sold to GOUDIE
on 201196
by Dave Helmoat 10:01:01
*** Doors Open 6pm ***
Issued on behalf of
HGE Ltd
P&O
TO BE RETAINED

THE WHO
EARLS COURT, LONDON
6 DECEMBER 1996
SARAH RAMSEY GOUDIE, GIRL FRIDAY

I have always loved music from an early age. It must stem from my late dad Brian, who was a professional musician with many of the greats from the Fifties, such as Billy Fury and Johnny Kidd & The Pirates. Anyway, I digress. Dad loved rock, as did I, and he used to say, à la Del Boy, "You can't whack a bit of The Who!"

So, when I met Simon in the Nineties, and discovered we had a mutual love of The Who, what better gift could I get Sim (and me!) other than tickets to see the loudest rock band in the world! I purchased tickets for the princely sum of £27.50 apiece and we rolled down to Earls Court on Saturday 6 December 1996.

We were both euphoric to be there, and Simon was even happier when I got chatting to the T-shirt man who said that, as he liked me, I could have two T-shirts for the price of one – happy days! Simon said he hoped we'd get the same deal when I went to get the beers.

We settled in our seats, with much excitement. The lights went down, then up again, and there they were: the three remaining members of the band, Daltrey, Townshend and Bonham. I'm not ashamed to say that tears streamed down my face at the opening bars of 'I Am The Sea'. I was in heaven, with my love and the best band in the world – what more could a girl want. Well, the song ended, and we screeched and clapped and hollered like banshees.

The next tune was 'The Real Me' and then I lost it. I'm only little, and as I did the 'Townsend windmill' with my arm, I promptly smacked the fella in front of me around the earhole! Oh, I was so embarrassed.

Well, the gig went on through the rest of the *Quadrophenia* set in a flash, and we sung our little hearts out, and what can I say other than the gig was perfection; everyone in the band was on top form and the support excelled themselves. As we left on a high, we also saw Chris Tarrant, I think, getting a T-shirt. I bet that he didn't get two for the price of one…

This gig leaves me with so many happy memories of great times, but it is also tinged with sadness, as both my dad and Simon left this mortal coil in 2016. To this day, I can still hear my dad say, "You can't whack a bit of The Who." Never a truer word spoken.

DORIS TROY
THE BACK BAR, SOHO, LONDON W1
DATE UNKNOWN, 1995
GORDON ROBERTS, PROPRIETOR

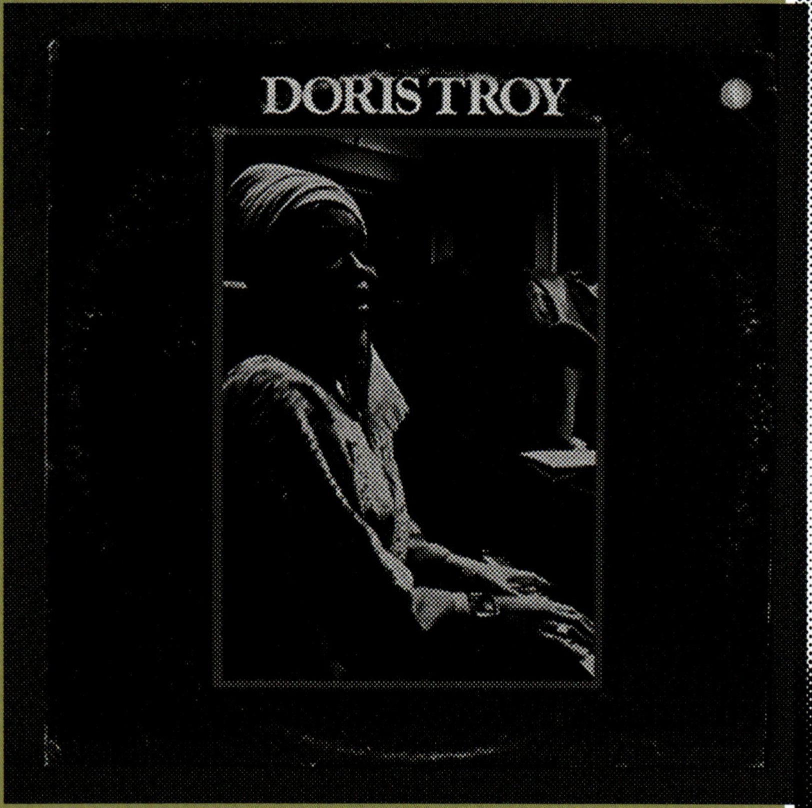

Back in the Nineties I ran a small live music bar in Soho with my then partner. It didn't start off that way, but after being there for the first year we decided that this was what was missing from that corner of the 'Dirty Square Mile', as they used to call it. One night, I had a chance meeting with an associate and for some reason Doris Troy's name came up.

Now, I have been a fan of Doris since the early Eighties, when I heard 'I'll Do Anything (He Wants Me To Do)' at an all-nighter somewhere up north, and watched the place go mad. Anyway, this chap mentioned that another associate knew Doris well from the old Rainbow Rooms days back in the early Seventies, and she was staying in Marylebone while performing at various places. Long story short, I obtained her telephone number and after a very nervous phone call she agreed to allow me to take her out to lunch to discuss a proposal I had in mind. I went to collect her in a very nice limo I'd hired for the occasion and took her to one of the restaurants at the top end of Portobello Road.

Once I had stopped gushing and listing out all her releases over the years (in case she didn't think I was a real fan) and following a fairly long lunch, punctuated with stories from back in the day, I plucked up the courage and asked would she do us the honour of singing at our music bar. She seemed hesitant at first, saying she was more used to the larger, more prestigious end of the market these days. Undeterred, I told her I hoped that for her it would be like being back in New York in her early days, and after a lot of persistence on my part, she finally agreed.

Back then the internet wasn't really up and running, so I made a fairly basic (and small 1/8 page) advert on my new PC for *Time Out* magazine, with black background and a few small white stars and white lettering stating 'One night only, Doris Troy'. I added the address and telephone number, saved it on a floppy disk and sent it over to the magazine.

Fast forward to the day of the event, and I was pretty nervous as I'd promised Doris a full house, but this was not the usual type of music my punters were used to, and I was having visions of Doris playing to a half empty bar. I needn't have worried. After a nap and a quick early dinner at Ley-Ons in Wardour Street (I was on seventeen-hour days back then), we headed over to the bar and I could see from a distance that there was a bit of a commotion going on outside. When we got near, I saw the agitated doorman (Dennis, I think he was called) trying to stop what I first thought was a load of tourists coming in. I then looked up the side alleyway and there were well over 100 people queueing up outside the bar, which was already almost full!

I had underestimated the power of *Time Out*, as well as Doris' popularity. People had come over from Germany, Sweden, Italy and all over the place, and were demanding to come in. We hadn't ticketed the event, since we thought it would be mainly regulars.

The band had dropped their gear off earlier and Doris arrived around 9 p.m. I spotted her limo and ran out and guided her into the fire escape to avoid the crowds. It was a filthy alleyway with a street door leading to the rear of the bar, which Doris found amusing. "Where is my dressing room?" was the first question. I led her to the small back room, which was more of a bottle store, and then I told her our resident MC would announce her. She came out about 9.30 p.m.

The bar, which was full to bursting point, erupted in cheers and applause as she was welcomed on to the stage. I think she opened with 'Just One Look', then went on for around 90 minutes with killer performances of 'I'll Do Anything', which she dedicated to me, 'Bossa Nova Blues', 'You'd Better Stop', 'School For Fools', 'What You Gonna Do About It' and 'You Are So Beautiful', among others. She had the crowd eating out of her hand with every beat.

When she took her final bow after several encores, it took her a good hour to get from the stage to the bar, as she didn't want to disappoint and signed every autograph asked for. Finally, when she got out the back, I could see she was exhausted, and so I got her a stiff drink. We then sat and chatted for quite a while and she recounted stories of when she first got started and her time at the Apollo, as well as tales about Pearl Bailey and others.

It felt like a dream come true for me. She thanked me for persuading her to come and perform and said it was the most fun she'd had in a very long time. I immediately asked if she would do it again, and she smiled and said, "I would love to, this was a really special night."

Doris was true to her word, and she performed on a few more occasions over the following weeks. We were savvy enough to sell tickets on the subsequent nights she came to us but even so, there were still crowds packing the alley outside and many people never getting in. But that first night will always stay with me.

I was told Doris passed away in 2004. I knew she had been unwell, but it choked me up, as I had always assumed I would see her perform again (she was only sixty-seven when she passed, so she was in her late fifties when I met her). The last thing she did after her final performance at The Back Bar was to hand me a CD. I went to pop it on when I got home at 4 a.m. and inside she had written on the sleeve notes "Gordon, you are so beautiful to me, Love, Doris Troy" (based on a line from one of her songs).

I have lived many years and moved several times since then and sadly cannot find that CD. But I will never forget my time there, and how one chance conversation led to one of the most amazing musical experiences ever.

YOUR TICKET to ENTERTAINMENT

axs.com

Brooklyn Bowl Presents

BOOKER T JONES

18+
Bowling Not Included

Friday, 8 July 2016 - Doors : 19:00
TICKET: £ 0.00

Standard entrance by the box office

GENERAL ADMISSION FLOOR

COMPLIMENTARY
ORDER NUMBER: 077-0295 8744
[GA1,666] #43/107

00573454000224

BOOKER T. JONES
BROOKLYN BOWL, NORTH GREENWICH, LONDON
8 JULY 2016
HILARY SEABROOK, MUSICIAN

My problem with selecting a ticket that tells a story in my life is twofold. First, I've been to a LOT of gigs and concerts, and second, I've been very fortunate in often being on the guest list and not having a physical ticket to keep. Add to that the fact that some tickets I did once have seem to have disappeared over the years and you can see the problem in undertaking my tiny part in this amazing project.

There are two gigs in the early Eighties that I remember particularly well, but there's no ticket – bari sax player Gerry Mulligan at the Royal Festival Hall (where I sat so close I could hear his live sound, not just through the PA) and Junior Walker & The All Stars at either Shepherds Bush Empire or Hammersmith Odeon (a group of us from Solid Bond Studios danced for hours).

Three of the tickets I have kept and treasured tell part of my story as a musician. I still can't quite believe that I actually saw Ella Fitzgerald and Oscar Peterson on 3 November 1980 at the Royal Festival Hall. The second ticket I've kept for all these decades is also almost unbelievable. Another Festival Hall trip, and this one for the epic trumpeter Miles Davis on 11 July 1989. This was in the time when the legend of bebop and some of the best jazz of the Fifties and Sixties reawakened his career and released the classic album *Tutu*.

Those five musicians – Mulligan, Walker, Fitzgerald, Peterson and Davis – spin their webs through my musical career, as I constantly return to their work and learn everything I can from them.

However, the final ticket I've found that tells quite a lot about my story as a musician comes from 8 July 2016. The significance of seeing Booker T. Jones at London's Brooklyn Bowl ("Bowling Not Included", apparently) remains huge. Just a few weeks earlier, a second tumour had been removed from my stomach and nearly four years of severe illness were behind me. Seeing Booker T. was my first real gig after the operation and it felt GOOD. That gig reignited my love of performing and sax playing, despite there being no horns on stage that night.

I loved that Booker T. was on stage with three of the young musical guns, including his own son, playing new tracks and some classics. His rendition of 'Green Onions' was simply stunning. I worked briefly with Steve Cropper years back and he told a great story about how that song came to life, becoming an overnight sensation that is immediately recognisable to most people from that moment to this – and the 2016 live version was no faint rendition of a past track, but a modern interpretation of a tune that everyone knows. With the subtle smile on his face, Booker knew he was pleasing the crowd and at the same time seemed to be enjoying that groove. That smile stayed on his face throughout the night – the smile that has formed part of his outward musical persona throughout five decades.

Although some of the tracks were included on the set list that night as crowd pleasers, it was clear from the musicians that they were really enjoying what they were doing. There were some great original Booker T. & The M.G.'s tunes, but also some fascinating versions of classics. Prince's 'Purple Rain' was something of a pleasing surprise and I loved the rendition of Gershwin's 'Summertime', which was particularly apt for a July gig. There were, of course, several Otis Redding covers – I remember particularly 'Respect'. The encore that night was 'Time Is Tight', another great Booker T. & The M.G.'s tune that encapsulates the great man's writing and playing skills.

The gig itself was stunning: it was clear that these were musicians of different generations who had worked hard to produce a show that absolutely rocked. They steamed through every tune with such a groove that it was impossible not to dance or tap a foot, at the very least. Booker's sharing the stage with such great young musicians seems to have been part of his musical soul since he was in the first house band for Stax Records and then the staggeringly brilliant Booker T. & The M.G.'s.

What with the Covid-19 hiatus, my sax playing has been on hold, but it's back with a vengeance now, and I can look back on that Booker T. Jones gig – even without the bowling – as a turning point for me.

EDDIE & THE HOT RODS/THE DAMNED
KENT UNIVERSITY
3 NOVEMBER 1976
TIM ROLLS, AUTHOR

It was October 1976. I was nineteen and a big Eddie & The Hot Rods fan – on the basis of three cracking singles and a load of positive music press, never having seen them. In early September they had been on *Top of the Pops* with the glorious 'Get Out Of Denver' from the *Live At The Marquee* EP (which charted at number 43) and during 1976 had fast built a reputation in the *NME* and *Sounds* as an excoriating live band. In some critical quarters they were seen as more of a fast R&B band and not really 'punk rock', though to be honest there were only about four or five 'punk' bands actually playing gigs at that point, and The Hot Rods were pulling in more punters than any of them, so any snobbery was a bit out of place. They were without doubt trailblazers for punk, and should be recognised as such. They made the cover of the November 1976 edition of punk fanzine *Sniffin' Glue*, which showed that editor Mark Perry rated them.

Arriving as a new student at Kent University in Canterbury that month, I was unimpressed by the Freshers' Ball headliner, Shakin' Stevens & The Sunsets, a magnet for every scowling middle-aged Ted in East Kent. The likes of Caravan, Gryphon (don't ask…), Procol Harum, Soft Machine and Steeleye Span had blighted the previous year's student entertainment, and nearly put me off going there.

Most of the bands already lined up to play that term did not impress me much either, but one date stood out: Eddie & The Hot Rods were playing in a college dining room in early November. I was greatly cheered that a real up-and-coming band had been booked, a slight shifting in the tectonic plates from the previous year, and I spent most of my first month in Canterbury boring anyone who would listen about how great they were, having bought my ticket at the first available opportunity. Reinforcing this, a few of us saw them at Margate Dreamland in mid-October, and they were a breath of fresh air, as good as the music press said they were. Barrie Masters was such a confident frontman, and the band so energised, it was possible to watch them and definitely believe they were destined for the toppermost of the poppermost.

The Damned, later announced as support, were already nurturing a notoriety that, in retrospect, was bound to cause ructions in such a conservative (small 'c') college environment. There was no debate: they were a punk band. It would be only their seventeenth-ever gig. 'New Rose' (the first punk single) had been out a fortnight and had sold 4,000 in the first week, without proper distribution. I had a copy, which I played to death before the gig. As I didn't listen to Peel and hadn't heard the Dolls or any NY punk, I'd never heard anything like it, or their cover of 'Help', which was short, frantic and mesmerising. I could not wait to see them live, though had little idea of what to really expect. The day of the Canterbury gig, the band were on the front cover of Sounds, fantastic exposure for such a new outfit. Somewhere I have a copy of that issue, with 'Bo**ocks From Sexist Rat' written across the cover.

I had joined the Student Union Entertainment Committee the previous night, hoping to up the ante with less Gryphon and more Hot Rods-type bands, so was very happy to help set up the gig, erecting the stage, clearing tables etc. This meant I got in free, so I presumably unloaded my ticket (I can't remember...).

Many of my fellow committee members looked in fearful disdain at our visitors, so my friend Martin and I were asked to look after Dave Vanian and Co in terms of food and drink. The dining room staff bluntly refused to serve them a meal. The bar staff even more bluntly refused to serve them a drink, after an entrance which certainly turned heads among the rugby shirt and cheesecloth brigade. I got banned from the bar for taking them in and arguing the case with the jobsworth head barman. We had to get some innocent-looking soul to buy food and beer and take it to their dressing room.

This nonsense really surprised me, as I'd assumed universities were liberal establishments, but in retrospect I was naive. And remember, this was a month before the Grundy/Pistols TV encounter that really got the punk witch hunt fired up. Martin chatted to Vanian at a gig decades later, and he laughingly remembered the food and drink nonsense. The leather jacketed but seemingly more benign Hot Rods were served without a problem.

The Damned's Captain Sensible and Vanian seemed decent blokes. Rat Scabies clearly thought he had to be as outrageous and objectionable as possible, and Brian James portrayed the moody wannabe rock star to perfection. The Hot Rods' frontman Barrie Masters was happy to chat. I don't remember talking to the rest of the band, but they must have seemed comparatively 'normal' to the audience compared with the supporting upstarts.

I recall little about The Damned's set, except that they were loud, the songs were brutally short, and they seemed to enjoy themselves, thriving on shocking a large part of the audience. They probably didn't expect much empathy so were unsurprised not to get it. There weren't many of us at the front of the stage by the end of their set, or in the middle or back of the hall, for that matter.

I don't remember too much about The Hot Rods' set either to be honest, though I do recall they played all the singles (unsurprisingly) and encored with 'Get Out Of Denver.' They went down pretty well and were afterwards appreciative of the audience response.

Looking back, that night was definitely a catalyst. The Damned were the first punk band to play in East Kent and as well as some of the more open-minded students, the bill drew a load of enthusiastic locals (mainly schoolkids). Among those there that night were whippersnapper schoolboys Simon Terry and Ben Challis, both within months frontmen in their own local punk bands, The Names and The Ignerents respectively. That night I proudly wore a Hot Rods T-shirt, which I am still mocked about decades later (it shrank and turned pink in the wash, but I still wore it for ages).

A Google search amazingly produced a copy of the gig poster. I also acquired one on the night, but a) it was inevitably not in good nick and b) I mislaid it years back.

I was mortified when the next Hot Rods single – 'Teenage Depression', released the following week – only got to number 35 despite a really positive *Sounds* review predicting a Top Five place. Worse, the in retrospect patchy, same-titled LP charted for only one week, just before Xmas. They were unlucky, as they were unarguably a brilliant live band, but despite a few top-class singles, including the anthemic 'Do Anything You Wanna Do,' they got largely pushed aside when 'proper' punk got going, and by early 1978 they were in decline. The Damned, despite being on the scene very early indeed, suffered from never being as fashionable as the Pistols or The Clash, but their first LP is still required listening and they are still going strong.

I remember The Damned were paid £50 – par for the course for support bands in those days – and The Hot Rods got around £400. Capacity was circa 600 and I think about 500 people turned up. At £1.10 a ticket it would have turned a small profit; unusual in an academic year where massive losses were incurred by legacy entertainment longhairs booking the likes of Larry Coryell (who?), Pat Travers (ditto), Babe Ruth and Frankie Miller. We did manage to put on The Stranglers, The Jam, The Damned, The Adverts and 999 by the following summer, so all was not entirely lost.

Forty-six years hence inevitably blurs the memory, so these recollections are sadly not as detailed as I would like. What is clear, though, is that the gig had a massive impact on me, and on a number of others there that night. It transformed the written page and my imagination to a glorious reality.

MANIC STREET PREACHERS
KARL MARX THEATRE, HAVANA, CUBA
17 FEBRUARY 2001
DARREN RUSSELL, PHOTOGRAPHER

The Manic Street Preachers were due to play the Karl Marx Theatre in Havana, Cuba, the first Western band to play in the communist nation in twenty years. I heard about it on the radio and really fancied it, as I had always wanted to go to Cuba and this was to be a historic occasion. Having previously had dealings with the band's management, I approached them and asked that, if I went out there, could I get a photographer's pass, and they were like yeah, fine. I wasn't really a diehard fan of theirs, but I like them; they've got principles and they're staunch. Financially, it also came at the right time, as I had a bit of dough behind me as a result of some advertising jobs I'd just done. Basically, I thought sod it, let's go. I teamed up with a mate of mine, Nigel, who was an architectural photographer. Cuba was somewhere he'd also fancied going, so we started planning. The idea was to go for three weeks and get a car and travel round the island before and after the gig.

We contacted the band's management, and they gave us instructions of where to go and so on. We arrived with our cameras, and this was in the pre-digital days, so we were using film. However, once there, we ran straight into the secret police. They pulled us over and said they wanted to check our cameras. We told them they were loaded with film, and they told us not to worry. We feared the worst and thought what the fuck are we going to do here, because we expected they'd open up the back of the cameras and expose all the film. But when they returned them, they were still on number one, the first frame. Welsh music journalist and big Manics fan Simon Price also got pulled over. He's a big guy and his head was shaved apart from two red-pink spikes sticking up. The look on the Cubans' faces when they saw him was priceless.

We didn't have tickets or passes, but a fluorescent green mark on our hands instead, but we finally got into the venue. It was then we discovered that this was a big place – sort of Havana's equivalent of the Royal Albert Hall, holding around 5,000 people or so, and it was packed, even though we'd only seen one poster advertising the gig in all the time we were there. We later learnt it was an invite-only thing and you only got in if you were connected, like having an uncle in the army or the government. Everybody who was anybody out there wanted to go – it was a huge event. They weren't all into the music, they were just curious.

The crowd were all seated, as though they were at the local Odeon cinema, and then the Manics appeared onstage, with Cuban trumpet player Yasek Manzano Silva. They played all their hits, and I remember 'If You Tolerate This Your Children Will be Next' went down really well. I'd seen the band a couple of times before that, and they were – and still are – an amazing band. Towards the end, everybody – and I mean everybody – in that place was standing and jumping up and down.

I got some great shots that night. We were allowed three numbers, and then off. As I was clicking, it suddenly went quiet and I realised Fidel Castro has just walked in, waving as he took a seat. I then moved to the back of the auditorium and got a shot of everyone sitting down, and then one of everyone standing up. We were also allowed to shoot the last song, which was funny. Sadly, I lost all those photos when the agency I was signed to went bust, and I never saw them again.

This gig was so monumental – that is the only way of putting it. It really felt special, like being there when the Berlin Wall came down. We were a part of history.

We had a great time afterwards in Cuba, too – a brilliant place, where we met some incredible people and went to some incredible places. The only problem was they see tourists as a walking dollar sign, a sort of 'cash point', if that makes sense? They offered us everything. I managed to learn the phrase "There's no business here", but a couple of them were very persistent. When I was offered a cigar or homemade rum, I'd say I had asthma, and slap my chest. When offered women, same reply: I've got asthma. Men? No, asthma. They perhaps had no idea what asthma was but probably thought fuck me, I don't ever want that…

At first it pissed you off, the constant asking, but the longer we were there and saw how most lived, the more we thought I don't really blame them. One thing, though, I never felt under threat at any time. Out there, you touch a tourist and you're dead. They understand that if a tourist doesn't feel safe, it's a real problem, since their economy relies on tourism. So, we always felt as safe as houses.

We eventually hooked up with a Cuban guy called Ricky, in his early twenties, who was white with blond hair. His German grandfather had been torpedoed off the coast of Cuba during the Second World War and he swam to the mainland. Ricky said his grandfather thought, "Germany's fucked, I'm staying here," and so he settled there. Anyway, one afternoon we taught this Ricky how to drive and in return for that he looked after us in shops. When the shopkeepers were talking about us in Spanish, about how they were going to make a nice profit off of us, he piped up and told them to back off. They never once suspected he was Cuban.

We travelled all over the island. We went up to the mountains where Castro had his base and also to the town of Trinidad. We even got to Guantanamo Bay, where you could see a whole complex full of US navy and military. We stayed mainly with local families, when not in hotels. There was a network out there organising all that. The families would give you a bed for the night and feed you and it only cost a couple of dollars and they were very happy with that.

Driving back one day, we picked up an older couple who were hitchhiking and gave them a lift home. We could hear this clucking coming from a bag, and the fella opened it to reveal a very feisty, mean-looking cockerel. Of course, we ran into some motorbike coppers, who I think were looking for a back-hander from us, only to find two locals and a cockerel in the back. They finally let us pass and pulled over a group of twenty pink-faced tourists instead, who were out on scooters. Obviously, there was more money available with them.

I heard later that the Manic Street Preachers had met Fidel Castro before the gig and warned him it could be loud, to which he replied, "Will it be as loud as war?" When they saw him again after the gig and asked, well was it? He simply said "Louder!"

U.K. SUBS
THE CITY ARMS, CITY ROAD, LONDON
29 APRIL 1978
DAVID ALEXIS SAUNDERS
RETIRED SOHO BOY

In the 1976/77 season, Tottenham got relegated from the old first division to the second division. I remember I was up in the old supporters' club, thinking gawd, I've just been made redundant from me first job, Tottenham have just been relegated and I ain't even hit eighteen yet.

The only glimmer was the new punk phenomenon that was just breaking through. It was wonderful, so much energy, some really good bands and tunes, and we didn't have to sit through those five-minute Cozy Powell drum solos anymore – what a load of old pony that was.

Anyway, it was the last game of the season, and Tottenham were supposed to play Southampton at the start of the season, but for some reason cup games got in the way and every time they rearranged they'd get cancelled again. We finally played them when if both teams drew, they'd both get promoted. So, we all went down to Southampton, and as soon as we got into Surrey, the Old Bill was all over us. Our coach was stopped and we all got searched, the police looking for weapons. When we finally got into the ground, they'd built a cage for us so we couldn't get on the pitch. Only thing was it was so flimsy, it only lasted till half time and then it came down.

The final score was predictably 0-0, both teams winning promotion. So, we had a bit of a dance on the pitch and then jumped on the coach back to London and were all having a great old time. On the way home, we stopped the coach a couple of times and picked up a couple of punk rockers who were thumbing it back to London, and then the bus got stuck on the grass – gawd knows how – and we all had to get out and push the bleeding thing off the grass to get it going again.

Then we got back to London, hit a chippie in Hoxton and then down the City Road, to the City Arms, N1. I'd been in there the night before and saw a couple of really good punk bands, and as it was my mate Steve's local, we decided to go back and celebrate in there. It was full of Tottenham fans celebrating along with a few Rangers fans, who had also just won their title, so we were getting well Mozart*.

It was then I noticed they had punk bands on again. The first one, name escapes me, were really good, and then I saw U.K. Subs' frontman Charlie Harper counting up to four. They were fantastic. They were raw, sharp, together, and the songs had terrific lyrics. It wasn't just me – the entire pub knew they were special. They were so much on form, on another level.

Even though I wasn't dressing as a punk, I was attracted to a three-minute song that was so vibrant and so alive, so in your face, so anarchistic. You've got to remember that at that time everyone had long hair and wore a pair of Lionels*, whether it be a judge, a solicitor or your bank manager. So, if you had a short, back and sides with a spiky top, tight trousers and a jacket with safety pins in small lapels, oh you could stop traffic. You didn't need to have a leather jacket and a Mohican, which came after – just being 'us' was different enough.

I can even remember the outfit I was wearing that night. It would have been a donkey jacket – pretty Tottenham (well, London) at the time – tight trousers and a pair of Dr Martens or motorcycle boots. My hair was also a bit quiffed up, though it was more of a flat-top, really – a spikier, punky flat-top.

After the gig I was talking to a bloke called Nick Garratt, who was the guitar player in the UK Subs, and it turned out he was born quite near to me – him in Leicester, me in Northampton. So that was it, I was in. After that we'd always go and see the Subs play whenever we could, and from 1978 to 1980 we followed them everywhere. Some of my favourite songs include 'T.V. Blues' and 'Stranglehold' – that was always a winner. They were regulars on *Top of the Pops*, too. Make a few appearances on that and release records at the right time, and you'd get in the charts.

I was living with my mum and dad in Northampton at the time, so I used to stay over in London and loved it, though it could be very rough, and I've got to say, it was very right-wing, with The (National) Front all over Tottenham at that time. However, I was very keen to move to London pretty much since the first day I saw the TV show *Budgie*. I really wanted a bit of that, to be a Soho boy. I was very lucky to get a job here in '78 and a flat, and so I bit the bullet.

I'll end with this. I was in my local in the late Eighties, the Kings Head on Gerrard Street, and it had the Dive Bar downstairs, which the Pet Shop Boys wrote about in 'West End Girls'. You'd also see The Undertones in there a lot. One Sunday evening, I'm in there and it's very quiet, and propped up on the bar is Charlie Harper with some little Norwegian groupie. So, I got a beer and said, "Excuse me, Charlie, not sure you'll remember me?" and we started having a chat. He said the bird's all right, she'll wait, and we started talking about all the gigs we went to, and he suddenly remembered me and mentioned I'd been mates with Nick Garratt.

I chose this gig for the book as it reminded me of such a happy day. The day I first saw the U.K. Subs I'd been at rock bottom, and just after that gig I managed to get a job in London, and a flat in Soho. And, of course, Tottenham got promoted. Being eighteen in 1977/78 – I mean, it was just all there.

** Mozart and Liszt = pissed.*
** Lionels, Lionel Blairs = Flares*

WEMBLEY STADIUM

Harvey Goldsmith
proudly presents

No ticket genuine unless it carries
a Lion's Head watermark below

THE ROLLING STONES

in concert plus guests

SAT., JUNE 26, 1982

GATES OPEN AT 1.00p.m.

Do not bring bottles or cans. Ticket holders consent to the filming and sound recording of themselves as members of the audience.

Access throughout Stadium.

TURNSTILES

J OR K

1475

Tickets £10.50 incl. VAT in advance

£11.00 incl. VAT on the day

TO BE RETAINED   ISSUED SUBJECT TO THE CONDITIONS ON BACK

YOU'LL NEVER WALK ALONE

TO BE GIVEN UP

4359488

27662090

Concerts West & AEG Presents

The Rolling Stones - SIXTY

09/06/2022

Gates Open: 4pm

Pitch

Area
Golden Circle

Adult
£169.95

TURNSTILE: T 1-4

Supporter ID: 20405912

The Rolling Stones – Sixty

174124144003089213020342

www.liverpoolfc.com/concerts

2167 AEG PRESENTS   Golden Circle

THE ROLLING STONES
WEMBLEY STADIUM, LONDON, 26 JUNE 1982
& ANFIELD, LIVERPOOL, 9 JUNE 2022
RAOUL SHAH, CEO, THE CASBAH PR COMPANY

It's 1982. I was in Our Price Records (formerly Oliver Crombie) on Golders Green Road, buying my copy of *Combat Rock* as well as collecting the empty sleeves used for the window display. But, for once, it was not The Clash who were my preoccupation and focus. In the background I heard Black Uhuru's 'Youth of Eglington', which stopped me in my tracks. Pure vibes with Duckie's vocals and the unmistakeable sound of Jamaican rhythm section Sly and Robbie on drum and bass. I left the store with their album *Red* in my bag and decided I had to see them live.

Cut to The Rolling Stones' Tattoo You European tour, with Black Uhuru opening along with The J. Geils Band – remember the 'Centrefold' video? Three for the price of one. Bingo! A postage stamp and £10.50 later, me and my three friends Matthew Green, Yul Desai, Matt Sage are set for a date at Wembley Stadium. Black Uhuru played a few tracks from *Red* as well as a couple from *Chill Out*, which I bought on the first day of release later that year.

It was one of those moments that only really took shape and proportion several years later. First time on the pitch at Wembley. First of many times seeing Black Uhuru. First tour T-shirt – I got a bootleg outside because I couldn't afford the official merchandise. First time smoking weed, which brought a new dimension to the proceedings. First time seeing The Rolling Stones and becoming a fan for life.

So here I am, forty years later in 2022 at another Stones' gig. The world has changed beyond recognition, yet live music and friendship bring us together again and provide the elixir to a good life and sharing love. On this occasion, I had the privilege of being a guest of Keith and David (thanks Bravado/Universal), my wife Sonia was my plus one (plus for-ever!) and we're standing on the hallowed turf of Anfield, my beloved team's home. This was the grand finale to a bitter-sweet season in which Liverpool came close to securing the quadruple.

The Stones were phenomenal, playing the greatest of greatest hits. Mick didn't stop running for two hours. Keith was funny ("Good to see you. In fact, it's good to see anything"). Ronnie provided another beautiful artwork for the setlist. And Steve Jordan was behind the drums, paying a fitting tribute to the late, great Charlie Watts. Echo & The Bunnymen opened the show and transported me back to another soundtrack to my youth.

This time I left on a natural high and with an official band T-shirt. And so, it goes. Four decades between two shows featuring one of the greatest and most enduring rock'n'roll bands of all time, and still playing the same Black Uhuru records bought in NW11.

P.S. Full circle. Drummer Sly Dunbar plays on 'Undercover Of The Night', which appears on the Stones' *Forty Licks* double album, released in 2002.

STAX PRESENTS "IT CAME FROM MEMPHIS" FEAT. BOOKER T. & THE M.G.'S/EDDIE FLOYD/ WILLIAM BELL/MABLE JOHN
BARBICAN HALL, LONDON
25 APRIL 2005
NEIL SHEASBY, MUSICIAN

It had been a while since I'd seen Brendan Lynch, the record producer best known for overseeing classic releases from Paul Weller, Primal Scream and The Young Disciples. We'd become fast friends a few years previous, in the mid-Nineties, largely due to his time spent up in Birmingham working with Ocean Colour Scene. We'd first met at Sweat Club, which was held at the Institute in Digbeth where we'd both occasionally DJ. He complimented me on my choice of tunes and ironically a Stax T-shirt I was sporting on that first meeting. We hit it off and hung out for the next eighteen months or so.

It would be several years until I ran into him again purely by chance, when myself and Jonesy bumped into Bren and Primal Scream main men Bobby Gillespie and Andrew Innes in the foyer of London's Barbican Hall, where we were attending an "It Came From Memphis" concert featuring Booker T., William Bell, Eddie Floyd and Mable John and celebrating Stax Records' legacy.

Bren, delighted to be reacquainted again, said he'd be able to get us into the aftershow party if we wanted to tag along. Of course we did! This time, for additional entertainment value, former Stone Roses bass player and now current member of the Scream Team squad, Mani, was part of their crew.

We hit it off famously. Mani and Neil Jones were an instant match over their love for Manchester United and Mani, somewhat comically, also shared our enthusiasm to attempt to meet our soul idols.

Once backstage and in the vicinity of a meet-and-greet type area, the three of us set off on a mission to try and get our tickets signed (this is pre-social media, so photos weren't the currency they are now back then – nobody carried a camera, which on this occasion is somewhat of a shame).

First up, we spy legendary M.G.'s guitarist Steve Cropper holding court to a gathering. We inconspicuously make our way to the rear of Mr Cropper as he regales his captive little audience with his tales of wisdom and wit, and merely lie in wait for a break off in conversation or indeed a punchline to be delivered; oh how we laughed! So much so that Steve Cropper almost shits himself as Jonesy, Mani and my guffaws bellow down his lug

holes. We didn't even know what the joke was, we just wanted his attention. It was like a scene from Alan Partridge… "Aha! Steve, that's so great! Lovely to meet you! What a gig! Can you sign my ticket please?" (x three). First one in the bag.

Oh Shit! Quick! There's Booker T. Jones! We promptly line up to utter some semi-audible babble about how much we love his playing and what his records mean to us, blah blah… He signs our tickets and shakes our hands. Booker T. actually has hands the size of an Action Man – tiny, like fucking Jeremy Beadle. Time may be tight but I bet his fucking gloves ain't.

And so it goes… We meet Donald 'Duck' Dunn, a bona fide bass love moment for myself and Mani. He comes over like some jovial old uncle who you feel you've met before.

Me and Jonesy take a detour across the other side of the room where we get a moment with Eddie Floyd. In fact, we find ourselves spending more than a moment with Eddie Floyd – it transpires that Eddie likes to talk. I've no idea who he thought we were but he wasn't letting us go in a hurry…

I tell him we tried to see him the previous year when he was out on the road with Bill Wyman's Rhythm Kings, but as it transpired we just got busy. "Man!" retorts Eddie. "Just how busy were you fellas? We did 153 dates on that tour!"

We tell him how much we love 'Never Found Me A Girl' and 'Big Bird' and he offers a detailed note-by-note account of how they were recorded and conceived, which of course is fine, but while he's talking at us, me and Neil can see that Donovan has just walked into view and is now sitting on his own, right behind Eddie. Now, me and the Jones lad are fairly intuitive and we both know we are suddenly thinking the same thought, which is something along the lines of – Eddie … haven't you got some wood you should be knocking on right now? And would it be rude of me if I stopped talking to you now and go and speak to him instead?

Fuck me, you think Eddie Floyd can talk? Meet Donovan. Book half a day off.

In Donovan's world it's still 1967. "Where you cats from? Birmingham? Oh, far out. I'm doing a show there soon, it's gonna be beautiful man, you cats should get along, you'll dig it man, beautiful."

Once we've exhausted the cosmic wheels of conversation with Donovan we spot William Bell walking out of the door. We know that the dressing rooms are right down the corridor so we hatch an instant plan to peg it down to the next available exit and head him off there before he departs. It works like clockwork, and we even manage to have something resembling a normal encounter with a soul legend. At this moment in our lives it would seem implausible that just over a decade later William Bell would sing on one of our songs.*

Jubilant and triumphant from our autograph hunt, we return to say our goodbyes to Brendan, Bobby and an equally excitable Mani, who we suddenly realise is famous enough to sign our ticket too.

What a night. Neil and I wander about in a state of disbelief at our adventures, trying to make sense of what's just happened while ambling about down dead ends in the depths of the Barbican, trying to figure out a way out of the building. Eventually we find a staff lift situated by a kitchen; we call it, knowing one level will lead us back out into the street.

As the lift opens we are greeted by a burly, bearded figure with long hair who barks, "Do you guys know the fuckin' way out of this place?" in a booming American accent.

I try to answer his question but all I can muster is, "Fuck me, it's Arthur Baker!" As if our evening couldn't get any more surreal we end up escaping the Barbican at one in the morning, and taking a Tube ride somewhere in the direction homewards with the guy who produced Madonna, New Order and Afrika Bambaataa's 'Planet Rock'. "Hey guys," Arthur says, "next time you're in London look me up and come eat in my restaurant."

Thankfully I still have my ticket, with the scribblings of Booker T., Steve Cropper, Donovan, Eddie Floyd, Arthur Baker, Mani and William Bell, so I definitely didn't dream it all…

* *'Strange People' featuring William Bell on vocals appeared on Stone Foundation's 2017 album Street Rituals.*

Issued By:
SEE Tickets - Agency

SJM Concerts present

21306820

TEENAGE CANCER TRUST
AT THE ROYAL ALBERT HALL

ROYAL ALBERT HALL

The Who
Plus special guest
Wilko Johnson

Thu, 26 March 2015 at 7:30 PM
Doors open at 6:45 PM

Door	11
Arena	E
Row	20
Seat	19

9900000210430136889820

Promoter
£ 100.00

Event by The Teenage Trust (Trading) Ltd
in support of Teenage Cancer Trust (reg charity: 1062559)

81775763
erowley 6 15TCAT04

THE WHO
ROYAL ALBERT HALL, LONDON
26 MARCH 2015
IAN SNOWBALL, AUTHOR

I found myself being escorted through the basement corridors of the Royal Albert Hall, and within minutes I had bumped into frontman and vocalist Roger Daltrey, manager Bill Curbishley, keyboardist Bob Pridden and guitarist Simon Townshend. It was around 4 p.m. and I was at this iconic London venue because I had been invited to The Who's sound check for the fifteenth Teenage Cancer Trust concert.

At the time I was deep into the research for my book *The Who: In the City*, which was my follow-up to *Keith Moon: There is no Substitute*, which Pete Townshend had kindly provided the foreword to. So, getting the invite to see The Who machine in process was gratefully accepted.

It wasn't long before The Who's tour manager, Rex, found me and ushered me in the direction of a door that led out into the floor area of the Albert Hall. Rex pointed and told me to sit wherever I wanted, so I selected a seat, about ten rows from the stage. Just as I got comfortable former Creation Records founder, Alan McGee, walked through the same door I had and, after nodding to each other, he plonked himself down in a chair a few rows behind me.

I sat back, watching on as roadies pushed and pulled The Who's equipment from one side of the stage to the next. It was all very exciting and fascinating, and I just couldn't wait to see one of my fave bands do a sound check. But I couldn't have predicted what I was about to witness.

Zak Starkey was first to enter the stage. My eyes fixated on him as he sat on his drum throne and picked up his sticks. Next up was Roger, dressed in black jeans, black shirt and a stylish-looking black waistcoat, with his glasses on. The stage then filled with the rest of the band, and an awesome projection of a mod target with the words 'Who 50th' appeared behind them.

I watched as Roger grabbed his harmonica and started to blow. It sounded OK to me, but he cried out to the sound desk "Too much top side!". Harmonica sound dealt with, he then picked up an acoustic guitar and began to strum 'I Can See For Miles'. It was brilliant, but it got even more so as Pete Townshend walked on stage. "Hi Pete," said Roger.

Moments later, Pete was clutching his red and white Fender Strat and launched into playing 'Who Are You'. The band joined in and Pete got right into playing the song; he even threw in a few of his trademark arm windmills as he danced around the stage.

'Who Are You' was followed by 'Eminence Front' and then 'I'm One' from 1973's *Quadrophenia*, which thrilled me no end as that track is from my favourite Who album. Before the sound check was over, the band had also run through 'Magic Bus' and 'My Generation'. Pete's last words were, "Well it sounds good to me up here." And just like that, one by one, Pete, Roger, Zak and the band put down their instruments and exited the stage.

I hung around for a bit, gathering my emotions and thoughts, and headed off to get some food, which was easier to digest than the experience I'd just had. A few hours later I was back for the full concert. The set included so many classics: 'I Can't Explain', 'Substitute', 'The Seeker', 'The Kids Are Alright', 'I Can See For Miles', 'Pictures Of Lily', 'Magic Bus', 'Behind Blue Eyes', 'Join Together', 'You Better You Bet', 'Love, Reign O'er Me', 'Pinball Wizard', 'Baba O'Riley', 'Won't Get Fooled Again'. But for me, amazing as the gig was, it was all about the sound check that day.

BLUR
LA2 ASTORIA, SOHO, LONDON
10 FEBRUARY 1997
BEN STANLEY, DEMON RECORDS

As was the way in 1997, when Radio 1 was still a thing in my life, I would avidly listen to the Evening Session. One Thursday night it was announced Blur would be playing a one-off gig in support of the release of their new self-titled album *Blur*, set for release on Monday 10 February.

In the pre-internet age, the only way to get tickets was to queue in person at the venue. I was up bright and early at LA2 on the Saturday morning before the show – which, considering I lived in Angmering, a small village in West Sussex, it seemed improbable I'd be able to get there for 9am and have a hope in hell of getting tickets. Asking around in the pub the previous Thursday, my two best mates Jamie and Alex were desperate to go – plus Jamie's sister, Vicky, who promised to drive if I got her a ticket. So, needing a plan, I managed to convince my sister and her then boyfriend that it would be a great thing for them to drive to London to go shopping for the day – and could they give me a lift? Amazingly, they agreed.

Lovely guy he was, but my sister's boyfriend wasn't a music fan. I distinctly remember listening to No Mercy's Europop banger 'Where Do You Go' on loop in his souped-up 205 GTI on the way up to London. But despite the pain of Spanish Europop, we got there, with the queue already round the block into Soho Square and security repeatedly warning us not to bother as demand was huge.

But I thought "fuck it"; I 'd spent two hours getting there and was happy to stand on my own all day. It was totally worth it to get to see Blur play such an intimate venue, considering where they were in their career trajectory.

At around 4 p.m. I got to the front and somehow was told there were a handful of tickets left. I was mentally counting how many people were in front of me. As luck would have it, I bought the last four tickets for the show. A result. As well as the tickets I was given two promo 'Beetlebum' posters that glow in the dark to spell Blur, one of which is framed and still hanging on my wall now. On the way home I asked if I could be dropped off straight to the pub and milked the euphoria – for a change, I don't remember buying a pint that night.

Then came Monday – first stop, a trip to Woolworths to buy the album. I quickly headed home to copy it to cassette, then off to sixth form. Mid-afternoon we rammed into Vicky's old mini metro and off we went, a solid three-hour drive ahead of us. We listened to the new album on loop for a few hours, then the usual Britpop mixtape with a rousing singalong of the Manics' 'You Love Us'.

Blur's 'Advert' came on the stereo, and when Damon sang the line "it's six o'clock … " it was precisely 6 p.m. on the car clock. I had a feeling tonight was going to be awesome.

We arrived in central London and it was like a scene out of *The Inbetweeners*, as we randomly left the car down a side road in what I can only remember to be Dean Street and hoped for the best – praying it would still be there later and not clamped.

I don't remember a support … I might be wrong, but I was too into it and didn't care about any other bands that night. We hung about at the back of the Astoria and then Damon, Graham, Alex, and Dave came on. The first chugged chords of 'Beetlebum' hit and within seconds we'd pogoed from the back to the front of the stage, and we were in. Apologies to anyone I elbowed – I was totally caught up in the excitement of the best band in Britain, living the most exciting moment of my seventeen-year life.

Blur played the entire album that night – fourteen brand new songs nobody had heard before – which for some is a bit of a no-no, but through the *Evening Session* and repeated listens that day, the songs were already like old favourites to us. The band were genuinely enthusiastic and passionately playing the new songs with real energy – before swaggering through a greatest hits encore.

Unlike the regional gigs we'd usually roll up to in Brighton, Portsmouth or Worthing, London offered up some famous faces that night. I remember seeing Z-list soap stars, a *Who's Who* of Britpop, and, randomly, Ginger and Sporty Spice got on stage – still the most Nineties moment of my life!

As the gig ended our gang were left wrecked but happy. I stood drenched in my Fred Perry shirt, Damon beads still intact, jeans caked in beer, and new Adidas Sambas destroyed through pogoing, and being trodden on. Post gig T-shirt purchased, someone had a bright idea to attempt to find the aftershow, and we ended up loitering outside for two hours in the hope of meeting the band. It was February and freezing. We had no coats and we were soaked in sweat. No doubt in sympathy, we were handed a couple of aftershow passes as souvenirs by security, although we weren't allowed in. We could see Damon and Graham and beckoned them out – but funnily enough they weren't feeling it.

Eventually, knackered and fucking freezing (I don't think I owned a coat until my twenties), we wandered around Soho for a while and managed to find the Metro, piled in and drove home. Getting in around 5, I remember crawling into bed, only to be woken a few hours later by the alarm clock for sixth form. I was exhausted, but extremely happy and sharing notes with my mates on what had been THE best gig.

GLASTONBURY FESTIVAL
WORTHY FARM, PILTON, SOMERSET
23–25 JUNE 1995
LORRAINE STANLEY, ACTRESS

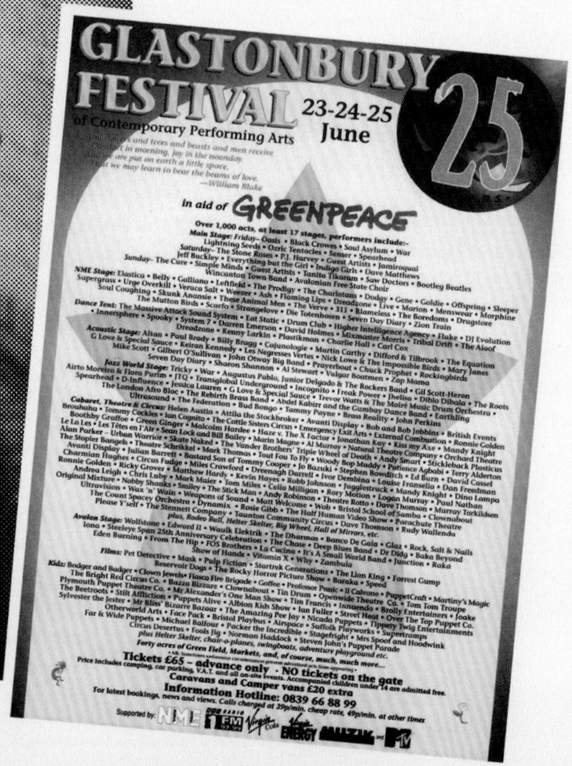

I was a student doing a BTEC in performing arts at Southdown's college in my hometown, Portsmouth. I was eighteen years old (twenty-eight years ago) and we all decided to go to 'Glasto' for the first time; my birthday is on 28 June, so it was a birthday treat to myself. Although we were all very skint students, we knew we could go on a tight budget, and in those days you could bunk in!

So off we went in Lee Cooke's car with my friends Louise Appel, Kevin Taylor, Richard Miller, Steel Wallis and Richard Cotter. There was a convoy of cars by the time we got close to Glastonbury, which added to the excitement.

We parked up and walked through a forest, trying to find a way in. Having trekked through bushes, climbed hedges and dodged security, we finally found two 6ft something big blokes that had dug a trench under the fence. We were like, "Yeeessssss, we're in!" It was £10 each, but me and Louise bartered and offered £5 each for two small ones, which they agreed. Happy days, the weekend had begun!

I remember looking from our tent across the festival thinking this is just where I needed to be. It was a hot weekend and we'd packed a few bottles of vodka in our rucksacks.

The first act I remember seeing was Oasis. They were at the start of their career, but I remember thinking these are going to be huge! They were brilliant; the crowd went nuts for them and they created such a wicked atmosphere. We were all big Led Zeppelin fans so seeing Page and Plant was another highlight. Old and young people were there together, all appreciating the same acts.

Jamiroquai was the best! I had the biggest crush on him back then and just loved his music. I knew every word to every song. I was in my element. Seeing him was really special – I think I cried tears of joy. He did a headstand on stage and I nearly wet my pants, hahaha! He didn't disappoint.

I also vaguely remember seeing Orbital, which was a crazy experience. And I think I caught the end of Portishead, another favourite band of mine back then. I'm sure The Stone Roses were meant to be there, but they cancelled due to John Squire falling off his bike.

We also saw Freak Power, who I loved; they were amazing! Very funky acid jazz. I remember the frontman was wearing a thick white fur coat and had a sweating bald head. I wondered how on earth could he wear that on stage, but he styled it out.

There were so many other bands there that we didn't get to see, or did see and just can't remember! We had drunk so much and partied hard, and I don't think I had any sleep the whole time we were there. Those were the days! It's all a massive blur to be honest. I'm kind of glad in a way that we didn't have phones back then as I don't think I'd be looking too great in the photos… I remember losing my friends for a day. I kept asking people, "Have you seen a green tent?" I mean, that's how mashed up I was … there were thousands of green tents.

I remember hanging out with some cool older hippies, like proper hippies. They had a fire and were dancing round it. It was all very tribal. I felt like I was in *The Doors* film*, haha! I remember buying some second-hand Seventies shirts, dancing with strangers and feeling completely free. The vibe there was unreal; I haven't been to another festival like it, and I haven't been back since. Not sure why, as I had the time of my life!

I got home and my mum said, "You stink!", and she was right. I looked a state, but I didn't care. It was the best weekend of my life!

I'm definitely going back maybe for my fiftieth birthday.

The 1991 musical biopic about The Doors, directed by Oliver Stone and starring Val Kilmer as Jim Morrison.

CELIA CRUZ & TITO PUENTE ORCHESTRA
HAMMERSMITH PALAIS, LONDON
10 JULY 1986
CHRIS SULLIVAN, WRITER/PROMOTER

Even though, I've seen thousands of live bands, especially during my eighteen-year tenure as host, booker director and co-owner of Soho's Wag Club, I would say that most live music leaves me as dry as powdered cinnamon. But, like theatre, when a fellow catches a great act, something that is pure class, it is magic in its truest sense – the creators nothing less than alchemists reading each other's minds, almost projecting the intense life force of each band member in one neat package.

For me it's always been big bands. I have little truck with the synth duos of the Eighties, the solo singer-songwriter or the four-piece rock ensemble. A band, for me, needs at least six members and features drums and percussion (the conga is a prerequisite), bass, no lead guitar of any description, nor necessarily a singer, but instead a piano and a few horns. Of course, a truly great singer with no amount of soul helps, but the focus for me has always been rhythm section and brass working in unison – the latter more like a percussion instrument than a horn. My old friend Pee Wee Ellis, The J.B.'s arranger and saxophonist, once told me that James Brown insisted everything should work like drum rhythm, that everything be percussive, punchy and syncopated – and, lest we forget, Mr Brown created some of the finest platters ever to grace a sound system.

This isn't a new concept. Afro-Cuban salsa bands are all about that. That said, for yours truly there is nothing that can beat a big salsa band of ten players and over. Ipso facto, one of my most memorable concerts was in the mid-Eighties, when my great friend, the recently deceased Stuart Lyons, put on an almighty salsa line at the Hammersmith Palais starring Celia Cruz & Tito Puente backed by a sixteen-piece band. In support were London's finest salsa outfit, El Sonido De Londres, led by Stan Rivera, who had a residency at the Wag Club on Wardour Street. I'd seen live salsa in New York and in London previously, but this was the Queen of Salsa, next to her King Tito and heir to the throne Mongo. And they blew the bloody doors off.

El Sonido De Londres delivered the best show they ever played. The horns, as arranged by saxophonist/band leader Stan, were as sharp as razors, Dawson's conga solos cut the curry while Kim's piano solo had the crowd in awe. And the proceedings were off to a flying start, dancefloor full to the gills, Latinos flashing their finest moves and what movers they were too.

Subsequently, Tito Puente spanked the arse out of 'Take Five', 'Oye Como Va', 'Ran Can Can' and 'El Ray De Timbal' while his timbale solos almost made me cry. It was sharp, it was tough, and it was real. And then came Celia who, backed by Tito and his confederates, performed her greats, such as 'Quimbara', 'Azúcar Negra' and 'La Negra Tiene Tumbao', and sang as if it was her last night on earth, her big, all-powerful vocal rattling the optics. She commanded the stage like General Patton, dancing up a storm in her huge dress, massive hairdo and over-abundance of make-up. This was quadruple DIVA territory. She was immense.

Every musician was the cream of the Latin crop, their product mesmerising in its eloquence – horns that could cut bread, a bass so fat it ached, the sprawling montuno piano hypnotic in its magnificence while the percussion – timbales, conga, claves, guiro, cowbell and maracas – almost made me take up religion ... but not quite.

The crowd, 99.9 per cent Latino, went absolutely ballistic. I'd never seen such unbridled joy. It was like VE day, a thousand birthdays and 100 New Year's Eves all rolled into one corpulent melange. The whole place exploded. Aside from the London Latin percussionist crew, such as Robin Jones, Sonido and a few followers, Wag DJ Steve Holloway and I were the only non-Latin folk in the ballroom, which made it all the better as we were so well accepted. I danced on my own for the entire four hours and, by the time the music finished, was wetter than an incontinent boxer's shorts. Everyone was smiling. Everyone was grooving. And everyone was jubilant. Indeed, it was the nearest I've ever been to a religious experience. This was most odd, as I hadn't taken any drug and hardly drank, since I was glued to the floor all night.

I left the Palais, my head spinning. Words could never express how thoroughly, gobsmackingly amazing this was. We were buzzing like blue bottles on the pull and equally as excited.

Sadly, the Palais was demolished in 2012 to make way for a luxury student hall of residence, so my appreciation of this event is also a lament for what we lost and are still losing. The first Palais de Dance in the UK opened in 1919 after the First World War and towards the end of the Spanish flu epidemic (which actually started in Kansas City, Missouri in 1918 and killed an estimated 100 million worldwide) it was the place that working classes went to dance the night away, lose themselves in the rhythm, meet each other and fall in love. It made millions happy as only a dancefloor can, but the Conservative Hammersmith and Fulham Council in their wisdom deemed that entirely negligible and gave permission to destroy it.

This would not happen in many other great cities such as Paris, Lisbon or Rome, as they appreciate the wealth of heritage over possessions. This is something the Tories would never understand.

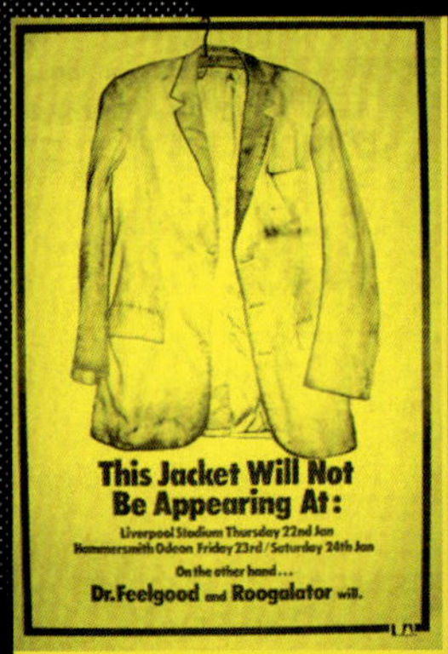

DR. FEELGOOD
HAMMERSMITH PALAIS, LONDON
19 DECEMBER 1976
MICK TALBOT, MUSICIAN

I first heard Dr. Feelgood on the Charlie Gillett show on Radio London, when he played the first single 'Roxette'. Charlie was a big patron of what would be called the 'pub-rock scene', and was particularly good at plugging gigs in the Greater London area. He was enthusiastic about the Feelgoods and knew a bit about them.

Not long after, around the release of the first album *Down By The Jetty* (1975), I saw the Feelgoods on *The Geordie Scene*, where they played the entire half hour. *The Geordie Scene* was mind-blowing. It was such a weird thing to see a weekday programme at 5.15 – essentially a kid's show – with the band playing a half-hour live set. I've since chatted to fellow musicians such as Paul [Weller] about it, who agree.

There was so much intensity coming through the screen on that performance, and a lot has been said about guitarist Wilko Johnson's psychotic thing, but Lee Brilleaux – he's a really commanding frontman, and together they were a real twin force. When Lee plays the harmonica, well, I've never seen anyone play it so aggressively. What Wilko does with a telecaster, Lee does with a mouth – he's playing like his life depends upon it. Such a visceral presence, which came across on the telly.

After that I began checking them out and I bought the single. I was telling my mate, who was really into The Rolling Stones, about the band. He knew Dr. Feelgood had covered a couple of early Stones tracks, including 'Walking The Dog'. He had a bit more money than me, so he bought the album. He said, "It doesn't sound like the Stones," so I said, "Why don't you give it to me?" He didn't see it again for another nine months. I think I listened to that album every day after school until he asked for it back, and then I finally had to get my own copy.

The NME was touting Dr. Feelgood as the 'Godfathers of Punk', which was emerging throughout the year, and they did indeed influence a lot of people from that scene, whether they said it or not. The Clash's Joe Strummer bought a Fender Telecaster because Wilko played one. I heard Malcolm McLaren would take John Lydon to see the Feelgoods to watch Wilko and really soak up his stage persona.*

**He also took him to see Ian Dury & The Blockheads, to study Ian's stance and attitude towards the audience. Both acts were very entertaining, but this wasn't old-school showbiz – it was a case of either like it or lump it.*

All this led me and my mates down the path of following the band, and I eventually got to see them live quite a few times. However, my favourite gig was at the Hammersmith Palais in December 1976. The Palais was a better gig to see Dr. Feelgood – much better than the Lewisham or Hammersmith Odeons, which they also played on that tour. The Palais was a proper old-school dance hall and had a flat floor, which enabled you to get really close to the stage if you wanted. The gig was billed as 'Dr. Feelgood's Christmas Party' and featured The Lew Lewis Band and Clover in support. Clover were an American band who seemed to turn up everywhere. They were usually third on the bill at Camden's Roundhouse, and Nick Lowe brought them in to play on Elvis Costello's first album.

Inside the room there was a mix of ages, but most of us down the front would have been around seventeen, eighteen. I can't remember what song Dr. Feelgood came on to, but I do remember them playing 'I'm A Hog For You Baby', during which Wilko was on his back and playing a one-note solo, which sounds ridiculous, but played with such power and intensity it made sense. And the set – well, by that stage they were on their third album and had a number one with the live album *Stupidity*, so the running order was based on the first two studio albums *Down By The Jetty* and *Malpractice*, plus a few R&B covers by the likes of Solomon Burke, a Bo Diddley number, a Chuck Berry thing, and a Coasters song.

There were some real funny moments with Wilko skittering about, and as he had a curly guitar lead it almost looked like he was on a coil that was throwing him around the stage. Visually it looked like a spring, or a jack-in-the-box, or Zebedee on speed, thrashing the guitar running all over the place. Lee was quite a versatile musician as well; he used to play lovely slide guitar on 'Back In The Night' and a lot of blues harmonica on songs that Wilko sung, such as the John Lee Hooker cover 'Boom Boom'. The band looked like they'd just done a bank job (coincidentally, one of the support acts at the Palais, their mate Lew Lewis, did do a bank job some ten years later!*).

All the while Wilko and Lee were captivating the audience visually, behind them was a no-nonsense rhythm section, with The Big Figure on drums and John B. Sparks on bass. They really were a solid foundation on top of which Wilko and Lee could fly.

When the band came out for the encore, Lee Brilleaux was wearing a great big hardboard cartoon safety pin round his neck, which was about 5ft long – nearly as tall as him! He remarked, "Someone said we're the Godfathers of Punk, but you're supposed to wear a safety pin for that ain't yer?" It was a mad gimmick but really funny looking back.

It was actually a post office job; in 1987, Lewis received a seven-year jail sentence for holding up a post office with a fake gun, stealing £5,000 and attempting to escape on a bike.

They'd come to the end of a tour and there was a thing in the *NME* where Lee stated it was really hard to stay looking sharp on the road (the *NME* seemed to get behind the Feelgoods before *Melody Maker* did; in particular, journalist Charles Shaar Murray was a big patron of theirs). Lee had a penchant for wearing white suit jackets onstage, and he said, "For the next tour I do, I'm going to get a white suede jacket – you try keeping that clean." I remember the *NME* held a competition to win Lee's jacket at the end of the tour, and he said, "As it's going to someone as a prize, I won't bother getting it cleaned." He must have worn it every night for about forty nights and the gig at the Palais, being the last night of the tour, was the final time he wore it. I recently googled images of the show to blow away the cobwebs of my ancient mind and he's in the jacket, and I have to say it looks pretty grubby. Him and Wilko must have been knocking things over all the time. In the images, Lee's often holding what looks like a pint of water, but it is in fact gin and tonic, I believe.

That gig was certainly an event, and it was something that really touched me. Amazingly, many moons later, in 2013, I got to work with Wilko, on the *Going Back Home* album with Roger Daltrey, and I was so chuffed to do so. I got to speak with him about that gig, and he told me it was the last UK gig he did with Dr. Feelgood, as he left the band in early '77 after they all fell out while recording the *Sneakin' Suspicion* album. It was a weird one to bring up with him at the time, especially as we thought he was dying as he'd been diagnosed with terminal cancer. We were staying at a hotel in Sussex, and I got up for breakfast and Wilko was sitting on his own, so I went and joined him. He was such an easy man to be around, given that he'd been given the death knell. He was a laugh and I felt I had to mention the gig and confess what a fan I was. He was quite enchanted and really glad to hear I'd enjoyed it so much. Thankfully, he made a miraculous recovery due to some pioneering surgery and is still going strong.

I'm really pleased the documentary *Oil City Confidential* (2009) was made about Dr. Feelgood, as it explains to those who never got to experience the band why they meant so much to so many people, including myself.

PAUL
WELLER
LAST U.K.
DATE OF '98
FINLEY
QUAYE
IAN DURY
& THE BLOCKHEADS
RIALTO
VICTORIA PARK
SAT. 8th AUGUST
C/C HOTLINE 0171 420 0066

PAUL WELLER/IAN DURY & THE BLOCKHEADS
FINLAY QUAYE/CARLEEN ANDERSON
VICTORIA PARK, LONDON
8 AUGUST 1998
DANNY WALTERS, EVENT PLANNER
WALWORTH ROAD LEGEND

On Saturday 8 August, in the summer of 1998, I found myself alone among thousands of people outside a Paul Weller concert on a sunny afternoon, stuck with four spare concert tickets after getting a last-minute blank from a new flame and her mates the night before.

I eagerly bought the tickets as a surprise to impress the then love of my life and her friends. Which didn't work, obviously. The concert was at Victoria Park in Hackney, East London, so I made my way there to try and offload the spare tickets. I must have looked like some dodgy tout as I offered them at half price, but after thirty minutes with no takers, I decided to give them away just as the concert was due to start.

I was getting in the mood and met some nice people in the process to hang out with. I was feeling better finally, and Paul Weller and his band were great as always, and all his guests were brilliant.

At the end of the concert, I was told there was going to be a soul event at the Wag Club in Wardour Street, so as it was on my way home, south wise, I thought why not just as I was being invited by new friends for the day to jump in a cab.

As we drove through London on the way to the Wag, I could see out on the street; it was all fun, with a nice natural buzz. After passing the doorman test, I walked up the stairs and when I got into a room one of the acts was about to start. I asked someone who was on next, and they said Prince Buster! He was brilliant, and I was only a few feet from him. It was so unexpected, but it caught a beautiful London musical vibe that I will never forget. I mean, Weller and Prince Buster and a brand-new friend who was cool as well.

All in all, simply amazing. It turned out to be one of the best musical concert days ever, just like that Kinks song 'All Day And All Of The Night'. My 'Heavy Soul' was 'Out Of The Sinking', and I was certainly 'One Step Beyond'.

I guess being stood up that day was a one of the best blanks I've ever had!

MAZE FEAT. FRANKIE BEVERLY
HAMMERSMITH ODEON, LONDON
6 MAY 1983
MARK WEBSTER, JOURNALIST/BROADCASTER

I'm writing here to give you some intimate details about a beautiful love affair. It happened a few decades ago now. So, all those involved were in their prime! Yet in spite of the passing years, time has not diminished the intensity of that flame of unrestricted joy and total commitment that burned so brightly back then. Although, to be fair, there's also been a couple of decent flickers since. Nevertheless, nothing will replace that first flush of love when the Hammersmith Odeon met Frankie Beverly and Maze.

In May 1983, Frankie and his band returned for a series of sell-out nights beneath the flyover, having made a one-off appearance there around a year before. Suffice to say, that went OK! Hence there was not an empty seat for nigh on a week, for a band who were barely known outside of the world of the soul heads, of which I was a fully signed-up member, being, as I was at the time, one of the handful of staff who brought you *Blues & Soul* magazine every fortnight, from its nerve centre over a souvenir shop in Paddington. To *Blues & Soul*, and its readers, Maze couldn't have been more 'them' if they tried. And I don't think they actually did have to try. Because if anything it just came naturally to this group; it was the music they made.

So, for us, Frankie and Maze's credentials were never in doubt. We'd heard the songs, and we were in! But these concerts by the roundabout had an extra dimension to them. An X factor that I have always felt contributed directly to how special these shows were. The fact that we were ready for them when they got here. The reason I feel these Hammersmith Odeon concerts were so special is because – I'll pretty much guarantee it! – everyone in the house had done the dress rehearsal at home.

A couple of years prior to the band's first trip to London, the album *Maze Live In New Orleans* was released. The essence of the group was formed in 1970, as Raw Soul. A few years later they caught the eye of none other than Marvin Gaye, who suggested the name change. From the mid-Seventies they became familiar to audiences as the support act to Gaye. Their talents were also spotted by industry individuals around this time, and in 1977 they released their debut album. But it was their incredible live prowess that captivated (in particular) black American audiences. So, when the legendary Saenger Theatre in New Orleans was refurbished and reopened, it was decided that the band's show there would be recorded for a live album, giving their label the best of both worlds.

Cut to a couple of years later, and me at the Hammy O, which remains my favourite concert venue in London. Yes, because it happened to be where I saw so many great shows (off the top of my head, James Brown, Anita Baker and Herbie Hancock could just as easily have been filling out these words), but also because its size and shape generates such a fabulous atmosphere. And so, it was on the night Mrs W. and I pitched up to experience what I had previously heard and felt on that live album.

And I wasn't the only one. If Frankie and his fellas were initially unsure how they'd be received by an audience beyond their natural borders, then that trepidation didn't last long. Maze were welcomed like long-lost friends by a few thousand Brits, who (and of course this is a piece of selective memory, seen through rose-coloured glasses) as far as I can remember, were pretty much person for person the teens, twenty and early thirtysomethings of our own black music scene. Thus, a sea of faces from the dancefloors of Blighty. And everyone knew what the score was.

If the band were welcomed like old familiar faces, then each song was hugged like it was part of the family. Songs such as 'Changing Times', 'Feel That You're Feelin'', 'Southern Girl' and 'Happy Feelin's' rode the crest of a roar from their opening bars. Indeed, the vibe that Maze and the Odeon created was such that on a subsequent appearance there, one of their real showpiece songs, 'Before I Let Go', was recorded and later released as a twelve-inch single. So, the UK had its own mini-New Orleans by the Thames.

Did I say showpiece songs? The track that seemed to catch fire on the live album positively burst into flames in West London. 'Joy And Pain' is Frankie Beverly's tour de force, a song that builds from a tiny riff, emerges into an irresistible groove then fills the air as a peerless anthem. Now me, I am not your natural joiner inner. I get it, and love it when an American audience does it that fits. But to be in the middle of it…? Not a bit of that when 'Joy And Pain' went to work. So BIG was this song, it became the whole building as the band joined us in singing the chorus. At the same time, by the way, we performed the full 'joy', 'pain', 'sunshine', 'rain' dance routine for the benefit of those on stage, and they just did the 'joy' bit.

Which is another reason this Maze gig was so special. Because Frankie Beverly was. Frankie wasn't Marvin; he's a small man who in 1983 sported a very full beard and a baseball cap (which has never seemed to leave his head over the decades). His songs are a string of pearls, which he delivers often from his piano or, when he was in cheerleading mode, centre stage at the mic. His arms and legs constantly tick along inside the rhythm.

Mind you, he wasn't the focus of my attention. Throughout the night my eyes were drawn to his long-term sidekick, the late McKinley 'Bug' Williams. Bug was a big fella, his face fixed in a permanent grin as he played percussion and joined in on the harmonies. And he moved. All of him did. There wasn't an inch of Bug that wasn't grooving. Unremittingly. His sheer enthusiasm seemed to be the glue that kept Frankie's incredible band on point. And it was Bug who really seemed to embrace what the Hammersmith Odeon was sending in Maze's direction on that night in 1983.

Since then, there have been other Maze moments for me. We took our young kids on another visit to the Hammy O, and they (I'm going to guess reluctantly) joined in with 'Joy And Pain'. I even interviewed Frankie in a café on Wardour Street for a TV show, during which he was a true gent, and actually spoke with a slight stammer. He told me he liked Donna Allen's cover of 'Joy And Pain' but hated the idea that it had been sampled by Rob Base & DJ E-Z Rock.

Then, around ten years ago, the Family Webster were in Vegas for my oldest son's wedding. One evening we went to the Blue Note club, which was quiet when we got there, although there was a DJ who was happy to take our requests, one of which was 'Joy And Pain'. And yep, we sang along and did the dance. Because we had to. Because it's part of us.

THELONIOUS MONK QUARTET/ART BLAKEY JAZZ MESSENGERS
HAMMERSMITH GAUMONT, LONDON
30 APRIL 1961
SPIKE WELLS, DRUMMER/VICAR

HAROLD DAVISON presents
FOR THE FIRST TIME IN GREAT BRITAIN
THE
THELONIOUS MONK
QUARTET featuring CHARLIE ROUSE
Plus
ART BLAKEY'S
JAZZ MESSENGERS
ROYAL FESTIVAL HALL
SATURDAY 29 APRIL at 6 p.m.
TICKETS: 6/-, 8/-, 10/6, 16/- & 20/-
NOW AVAILABLE FROM HAROLD DAVISON LTD., EROS HOUSE 29-31 REGENT STREET, LONDON, S.W.1. Stamped addressed envelope with postal applications, please.

A young chorister singing the choral repertoire day in day out at Canterbury Cathedral. That was my introduction to the world of music. One Christmas, the organist gave me a Glenn Miller LP. Then I heard Louis Armstrong. And finally, I acquired a Dizzy Gillespie EP. That was the turning point. From then on, be-bop and beyond was my religion.

I started trying to play the drums. I played with and to friends at parties on a crappy kit. I adorned the front of the bass drum with the legend, in clumsy black sticky tape letters, 'ALIAS MAX ROACH OR ART BLAKEY'. The chutzpah of it!

Anyway, the opportunity soon arose to see the real Art Blakey in the flesh.

This concert was that opportunity. Although I had turned fifteen, my upbringing and circumstances were such that I would need my parents' blessing to undertake such a venture. I pleaded with my father not to make me miss this event. I knew he was worried by my growing passion for jazz. In the end he decided that I should go but that he would come with me to satisfy his curiosity and hopefully allay his fears.

We lived in Tunbridge Wells. So, it was a day return to Charing Cross (hauled by one of my favourite locos (I was still a keen trainspotter) – a 'Schools Class' 4-4-0), half an hour of cartoons in the Charing Cross terminus News Theatre (since we were early), and then a Tube to Hammersmith.

The Gaumont, renamed the Odeon the following year and subsequently again renamed the Apollo, is that huge auditorium with the gaudy façade at 45 Queen Caroline St. in the middle of the one-way system. Not to be confused with the dance hall just up the Shepherd's Bush Road, called the Hammersmith Palais.

I had never been in such a huge cinema/theatre/music auditorium before and was suitably gobsmacked. (Modesty, I fear, fails to prevent me from mentioning that I played there myself years later with Humphrey Lyttelton, Jay McShann, Buddy Tate and Charlie Shavers.)

This 1961 concert was a landmark in my musical education. The two bands had just started the brief British part of a European tour – they had opened the night before at the Royal Festival Hall and this show was reviewed in the June 1961 copy of *Jazz Journal*.

The Thelonious Monk Quartet was top of the bill and played the second set. My abiding memory is visual – that of Monk getting up from the piano during the tenor, bass or drum solos to do a lumbering dance round the stage. I believe he might also at one point have taken his shoes and socks off and waved his feet at the audience, but I may be fantasising! I was fascinated by the way he attacked the keyboard with splayed fingers and flattened palms (I was too young to have yet witnessed Stan Tracey live). Charlie Rouse on tenor had a nice distinctive sound but was rather repetitive. With hindsight, I've always wished that Bobby Wellins could have been in Monk's regular quartet – that would indeed have been a marriage made in heaven!

My father was slightly distressed at Monk's eccentric dress and antics but, when both bands had finished, he said he thought Monk's drummer (the conventional and stolid Frankie Dunlop) had "stolen the show"! I was still recovering from the brilliance, subtlety and dynamics of Art Blakey, so this comment floored me.

As far as The Messengers were concerned, we agreed on Lee Morgan's superb trumpet playing and Bobby Timmons' fluent and driving piano. However, Wayne Shorter was a step too far. I was captivated by the astringency of his tone, his harmonic originality and the pithiness of his solos. My father, on the other hand, expressed the regret that those obviously competent enough to entertain us in the Coleman Hawkins style would spend their time instead making deliberately ugly noises.

Well, there it is.

I am eternally grateful to my dear late father for sharing this day with me despite his disappointment at the experience. I like to think he was at least partly reassured about my career choice when he later witnessed the size of the crowds pouring into the Fairfield Halls in Croydon to see the Roland Kirk quartet with me on drums…

Hammersmith, 30 April 1961, was a red-letter day in my life. It feels like a *coming of age*, both as an aspiring musician and as a son.

Harvey Goldsmith proudly presents
DAVID
in concert + guests
MILTON KEYNES BOWL

DAVID BOWIE
MILTON KEYNES BOWL
JULY 1983
JASON WOOD, BFI

Memory can be unreliable. I have spent my life up until the moment I sat down to write this convinced that the first ever live music concert I attended occurred on the occasion of my thirteenth birthday, 5 July 1983. I have since discovered that it would have been on either 1, 2 or 3 July, so just before the flowering of my teenage years. What is fact is that the artist was David Bowie, and the venue was a sweltering and densely packed Milton Keynes Bowl. Icehouse and The Beat were the support acts. I draw a veil of silence over Icehouse; The Beat I loved, and still do.

I was fortunate enough to have an older brother with a coterie of switched-on friends, all of whom were very passionate about music. It wasn't through any form of snobbery, but while my contemporaries were having their tastebuds tickled by mainstream pop, I was being introduced to jazz, reggae and post-punk, as well as artists such as Annette Peacock, Captain Beefheart and Can. David Bowie was the glue that held it all together, and the artist through which all the constellations in my universe coalesced. Even my football mates liked David Bowie. He was an outsider and a little bit avant-garde, but he still had number one singles, 'Ashes To Ashes' being the most recent. He also had a South London accent. Which is good when you live in Streatham.

At my then tender age I owned every single David Bowie album. I actually enjoyed school, but I'd play the title track from *Heroes* before beginning my daily walk to the foreboding Victorian gates. I considered *Young Americans* Bowie's best album; today I think it is *Lodger*. When the post-Eno *Scary Monsters* (*And Super Creeps*) LP hit I was peak Bowie and voraciously surfing his cultural zeitgeist.

Summer, 1983. I was playing five-aside football in the school gym after hours. There was a viewing balcony and someone up there had a cheap transistor radio tuned to Radio 1. Word filtered down to the pitch that the DJ was about to play for the first time the new Bowie single, 'Let's Dance'. We all stopped playing immediately. The radio was turned up to maximum volume and we stood like statues, utterly transported. Music can do that.

Later, following a press conference at Claridge's during which a tanned and relaxed looking Bowie appeared and announced the *Let's Dance* album, dates were ceremoniously revealed for the UK leg of the Serious Moonlight Tour. It was obvious Bowie was entering what would be an imperious commercial period. My brother and his clan were suspicious. They'd seen Bowie at Earls Court on the Station To Station Tour and had also seen him playing keyboards as a sideman in Brixton with Iggy Pop. But I begged, pleaded and cajoled. They capitulated and agreed to take me to see Bowie at somewhere called Milton Keynes as my thirteenth birthday present. We travelled down in a VW campervan in the wee small hours on the morning of the concert, spending many an hour in traffic, a few more hours exiting a motorway slip road and then some more time trying to find space in a car park. The glamour.

I had never seen so many people in one place at once. The attendance has subsequently been recorded as something like 65,000. I found it intimidating. It was also unbearably hot, and I was almost instantly interminably bored. The ennui stretched on and on ahead of me. The torpor incorporated Icehouse. I sensed the general air of anticipation and celebration, but I was utterly immune to it. I was also too young to drink, which for my brother seemed to be helping to take the edge off. And then the sun began to set, and a hush descended. Bowie's name was chanted by the crowd, which reached a crescendo as the band ran out on to the stage. When Bowie appeared, there was a wall of noise so strong that I thought I was going to lose my footing. The first song out of the blocks was 'Jean Genie'.

I distinctly recall spending the next two hours or so in a state of reverie as a band featuring Earl Slick and Carlos Alomar raced through a set list that incorporated the four singles from Let's Dance (yes, I am including 'Cat People (Putting Out Fire)'), but also pivotal back catalogue tracks including 'Station To Station', 'Fashion', 'Rebel Rebel', 'Life On Mars', 'Breaking Glass', 'Fame' and 'Space Oddity', during which a huge inflatable half-moon balloon was released, floating up towards the star-filled night sky

This concert was seminal for me. It cemented a life-long connection to Bowie, to live music, and to the notion of culture, self-expression and creativity as a potent binding element, bringing people together in an act of celebration and communion.

Acknowledgements

To all the contributors and my gig-going friends and family over the decades – Lock & Jonesy, Nicole, Sean Robbie, Al Peasey, Simon Kortlang, Fred Wong, Simon Kelly, Rory Blaney, Paula, Paul Miceli, Al and Billy Sullivan. Thanks for your time, company and keep on rockin' in the free world.

Stu

Big thanks to all those who said yes to my approach with the book idea and then delivered some great memories and photos to illustrate them. It was a real pleasure working with you all.

Bax x